Herbert Hoover

Forgotten Progressive

Joan Hoff Wilson

Herbert Hoover
Forgotten Progressive

Edited by Oscar Handlin

WAVELAND

PRESS, INC.

Prospect Heights, Illinois

For information about this book, write or call:

Waveland Press, Inc.
P.O. Box 400
Prospect Heights, Illinois 60070
(847) 634-0081

For

Edith and Charles Wilson
with love and respect

Editor's Preface

HERBERT HOOVER's place of birth was the American heartland; but for much of his life, he was a stranger to his native country, and never more so than while he was its president.

His career followed a pattern familiar in the history of the United States — not quite the log cabin to the White House, but almost. Humble birth, hard work, the desire for achievement and finally, wealth, public service and the presidency formed a progression recognizable in much of the national experience. There was continuity with the past also in the values Hoover acquired in his youth and which stayed with him through life.

The great crisis of Hoover's life was the depression, which ironically began soon after he took office in 1929. He then had to ask whether those values were still appropriate; and the answer he gave differed so markedly from that given by his countrymen that a gulf opened between him and them that was never to be bridged in his lifetime.

Hoover had been too much away. Shortly after he left college, work took him to remote parts of the world; not until 1920 did he finally return to live in the United States. He advanced to the presidency after less than a decade's residence in the country. In his absence, the United States had changed. The massive industrial organizations and great cities of the 1920's and 1930's were far removed from the rustic landscape of West Branch, Iowa or even of Palo Alto, California; the places most familiar to him. He was widely respected in 1929, but there was little comprehension between the president who then took office and the people who looked to him for leadership.

Perhaps because he felt that the burden of blame for the depression thrust upon him was unfair, he remained out of step. In the years of the world's peril after 1939, he fought a lonely battle against the dominant opinion that the fate of the United States could not be detached from the fate of men elsewhere. He died unpopular and isolated — largely disavowed by his own party and embittered by the lack of understanding.

His career therefore mirrored in reverse the forces of the times in which he lived. In 1975, when the United States again feels the urge toward withdrawal, readers may be more sympathetic than they were a quarter of a century earlier. Professor Wilson's account may throw light not only on his career but also on the changing nation which rejected him.

OSCAR HANDLIN

Contents

Herbert Hoover
Forgotten Progressive

I

The Quaker
as Man of the World

*". . . if he is shy, so is a steam shovel."**

HERBERT CLARK HOOVER (1874–1964) was the second of three children born into the Quaker family of Jesse Clark and Hulda[h] Minthorn Hoover. He exhibited so few distinguishing characteristics as a child, except for an inordinate shyness and reticence, that after he became famous neighbors and relatives remembered his early years with difficulty. Mollie Brown, his first teacher in West Branch, Iowa, recalled him as a "sweet little boy," chubby and round-faced, with unruly straight hair. He showed no particular interest in learning, but nonetheless progressed satisfactorily under her tutelage. Aside from being very bashful, "Bert" was in no way memorable as a child, and he was no less awkwardly reserved as an adult. Characteristically, Hoover never stood out in crowds, even when they gathered in his honor.

His parents were practicing Quakers, as both sides of the family had been since the colonial period. Jesse's ancestors came from Switzerland in the 1730s after living for one generation

---

* All chapter epigraphs appear elsewhere within the chapter with source information.

in the Palatinate, while Hulda's had come a century earlier from England and migrated to Canada after the American Revolution. Although Jesse and Hulda belonged to a "progressive" faction in West Branch that permitted some organ music and gospel hymns at the Quaker meeting house, their second son's religious training was still quite rigorous. Hoover would later recall plain clothes and plain speech, daily Bible readings, and long Sunday meetings "waiting for the spirit to move someone." The community prohibited most worldly pleasures — fancy dress, drinking, dancing, smoking, card playing, and novels, except those, he noted, "where the hero overcame demon rum." Boisterous play was encouraged, but direct fighting, verbal or physical, was considered sinful.

Except for his conservative style of dressing, as an adult Hoover retained few outward signs of his boyhood faith. Not only was his personal and professional aggressiveness as a mining engineer inconsistent with the Quaker ideal of moderation in all things, but he also could swear with the roughest of the miners he directed, was a habitual smoker, enjoyed a good drink, and often fished on Sundays. Yet there is little doubt that his later rejection of moral relativism and his rigid commitment to unchanging laws of progress (whether moral or scientific) stemmed from his Quaker upbringing. The same is true of his idealism, stoicism, pragmatism, and general social inhibitions, but to a lesser degree, for like any child Hoover experienced environmental conditioning other than religious training.

Perhaps the most important such factor was that he was left an orphan at the age of nine. First, his father died of pneumonia in December 1880, and then his mother of typhoid in February 1884. As a result, he quickly learned what it was like to work hard at being self-reliant and yet have to submit to the arbitrary authority of well-meaning relatives. The exact effect this had on his adult personality is difficult to determine, but his reputation as a loner and his secretive defensiveness about what he considered personal matters could have been a result of his orphanhood. It also may well have influenced his later philanthropic concern for underprivileged children.

There is no doubt that the transient nature of Hoover's life as an orphan influenced his personality. Most important, it intensified the reticence he had already displayed before his parents died. Even in the course of the three years from late 1880 to early 1884 during which his mother survived his father, the child was often uprooted because Hulda's eminence among Quakers increased along with her religious zeal. She was often away from home preaching, leaving the children with relatives in West Branch for two or three weeks at a time. Her absence became all the more frequent after she was officially ordained a Quaker minister in 1881. Once, Bert even spent eight or nine months on an Indian reservation with his Uncle Miles Laban. Thus began his itinerant life among Quaker relatives and friends of the Hoover family, and during the process his natural shyness apparently hardened into a defensive shell that he was to carry with him for the rest of his life. Because his impersonal, dogged determinism and ambition so masked his vulnerability and diffidence, Herbert Corey both defended and tried to explain Hoover's complex personality in his 1932 biography by saying: "If he is shy, so is a steam shovel."

Other than Quakerism and an orphaned existence, however, life in West Branch meant for Hoover a typically rural-American, semifrontier childhood of the last quarter of the nineteenth century. Most of the town's two hundred or so citizens faced an austere, subsistence-level existence inevitably accompanied by a short life expectancy. By the time he began to write down some autobiographical sketches before World War I, Hoover privately acknowledged that "progressive men never go backward," and later in his published *Memoirs,* he denied any desire to "return to the good old days" of subsistence farming in West Branch, which he compared to a "Montessori school in stark reality." His brother Theodore, being less taciturn and dour than Hoover, recalled in his more colorful autobiography that the Hoover children grew up in an "atmosphere of rigid economy," which carried with it a dread of waste and developed in them habits of thrift, temperance, and tenacity. Despite the fact that they "suffered from typhoid, malaria, diphtheria, tonsils, toothache, and considerable malnutrition due to an abundant but faulty diet," Theodore proudly noted they "had a high ethical standard . . . and no venereal disease." Except for his Quaker upbringing and the early deaths of his parents, therefore, Bert's childhood was not much different from that of most native-born American males of his generation. And despite his rejection of its poverty and physical harshness, he too later idealized the values of his rural upbringing.

But his rejection of the substandard material existence of the West Branch Quakers in their weathered brown-frame homes did not prevent Hoover from being influenced by their prevailing sense of community. As a youth and later as a public figure, he was strongly impressed with their ability to act as socially responsible individualists. "The Friends have always held strongly to education, thrift, and individual enterprise," he approvingly wrote in his *Memoirs*. "In consequence of plain living and hard work, poverty has never been their lot. So far as I know, no member has ever been in jail or on public relief. This is largely because they take care of each other."

This sense of the harmony and unity of voluntary community cooperation, what Hoover later called "progressive individualism," was probably the most important legacy of his Quaker upbringing. Even the "ruthless righteousness" with which Hoover pursued his private and public careers was based on this cooperative work ethic, whereby all members of the community did their best in their particular "callings" in life for the good of everyone. A far cry from the Darwinian concept of survival of the most rugged individual, this nonetheless did entail the public ridicule or ostracism of both those who shirked and those who were too acquisitive.

Such community achievement and cohesiveness required not only dedicated individual industry at all levels, but also leaders who could provide socially responsible professional guidance. Hence, Hoover's Quaker background engendered in him an abiding faith in a very specific kind of individualism. On the surface, his general statements about the term sounded familiar to most Americans, but his specific definition and intended application of it were not. When he said in his public statements and writings that each individual should be "given the chance and stimulation for development of the best with which he has been endowed in heart and mind . . ." or that it was "the right of every individual to attain that position in life to which his ability and character entitle him," he was not equating these goals with "ruthless individualism." Instead he denounced any "individualism run riot," untempered by social responsibility. He called for "ordered liberty," a compromise between the individual's advantage and that of society at large. American individualism, as Hoover came to refine its definition, was based first on his Quaker training and later on his wartime experiences. It required a balance of perspective, "a sensitive adjustment of conflicting rights and interest through a spirit of decency and cooperation in human relationships, reinforced by government restraints to the end that men may enjoy equal opportunities." Anything less was false liberalism, and would result in either bureaucracy or monopoly, and the destruction of the "driving force of equal opportunity." So he would say later in the 1928 presidential campaign.

Such a demanding yet balanced and restrained individualism was practiced imperfectly at best by most Americans, including Hoover, especially during his extremely competitive years from 1897 to 1912 when he was establishing his reputation as the world's most successful engineer. Yet it was this Quaker ideal which would be a recurring theme in his attempts to restructure the American political and economic system in the 1920s.

None of the several relatives who sheltered the orphaned future president could have anticipated the impact their Quaker influence would have on his later thought. These relatives included, first, Allan Hoover of West Branch and, later, Dr. Henry John Minthorn of Oregon — neither of whom was overly harsh with him, although his Uncle John was much more of a disciplinarian. The women in whose houses he lived (Aunt Millie, Allan's wife; and Aunt Laura, John's wife) and those who taught him anything from how to read to how to typewrite (Mollie Brown in Iowa and Jennie Gray and Laura Hewitt in Salem) are singled out in his *Memoirs* for their kindness and attention. While Hoover's *Memoirs* do not detail much of his early life, they do reveal some of the less philosophically important, but nonetheless durable, influences these Quakers had on his thought: a life-long interest in education, an emphasis on a stable homelife, an aversion to public relief, a belief that hard work inevitably led to prosperity, and an inclination toward the Republican party. (The only Democrat in West Branch during Hoover's childhood was the town drunk.) In addition, there were many prohibitionists among the Hoover women — his great-grandmother Rebecca Hoover, the family matriarch, who lived until 1896; his own mother; and Aunt Hannah, the leading elder among the Quaker women he knew. Although he was certainly not a teetotaler, Hoover's views on prohibition while president were at least partially rooted in the temperance attitudes of his female relations.

The single most important Quaker belief that Hoover did not share as an adult was their commitment to pacifism. While his early career as an engineer certainly did not reinforce any pacifist tendencies in his character, it was also generally recognized that no man aspiring to high public esteem, as Hoover was by 1914, could be an avowed pacifist in time of war. Nor, by his own admission, was he a pacifist after the First World War. Nonetheless, like many other Quakers, Hoover was predisposed to accept any plan which could perpetuate peace through nonviolent means. In particular, his foreign policy as president was heavily weighted in favor of peaceful settlement of all controversies. This accounts for his later support of arms limitation, international arbitration, world organization, moral suasion in foreign relations, and minimum cost for minimum preparedness. These political positions can be viewed as consistent with Quaker attitudes, if not with their strict adherence to pacifism.

Armed with his Quakerism, his defensive diffidence, and an ingrained sense of Jeffersonian agrarian idealism, Hoover came as a teenager to the Pacific coast in the late 1880s. He matured rapidly under his uncle's strict tutelage in Newberg and Salem, Oregon. Dr. Minthorn was a jack of all trades. As Hoover accompanied his uncle on long trips to treat patients, he became familiar with the rudiments of physiology and learned as well about condescension — Minthorn referred to his poor non-Quaker patients as "white trash." From Minthorn's past experience supervising reservation schools in Oklahoma and Oregon, driving teams for the Underground Railway in Iowa, and serving briefly as a doctor in the Civil War, Hoover gained information about Indians, slavery, and a limited amount of American history as it related to the Battle of Shiloh. Since Minthorn belonged to a very liberal Quaker faction, Hoover also had access to secular novels for the first time. But the most important learning experience for Hoover was the business education he received when Minthorn decided to open a land-company office in Salem in 1889.

Bert became an office boy for the Oregon Land Company, a firm that sold land suitable for orchard plots to easterners. His uncle was not above writing exaggerated descriptions of his real estate, and soon had Hoover preparing such ads, meeting prospective customers at the railroad station, and accompanying them to prearranged boarding houses to keep them out of the reach of competing realtors. Although only fifteen when he arrived in Salem and seventeen when he left, Hoover became indispensable to the operation, possibly even investing some of his meager savings in acreage. An office secretary considered him "the quietest, the most efficient, and the most industrious boy" she ever knew in an office, noting that "he was a funny-looking little fellow, with a short neck and a round head which was always surmounted by a funny little round hat." Otherwise she recalled nothing particularly striking about him except that he somehow found time to read the geometry and geology books piled on his desk.

Hoover's serious interest in engineering and mining began at the very time his business sense was developing. Mining engineers periodically passed through the office of the Oregon Land Company; one of them, Robert Brown, particularly impressed Bert with his scientific jargon and descriptions of exciting outdoor life. He began to collect university catalogues and studied all the harder in his evening math classes at a new Salem business school.

The university Hoover finally decided upon had not yet opened. It was the progressive project of Senator Leland Stanford of California, intended as a memorial to his only son. After Hoover convinced his relatives that he did not want to attend a Quaker college, he found himself faced with another obstacle: he was woefully unprepared for the entrance examination. (Although Quakers placed great stock in education, their ideal was seldom realized in rural, frontier areas. Even Dr. Minthorn's Pacific Academy at Newberg, which Hoover had attended when he first arrived from Iowa, provided a typically substandard level of education.) Hoover was particularly deficient in English grammar and composition; the laborious, often unintelligible writing style that characterizes almost everything he wrote between 1897 and 1963 is proof that this plagued him throughout his life.

Fortunately for Hoover, Stanford University was more interested in recruiting students its first year than in obtaining highly qualified ones. When he failed the entrance exams given in Portland in the spring of 1891, he was given a chance to take them again in the fall. After a summer of special tutoring in Palo Alto, he was admitted on a conditional basis to Stanford's pioneer class.

The school suited Hoover perfectly. It was in an incomplete, formative state, and so was he. Its progressive academic atmosphere represented a curious blend of idealism and practicality that, from the beginning, appealed to his Quaker instincts. "Stanford," his classmate Will Irwin later wrote, "became a kind of complex with him." And just as his four-year stay there left an indelible mark on his character, so did he help to shape the school's destiny after 1912, when he became a member of the Board of Trustees.

Hoover's academic career at Stanford was as undistinguished as his person was inconspicuous, but he did succeed in impressing his immediate superiors: Dr. John C. Branner, head of the geology and mining department, and Dr. Waldemar Lindgren of the United States Geological Survey, for whom he worked during his sophomore and junior summer vacations. Furthermore, his extracurricular activities, especially those in student government, brought out all of his latent administrative talents.

Never popular among his fellow students, Hoover wandered about the campus with his eyes riveted on the ground, seldom speaking unless addressed first. "Affection for Hoover [was] not a sudden dazzling discovery but a gradual dawning," observed Will Irwin. "The crown of his personality was his shyness." He was just under six feet and walked with a slight stoop, carrying his head slightly to one side, and, as Irwin also noted, had the habit of standing "with one foot thrust forward, jingling the keys in his trousers pocket" and of chuckling but rarely laughing out loud.

Though not popular, Hoover did establish a positive reputation among the poorer working students as a member of the "Barbs," a political faction that opposed the richer fraternity crowd, the "Frats." The Barbs gained control of the student government during Hoover's senior year. While his political friends shared the limelight and did most of the public speaking, Hoover worked effectively, if colorlessly, behind the scenes. Elected treasurer on a party ticket, he devised a book-keeping system that straightened out student finances, and he helped to draft an improved constitution.

Hoover's experience at Stanford tested his physical stamina as he struggled to support himself financially and still partici-pate in school politics. His years there also developed his administrative ability, as well as sharpening his natural tal-ents for quickly retaining facts and reorganizing existing structures. He was to draw repeatedly upon these capacities in the course of his private and public careers.

When Hoover left Stanford University in May, 1895, he had forty dollars in his pocket and an A.B. in geology. The country was in the midst of a severe national depression. Early in 1896, after working as a common miner for several months in Nevada City at $2 to $2.50 a day, he obtained a $150 a month engineering job from Louis Janin, a prominent San Francisco mining expert. A little over a year later he left, upon Janin's recommendation, for his first engineering assign-ment abroad; the London mining firm of Bewick, Moreing & Company had offered him an annual salary of $7,200 plus expenses. He was then twenty-three.

He arrived in Australia in May, 1897, to do field work as a "mine scout" for this old English firm. Within a few months his salary rose to $10,000 a year and he became manager of the fabulously profitable Sons of Gwalia gold mine in Leonora. Although he was not solely responsible for discovering its value or purchasing it, as his *Memoirs* imply, the mine was Hoover's first major investment recommendation to Bewick, Moreing & Company. Their initial investment of $50,000 netted them $55 million in gold and $10 million in dividends over the next fifty years. In the fall of 1898 he accepted, upon the suggestion of C. Algernon Moreing, an offer of $20,000 plus expenses to become the chief engineer for the Chinese Engineering Company, the largest single commercial under-taking in China. By the turn of the century Hoover had earned the title of "the Chief" among his friends and was well on his way to establishing a legendary reputation as the Great Engineer. (This appellation of "Chief" referred to the engineer in charge of any mining operation, but his old engineering friend Edgar Rickard continued to use it during their Food Administration days from 1917 to 1918. "This singled him out from heads of other [wartime] agencies," Admiral Lewis L. Strauss later recalled in an oral interview, and from then on his personal staffs always referred to him as Chief rather than Mr. Director, Mr. Secretary or Mr. President.)

The Boxer Rebellion of 1900 soon ended the Chief's impressive employment record with the Chinese Engineering Company. But the revolution was fortuitous as well, allowing Hoover to participate in the conversion of this Chinese firm into an English limited-liability corporation. This deal was made by Chinese officials under duress as foreign armies began indiscriminately to confiscate the holdings of the Chinese Engineering Company. Operating as an agent for Moreing, although officially an employee of the Chinese government, Hoover performed the transfer and received between $150,000 and $250,000 in shares of the reorganized company. (His political enemies would use his involvement in this transaction against him in the 1928 and 1932 presidential campaigns.)

During these early successful years as a young engineer, Hoover came to symbolize the rugged individualist, although he used the term rarely in his later philosophical writings and did not equate it with his definition of progressive or American individualism. At best he identified rugged individualism with variety in American life, a protection against conformity but not a substitute for the "absolute equality of opportunity" which he thought the right of each American. This could only result from the inculcation of cooperative, socially responsible individualism at home and through the educational system. Thus, despite the individual drive he exhibited in his very competitive early career as an engineer, his Quaker upbring-

ing prevented him from becoming a lifelong advocate of
ruthlessly rugged individualism, contrary to the claims of both
his friends and enemies.

This misunderstanding arose in part from his almost con-
tinual absence from the United States between 1897 and 1917.
However, his later philosophical ideas did not arise exclusively
from his experiences abroad as a young, ambitious engineer
whose sense of social responsibility may well indeed have been
temporarily subordinated to the temptations of establishing a
world-wide reputation while succeeding financially beyond his
wildest dreams. At most, his rapid rise as an engineer reinforced his already established Quaker belief in the rewards of
individual exertion within one's chosen profession. But it
never killed his equally strong Quaker belief that one must
serve society to the degree that one is enriched by it. There
was simply little time or opportunity to practice this ethic
abroad, when Hoover was out to prove himself quickly in a
cutthroat profession.

As a partner of Bewick, Moreing & Company, for example,
Hoover was both an engineer in the field and an administrator
in London from November 1901 to July 1908. By 1907 he had
acquired 30 percent interest in this managerial firm and was
one of the highest paid men in his profession — a profession in
which he was increasingly operating more as a financial expert
and promoter than he was as a mining engineer. Hoover
reorganized mines all over the world, but primarily in Australia, because three-quarters of the firm's operations were
there. Traveling exhaustively, he "worked like a dog" by his
own private admission, and the results of these strenuous
efforts were impressive and rewarding for his company and for
him. They were not, however, as completely within the
bounds of Quaker moderation and ethical priority or as
efficient and profitable as Hoover later recalled in his *Memoirs*. In truth, there were a few notable failures, such as the
Great Fitzroy copper mine near Rockhampton in Queensland
and the Australian Smelting Corporation. The *Memoirs* also

neglect to mention the early financial failures of the Broken Hill field (Zinc Corporation) up to 1910. This tendency Hoover had of ignoring, dismissing, whitewashing, or even falsely claiming success for those inevitable financial failures common in any speculative profession like mining engineering, is a significant character trait. His capacity for self-delusion where failure was involved, or exaggeration of what was only average achievement, can be documented in every stage of his private and public development. It reached a tragic climax, of course, when he found himself president during the depression of 1929.

Whether such self-delusion stemmed from his emotionally and materially insecure childhood, from the emphasis the Quakers placed on the spiritual significance of failing at one's calling, or from his own sense of guilt at having violated certain Quaker ethics in his extraordinarily rapid rise to the top of his profession is a moot issue. What is significant is that Hoover never admitted failure and exaggerated the successes of most of the projects he undertook during his long and varied life. On occasion he also took credit for technological and organizational innovations as an engineer and an administrator that were not his.

None of this is meant to detract from the impressive fact that Bewick Moreing's business tripled during the years that Hoover served as an active partner. At the same time he took advantage of his field work for the firm to begin investigations of lead, silver, and zinc mining developments in Burma. His private investments here laid the foundations for his personal fortune. In order to take full advantage of the financial potential of the Burmese situation, and at the same time to purchase and operate other mines without being limited by his partners' strictly managerial approach, Hoover sold his interest in the firm in 1908 at the age of 34, just as his contract was about to expire. In an unpublished autobiographical sketch written during 1913 or 1914, he recalled that he sold out "for about $225,000 cash as I could not stand Moreing any longer

than necessary having given practically 5 years to that mess
. . . [and] accumulated about $200,000 more from outside
business."

Upon leaving this British company, Hoover immediately
established his own consulting offices in London, New York,
San Francisco, and later in Petrograd and Paris. From 1908 to
1914 he headed what he proudly called a team of "engineering
or mine doctors," who turned sick operations into healthy
ones for a fee based on a percentage of increased profits from
the reorganized and revitalized firms. Although these years
were probably not as creative as those he spent with Bewick
Moreing, they were profitable. Again, however, his *Memoirs,*
published in the early 1950s, exaggerate his accomplishments
as a managerial doctor and minimize his less successful efforts.

One example of such self-delusion, ironically, was later used
against him by his political enemies. In a single chapter he
devoted much space to his alleged activities in Russia, apparently because of the widespread popularity of some magnified
accounts by friends who in the 1920s had written biographies
of him claiming that he had created a great mining empire
there before World War I. Yet this was not true. Thus, while
his *Memoirs* lend credence to his mythical Russian accomplishments, it was a Scotsman, Leslie Urquhart, an innovative
entrepreneur, who actually developed several successful
copper-smelting operations in Kyshtim and Irtysh. Hoover was
simply one of Urquhart's bright consulting engineers, and
had never held extensive shares in any of Urquhart's London-
based Russian corporations. Most of what he did own he sold
in 1916 before the Bolshevik Revolution.

In fact, in 1932, long before time had distorted the memory
of his relatively limited Russian activities, when questioned
on the economic value of recognizing the USSR he was quoted
in *Literary Digest* as saying disdainfully that "there are more
minerals in Montana than in the whole of Russia." Hoover
never intimated then or later that any of his own limited
Russian mining holdings ever influenced his opposition to

recognition, but there were those who accused him of this. There is no doubt, however, that his brief career as an engineer in Russia for Urquhart had privately convinced him of the vast natural resources of the Soviet Union (despite his 1932 politically inspired remark), and he preferred a non-Communist regime to be in control of them.

Although his fortune was probably never as small as his own private estimate, nor as large as public speculation about it, Hoover was a millionaire by 1914 at the age of 40. In 1932, *Fortune* magazine published the most objective and detailed report of his finances to date, estimating that he was worth something in excess of four million dollars by the time he officially retired from his dual profession of engineer and financier in 1914.

While amassing this personal fortune, Hoover became a husband and father. On February 10, 1899, between his first Australian and Chinese assignments, he had married Lou Henry, the only female geology major at Stanford when he was a senior. Their relationship lasted almost fifty years until her death in 1944. She was the only woman in his life except for Quaker "Friend" Daisy Trueblood to whom he had scrawled a love letter when he was thirteen or fourteen.

Lou Henry was an independent and gregarious out-of-doors person whose banker father, having no sons, had raised her as a tomboy. As a result, she matured into a lithe and athletically inclined woman who still retained an "unladylike" enthusiasm when she met Hoover her first semester at Stanford. They soon discovered they had been born in the same year in the same state, and that in many ways their personalities complemented one another — her outgoing social graces compensating for his awkward shyness. In addition, Lou Henry turned out to be an avid antique collector, an accomplished horsewoman, and a patron of the arts and music — all of the cultivated things Hoover was not. Even though she originally came from a Quaker family less than a hundred miles from West Branch, she had experienced neither Hoover's economic and cultural deprivation nor his uprooted childhood. Her family had become Episcopalian following a move to California in 1884. After first attending the State Normal School in Los Angeles for one year (1891) because her mother insisted that it "had the best gymnasium west of the Mississippi," she switched to the one at San Jose, thinking that she would wind up teaching school. Instead, after graduating in 1894, Lou Henry worked in her father's bank. Then, upon hearing Hoover's mentor, Dr. Branner, speak at Pacific Grove in the summer, she decided to attend Stanford and major in geology.

Since this was a most uncommon career for a woman at that time, Lou Henry had a lot of explaining to do when she arrived on the campus. "It isn't so important what others think of you as what you feel inside yourself," she defensively told another female student in her freshman dorm. "I love the out-of-doors and want to know how the world is made and that is what I'll learn in geology." According to her only biographer, Helen B. Pryor, she answered questions about who might marry a woman geologist with the assertion: "I want a man who loves the mountains, the rocks, and the ocean like my father does." Hoover obviously fit this description, and was one of the few men at Stanford who was not put off by her professional interests.

Because she was a superb horseback rider who could "rough it," and because she understood the technical side of her husband's work, Lou often traveled with Hoover after their marriage. When conditions did not permit this, she often helped him by researching problems he encountered in the field. Thus, at least in the beginning of their life together, she was an intellectual as well as an emotional companion to the Great Engineer. Even after their two sons were born — Herbert, Jr., in 1903 and Allan in 1907 — she continued to accompany Hoover on his seemingly endless trips, despite her own longing to settle permanently in California.

They prided themselves on being a modern, progressive

couple, always using the latest means of transportation and labor-saving devices. Lou Henry Hoover planned their numerous trips with the efficiency of an engineer, accounting for everything from the exact amount of prepared baby formulas to getting the family "doggie" through customs. One article in the *Ladies Home Journal* noted a "surgical honesty about everything that the Hoovers [did]," from setting up households all over the world to entertaining guests. In 1900, right after they were married, Lou refused to leave Tientsin during the Boxer Rebellion, staying to organize hospital services for the wounded while Hoover directed food relief. Hoover fondly recalled in his *Memoirs* that she developed a habit of speaking to him privately in Chinese during this first trip abroad together.

Throughout their marriage Lou Hoover continued to develop her own interests, collecting artifacts and attending concerts and the theater. She also urged women to use their newly won right to vote and to choose independent careers even if they were married, once telling a 1926 Girl Scout convention that the woman who used her children as an excuse for not pursuing professional interests was lazy. Although she did not exactly follow her own advice — she never practiced as a geologist — she nonetheless was a national organizer of women and a positive model for them, always insisting that women could and should control their own lives. Under her leadership, for example, Girl Scout membership increased from 100,000 in 1921 to almost one million in 1933; and she encouraged all types of women's organizations and funding campaigns, from the PTA and peace groups to the YWCA.

Although Lou Hoover's feminist activities would be considered moderate by today's standards, they were advanced and innovative for her time. In 1923, as the only female officer of the National Amateur Athletic Association, she organized a women's division for the promotion of new opportunities for women in amateur sports programs, particularly in educational institutions. However, she opposed highly competitive professional athletics for women for physiological reasons and because she believed it would destroy "play for play's sake." In 1924, in the wake of the Teapot Dome scandal, she called a national women's conference on law enforcement, saying in her opening address that it was up to women to "arouse the whole country to an understanding of the dangerous significance of continued evasion of the law" by public figures.

Despite her independence and public activities, it became clear in the course of the 1920s that privately Lou Henry Hoover was no longer the intellectual companion and equal partner to her internationally famous husband that she had once been. Her role as the wife of a successful public figure became increasingly centered around providing "a background for Bertie," wherever they happened to be living. Initially this simply meant surrounding him at mealtimes with people he was interested in, usually business associates. But she continued throughout their marriage to manage Hoover's home life with great precision, and they seldom dined alone except on their anniversary every February 10.

At first she provided this expected domestic function almost perfunctorily, whether it was in Tientsin, Sydney, Kalgoorlie, Melbourne, Mandalay, London, Palo Alto, or finally Washington, D.C. When accompanying Hoover on many of his trips, she also aided him in his work, because of her geological training and her greater ability to master languages. Often she took up complementary relief activities when they lived in areas suffering from natural disasters or war. As her husband's success mounted, however, and they were separated more often, her primary marital role increasingly became one of raising their sons, managing large formal dinners, and dutifully filling in the awkward silences produced by her husband's unsociable nature and inaudible comments.

Their constant entertaining while at the Red House in London before World War I and later in the White House in Washington could have stemmed from Lou Henry Hoover's own social needs. Evidence suggests, however, that Hoover dreaded eating alone, or at least that his wife came to this conclusion and arranged large dinners where he was protected by a subtle yet rigid wall of social decorum in dress and manner. Or possibly Hoover simply thought it was a waste of time not to conduct business, even during meals. Whatever the reason, he steadfastly refused to engage in social chitchat at the table or elsewhere, so his wife perfected the art of allowing her husband to avoid personal participation in social events by increasing the formality of their entertaining, especially after he was elected president in 1928.

Before that, the Hoovers had had little patience with the pretensions of high society, although Lou was certainly better suited to entertaining when it could not be avoided than was Herbert. Their many years abroad had been quite informal; personal friends later recalled in oral interviews that while she did play the role of the socially refined hostess extremely well, Lou was also a "very home-type person . . . extremely easy to be around," and would rather go on a picnic than to a banquet. But the formality of the Hoovers' entertaining increased and became almost compulsively elaborate during the depression years despite widespread public disapproval as unemployment skyrocketed. There were always guests both at lunch and at tea every day, and each evening 15 to 30 people attended seven-course dinners (paid for out of the President's private funds). Lou Henry Hoover organized these White House dinner parties with an almost excessive precision. For example, she used subtle hand signals (perhaps reflecting her interest in dressage horsemanship) to instruct servants at a distance from a seated position, and she demanded the strictest formality from all butlers and footmen, all of whom were exactly the same height and were forbidden to talk in the pantry or to allow the silverware to strike the china when they were removing dishes.

In part, this elaborately engineered entertaining may have been to compensate for the lack of social life during the

Coolidges' stay in the White House, or simply to put up a brave front as the depression worsened. Most likely, however, it was simply Lou Henry Hoover's way of protecting her husband from an increasingly hostile Washington society. Nonetheless, there is something pathetic in the image of President Hoover struggling through endless official dinners saying nothing more than "Good evening" and "Good night," while press releases about him reported that his favorite song was "Hail! Hail! The Gang's All Here!"

Lou's great role in Herbert's social life had been equalled in quality by her participation in his intellectual interests — at least before the First World War. For example, she started translating Chinese mining laws for him in 1899 when he expressed a desire to standardize them and to catalogue the mining laws of the world (one of the few tasks that Hoover never completed). And she translated the difficult *De Re Metallica,* a sixteenth-century manual on mining, metallurgy, and industrial chemistry. Compiled over a twenty-five year period by the Renaissance scholar Georg Bauer, the first Latin edition of 1556 had never been satisfactorily translated into any other language because Georgius Agricola (Bauer's Latinized pseudonym) had coined so many technical terms. After five years of teamwork, which included laboratory tests to determine if their translations of certain words and chemical processes were correct, the Hoovers published the book privately in 1912 complete with reproductions of the original woodcuts. It was the most ambitious of their joint scholarly endeavors. Hoover provided the introduction and elaborate, technical footnotes — some of which inadvertently revealed his emerging political and economic views.

During the years they worked on the translation, the Hoovers collected what Lou called their "pseudo-scientific library" of over 2,500 rare books on ancient mining and related topics. This library remains one of the best private collections of its kind; the bulk of it is currently housed in the Honnold Library at Claremont College, California. In 1909, while they were collaborating on Agricola's *De Re Metallica*, Herbert delivered a series of lectures at Stanford and Columbia, which Lou helped him organize and publish later that same year as the *Principles of Mining*. This became the standard textbook in the field for several generations of engineers.

With his wife and on his own, Hoover consistently tried to broaden his intellectual horizons after he left Stanford. "I am sure I'd have made myself a better all-round man," he once complained to a friend in recalling their college years, "if I hadn't lost so much time just making a living." He read voraciously, especially from 1904 to 1907, and later recalled in an unpublished, undated autobiographical fragment: "[I] undertook a re-education of myself — history, economics, sociology, politics, [and] government. [I] read literally thousands of books giving at least two hours nightly and all spare time on long voyages." His reading was varied, extending so far outside his own field of engineering that in 1932 Christopher Morley would comment, "There can hardly ever have been a President who has read so much and said so little about it." He also broadened his awareness by participating between 1907 and 1912 in several archaeological digs in Egypt and northern Italy. And he found time during his frantic World War I relief activities to start collecting vast quantities of war documents. These papers later laid the foundation for what is now the Hoover Institution on War, Revolution and Peace at Stanford University. He collected foreign documents after World War II as well.

Like Agricola, Hoover seemed to aspire to become a renaissance man, with knowledge in all areas. Most of his friends recalled his "titanic intellect" and his ability to comprehend on sight whole pages of charts and figures. During these years of self-education and self-examination before World War I, Hoover was speculating about wealth and individual purpose much as Agricola had when the sixteenth-century scholar quoted a Greek philosopher: "Now, by the gods, why is it necessary for a man to grow rich? Why does he possess much money unless that he may, as much as possible, help his friends, and sow the seeds of a harvest of gratitude, sweetest of the goddesses?" Accordingly, Hoover discouraged a young American from going abroad to seek his fortune, saying that he himself should have established his fame and wealth in the United States instead of as an alien in foreign countries. "It might have been less imposing," he wrote, "yet one would be among one's own people; and the esteem that one hopes to build among one's associates would not be wasted by leaving it and them behind, only to go home later and then try to build it up again."

Obviously there was something more he wanted out of life — something involving gratitude and esteem from his fellow Americans — something that his financial success as an engineer had not brought him. Periodically between 1907 and 1914 he talked about retiring to the United States to take up some kind of public work, telling close associates that even though he was a rich man, "just making money wasn't enough." In 1907 he intimated to his pacifist friend David Starr Jordan, the first president of Stanford, that "he had run through his profession" for it could offer him only more money. Hoover also talked about going back to America to find executive work in which he could be of service. He was still contemplating "some job of public service . . . in government and all that sort of thing," when he talked to Will Irwin in London in 1912. When Irwin asked him to be more specific, he found Hoover uncharacteristically vague: "I don't know yet what it will be — but something." No doubt the idea of going into public service was slowly surfacing from his Quaker subconscious.

In these years of his greatest success, Hoover faced a crucial decision about his life style. Given his reticent, asocial personality, how could he best use his demonstrable talents and broad knowledge in public service? For a time he contemplated becoming a professor or dean of a mining school, possibly even president of Stanford, in the hope that as an educator he could satisfy the unfulfilled part of himself.

Partial fulfillment first came from an offer to promote the Panama-Pacific Exposition. In April 1912 he became an overseas agent for the exposition, which was an attempt to attract international commerce to the Pacific Coast. The outbreak of World War I in the fall of 1914 ended his work on the project, but Hoover deemed it a successful exercise in public relations. Specifically, his job had been to convince the British government to endorse the exposition. Contrary to the impression conveyed in his *Memoirs,* Hoover did *not* succeed in obtaining a reversal of the joint decision by England and Germany not to participate. He had, however, organized a publicity campaign with the aid of English journalist William A. M. Goode that finally convinced a majority of the members of the House of Commons to petition the government to change its mind on the eve of the war. He had also demonstrated his ability to negotiate privately with high European officials without attracting public attention to himself or experiencing any encroachments upon his well-guarded privacy.

This work for the Panama-Pacific Exposition represented the first time that Hoover had engaged in the kind of "behind-the-scenes" public relations activity that suited his personality as well as his talents. It also satisfied his vague but growing desire to educate the public and serve his country. In a conversation with former prime minister Arthur Balfour he rationalized his promotional work, saying that British participation would indirectly cement relations between the two countries and end the "sacred policy of political isolation" espoused by most Americans. His tendency to exaggerate his actual accomplishments, made evident in his engineering career, remained a part of Hoover's personality — it is highly unlikely that any commercial endeavor like the exposition could have significantly altered American attitudes on foreign policy.

In any event, Hoover was so impressed by the two-year experience of working for the Panama-Pacific Exposition that he negotiated the purchase of some newspapers in the United States. (He purchased the *Sacramento Union* and bought an interest in the *Washington Herald,* but sold both in 1921.) This was the best means of influencing American public opinion, and possibly government policy, without directly exposing himself, and it also held some promise of earning esteem among his fellow Americans. Hoover's reticent nature, his obvious ambition to go beyond his career as an engineer, and his personal dissatisfaction as an alien abroad, were leading gradually to the influential role he was to play at home, as an effective, unobtrusive, public relations–oriented administrator.

Public-relations techniques protected his person from public scrutiny, but did not compensate for his inability to write or speak in a commanding and persuasive manner. One kindly review of his textbook *Principles in Mining* noted that "the book would have gained from closer editing and rearrangement of involved sentences." The same criticism could be levied against almost all his writings, although in the 1950s they were more carefully edited than this first book. The same involved, almost pretentious style can be found in most of the longer personal letters he wrote throughout his private and public careers. Even his most sincere pronouncements, especially those made during the Great Depression, sounded stilted and unconvincing. Yet throughout his long public career he stubbornly resisted using ghost writers for his correspondence, interpretive writings, and major public addresses — preferring to subject his audiences and readers to his own unclear statements, reflected in many of his phrases quoted in this book.

For all his awkward phrasings and constructions, Hoover wrote and spoke carefully. He personally and painstakingly edited his speeches and published works, trying to say as precisely as possible what he meant in his effort to educate the American people. "He'd use involved grammar sometimes," his niece Hulda Hoover McLean has said, "but exactly the word he wanted whether it was a word that anybody else understood or not." Unfortunately Hoover often used clichés and common terms like "American individualism" and "American system," which his contemporaries and later generations chose to define as they pleased. He failed, consequently, to successfully propagate the ideas he had formulated so carefully.

One such idea was his belief that only through consciously cultivated cooperative individualism could the United States succeed in the twentieth century as a modern, technological nation and still preserve some of its best nineteenth-century, rural values. For Hoover, a successful American system would demand of its citizens extraordinary energy, self-discipline, moderation, ruthless righteousness, and social responsibility — all the characteristics that had made the Quaker communities of his youth successful. The potential conflict of his two dominant drives as an adult is clear: to achieve concrete, statistically verifiable results through hard work, while remaining within the parameters of a personal philosophy based on moderation in all things and on the old Quaker Query exhorting the Friends "to create a social and economic system which will function to sustain and enrich life for all."

It was to prove most difficult for a man with Hoover's diffident personality and writing deficiencies to explain clearly the subtle difference between the uncontrolled, individual acquisitiveness and open-ended national expansion so characteristic of nineteenth-century America and his dream of a humane, voluntarily controlled capitalistic system based on cooperatively sharing the abundance produced by technology. Hoover was beginning to sense what most Americans have never wanted to face: that in the twentieth century the United States had to reach a compromise between individual advantage and public right, the essence of which, he insisted, was "justice, self-restraint [and], obligation to fellowmen." Men with greater personal charisma, philosophical training and oratorical skills had failed before, and have since, to reconcile the contradictory aspects of individualism with collectivism in their theories about political economies.

Hoover's persistent and futile attempts to make the American people understand the most crucial, dialectical socioeconomic problem of modern times approached heroic proportions. In the process he never deviated from what he thought was the best progressive solution based on the unalterable laws of science and morality. He consistently held that cooperative individualism and a voluntary, decentralized version of corporatism were absolutely essential to public and private survival in the twentieth century, characterized as it was by economically interdependent, yet ideologically hostile nations, and technologial, urban centralization.

Because of his difficulty in expressing himself even on simple matters, Hoover developed a "memo mania" to communicate more efficiently with his subordinates. It was also, of course, perfectly in keeping with his lack of affability and aversion to personal, verbal communication. But he could not communicate with the American people through memoranda, and, try as he might, Hoover never developed into an effective speaker. Perhaps the most succinct description of Hoover's inadequacies as a public personality is by Henry Pringle, historian and journalist, who said that although Hoover did well before small groups, he was "lamentably bad" in front of large audiences because "inhibitions seem to rise in his throat and to choke his vocal cords." Furthermore, according to Pringle: "One hand is kept in his pocket, usually jingling [coins or keys] placed there to ease his nerves. He has not a single gesture. . . . He reads — his chin down against his shirt front — rapidly and quite without expression. . . . He can utter a striking phrase in so prosaic, so uninspired and so mumbling a fashion that it is completely lost on nine out of ten of his auditors." During personal interviews Pringle noted that Hoover's "answers are given in a rapid, terse manner and when he is finished he simply stops. Other men would look up, smile, or round out a phrase. Hoover is like a machine that has run down. Another question starts him off again. He stares at his shoes, or at the desk in front of him, as he speaks, and because he looks down so much of the time, the casual guest obtains only a hazy impression of his appearance."

This characterization confirms that Hoover's personality and his political and social liabilities did not change much after his Stanford days. Nor did they after he left the presidency in 1933, although he became ever so slightly more affable after leaving public office. His young, round "bull-terrier" cheeks sagged into "mastiff-like" jowls as he grew older and stouter, and he took to wearing heavily framed glasses which invariably slipped down on his short nose. Otherwise he was much the same. He continued to work incessantly, and to be ill at ease in the company of all but a few close friends, always looking down, jingling coins or keys in his pocket. He still paced back and forth in front of interviewers; if sitting down he doodled a circular, geometric design resembling a spider's web, or absentmindedly massaged his right knee as though it were sore. At least until World War II, he continued to wear the standard outfit of a bygone era, a conservative dark blue or brown double-breasted suit with high black shoes and a stiff white collar. His friends later recalled that he often wore these veritable "neck vices" when engaging in his favorite relaxation — fly fishing. Throughout his life, Hoover also enjoyed "clean" jokes, cigars (later in life he switched to a pipe), martinis, any dish made of corn, driving fast, and reading mystery stories before going to bed.

Although by 1914 Hoover appeared to have left behind the effects of his Quaker heritage and orphaned background through education, material success and professional acclaim, he had not succeeded in becoming an urbane, personable man of the world. Instead he had developed into a very private, highly principled individual who, despite his international business interests, idealized rural values and demanded as much of others as he did of himself — all in the name of a

unique brand of American individualism which most never
came to understand, let alone practice. Moreover, this taciturn, asocial engineer coveted the public esteem and gratitude
that he was incapable of courting. Thus, Hoover began to try
to find or devise a type of public service that would suit his
own personality. Like his engineering achievements, his public
successes were to be neither entirely fortuitous nor totally
altruistic, and his approach would be characteristically intellectual rather than emotional. On the eve of World War I,
however, not only did he lack the personality with which to
capture the public's imagination, but also he had neither the
experience nor the complete economic, political, and ideological data necessary to articulate his "American system." The
war would soon clarify his Quaker-bred theories on cooperation and voluntary community activities, and his still largely
unformulated views on a new conception of the modern
corporate state — one in which centralized decisions would be
executed in a decentralized fashion.

Fortunately for the personal dilemma in which Hoover
found himself in 1914, he had already discovered the effectiveness of carefully orchestrated publicity techniques during his
short-lived experiences with the Panama-Pacific Exposition.
Also, he would return to the United States after a long
absence to find that many of his half-thought-out socioeconomic ideas were already being refined and acted upon by
certain wings within both his own profession and the progressive movement. These developments, along with his varied experiences during World War I, would ultimately complete his professional education and add the ideological
ingredients still lacking in his intellectual make-up. The war
provided Hoover with his first opportunities to apply his
engineering training in philosophical and public-service endeavors. Some of these experiences would take him further
from his Quaker origins; others reinforced them. But he would
never free himself totally from his rural, West Branch heritage.

The Engineer
as Progressive

". . . he has lifted engineering to its highest level."

HERBERT HOOVER became an engineer in the "golden age" of American foreign mining exploits, a period between 1890 and World War I. Paradoxically, this highly speculative and competitive career ultimately reinforced his childhood exposure to the progressive Quaker philosophy of cooperative individualism.

Hoover did not owe his phenomenal success as an engineer to an uncanny "sixth sense" about ore deposits, as his apologists have maintained. A trained geologist, he was highly skilled in the analysis of drifts, lodes, and veins. He was an able administrator and coordinator, with a knack for introducing technological innovations. He also had considerable luck. When he left the firm of Bewick Moreing in 1908, Hoover's reputation in engineering was so great that the remaining partners made him sign an agreement stating that he "would not act as general manager of any mine within the limits of the British Empire for a period of ten years." Hoover further agreed to select Bewick Moreing as managers of any mines he might finance. Two years later C. Algernon Moreing sued Hoover for breach of this agreement, but later withdrew his suit; Hoover reportedly had made a cash settlement of the damages claimed.

A demanding taskmaster, Hoover drove himself as hard as he drove his men and machinery. He literally destroyed a typewriter through excessive use while on his first assignment in Coolgardie, Australia, and he left the machinery at the Sons of Gwalia works in a nearly exhausted condition through lack of repair. These were overly energetic, youthful applications of a principle he later stated more moderately in his textbook on mining engineering: Money saved on replacing crude labor "is not so great but that it quickly disappears if the machine is run under its capacity."

Partially as a result of such extreme tactics, Hoover had his fair share of labor problems. During his first job as manager at the Sons of Gwalia gold mine, he dealt summarily with workers who opposed his demand for labor-saving devices and efficiency techniques. He sometimes dismissed entire Australian crews and held imported Italian laborers in reserve "to hold the property in case of a general strike." While Hoover talked publicly about the "saucy independence and loafing proclivities of many of the Australian miners," his strongest criticism over the years was directed at Asian and African workers. On June 19, 1902, in a paper about a Chinese operation read before the Institution of Mining and Metallurgy in London, Hoover described the "mulishness of the native miner . . . his capacity for thieving," and emphasized his "phenomenal capacity at bribery." He callously added: "The disregard for human life permits cheap mining by economy in timber, and the aggrieved relatives are simply compensated by the regular payment of $30 per man lost."

Although such attitudes were common in Hoover's early professional career, he did not always respond harshly to the laborer's situation. Nor was he guided as Secretary of Commerce years later by the assessments he had made as an impatient, ambitious young engineer. Instead, Hoover's general practice after 1900, as most of his articles on mining show, was to raise the wages and improve the living conditions of his workers. He did so for very practical reasons: It was a good way to attract labor to unattractive locations, and satisfied workers were more efficient as well. As Secretary of Commerce, he would add another reason for his support of high wages: They increased the purchasing power of workers.

But because of efficiency statistics he compiled, combined with an average amount of contemporary racism, throughout his engineering career Hoover held nonwhite foreign workers in lower esteem than their white American counterparts. He considered practically everything American to be better. His associates in Australia were not entirely joking when they took his first two initials and began to refer to him as "Hail Columbia" Hoover — a nickname inspired by his chauvinistic faith in the superior quality of American technology and American workers. He especially downgraded the technical skill of the Australian mining industry, when in fact it was probably more advanced than that of the United States at the turn of the century. Hoover never acknowledged this fact, and during his fifteen years as an international engineer, he insisted on Americanizing the mining industry wherever he went. Probably the most positive aspect of this indiscriminate chauvinism was Hoover's resulting progressive position on the rights of American workers by the time he finally returned to the United States to take up a public service career.

In the first two decades of the twentieth century Hoover asserted that efficiency, based on the coordination of work by "human units," was the key to handling labor profitably; unemployment and unrest were technical problems that could be solved through engineering principles. Both these ideas were taken up independently by the progressive wing of the American engineering profession before 1914. In his 1909 textbook on mining, Hoover also endorsed compulsory arbitration, and stated that nonviolent labor organizations were "entitled to greater recognition [because they] are normal and proper antidotes for unlimited capitalistic organization

. . . [and because] the time when the employer could ride roughshod over his labor is disappearing with the doctrine of 'laissez faire' on which it was founded." As a student at Stanford he had disapproved of the coercive methods used by the United States government in the Pullman workers and American Railway Union Strike of 1894; by 1920 he was a public advocate of collective bargaining. By insisting that "the real controlling factor in wages is efficiency," rather than viewing wages as the result of supply and demand, Hoover had clearly allied himself with those in the Progressive movement who favored scientific management techniques.

The best scientific manager of business, according to Hoover, was the engineer, who stood as a buffer between labor and capital. Only the engineer, he declared in 1920 to a national engineering conference, could insure "the human right to consolidate the worker in the proper balanced position . . . against the consolidation of capital" in order to avoid economic disruption and achieve social justice. Although he agreed that labor and management had many common concerns, he could not completely endorse the "welfare capitalism" of the large corporations, as it would eliminate the nominal countervailing force he had in mind for loosely organized unions. He wanted the demands of labor to be backed by the force of public opinion and the voluntary cooperation of individual workers, rather than by highly disciplined strike action under union leadership. His views on labor, unions, and collective bargaining never advanced further, however, because he shared with most American Progressives a stronger suspicion of big labor organizations than of big business.

By 1920, Hoover's pragmatic, progressive position on American labor was consistent with his other socioeconomic views — largely because of changes within the engineering profession. Hoover had become a mining engineer in 1896, on the eve of unprecedented American exploitation of foreign mineral wealth. His profession was in a crucial period of growing pains and self-evaluation. Between 1890 and 1930 the proportion of engineers in the United States increased dramatically — over 400 percent. From 7,000 engineers in 1880, the figures rose to 43,000 at the turn of the century; 136,000 by 1920; 226,000 by 1930. It was the most rapidly growing American profession when Hoover embarked upon his engineering career, and the one which offered the greatest opportunity for upward mobility. In fact, prior to World War II, vertical rise in socioeconomic status was the major distinguishing characteristic of the successful professional engineer.

This created in turn an anomalous situation. An engineer's success now was measured in large part by the extent to which he ceased to be an engineer. The truly prominent engineers almost invariably ended up as corporation executives. Out of 284 top businessmen in 1900, 12.5 percent were originally engineers; out of 319 in 1925, 15.6 percent; and out of 868 in 1950, 19.5 percent. A young engineer was expected, therefore, to start at the bottom of his profession, but success was determined by how quickly he moved into other enterprises. On an accelerated scale, Hoover's career was a perfect example of the life cycle of the twentieth-century engineer before 1950.

Hoover's background was also typical of the majority of engineers. The sons of skilled workers, farmers, and small businessmen, they tended to be the poorer and less literate groups within the lower-middle-class stratum of American society. Young engineers like Hoover drove themselves mercilessly to overcome their backgrounds and to meet the standard of success tacitly set by their professional elders. On any achievement scale, however, few compared to the silent Quaker from West Branch. And few were as committed as he to hard work, personal initiative, self-reliance, thrift — all characteristics that made his early engineering career a symbol of nineteenth-century rugged individualism and which, in an earlier age, would have produced a master craftsman of a guild.

The rapid expansion and upward mobility of the engineering profession after 1900 posed many unanswered questions for both the country and the men involved. While promoting technological development in the name of progress, young engineers began to sense that the modern America they were helping to create threatened the very mores and values — particularly those associated with competitive individualism — that were the guiding principles of their lives and careers. Caught up in the search for a new organizational order to meet the demands of rapid industrialization, many engineers thought they had found the answer in the concept of social responsibility.

Just as Hoover approached the pinnacle of his career, a movement began within the four major engineering societies (the Founder Societies), urging that the profession assume a collectively responsible role. Their aim was to employ technology in a manner both humane and efficient to improve economic conditions for Americans while generally enhancing the social status and power of engineers in particular. This appeal to his social conscience had little effect on the young man just starting out in the profession. Until he had achieved some prominence, the average engineer did not pause to think about social responsibility. So it was the relatively young but established engineers within the Founder Societies who assumed the profession's burden of social responsibility between 1908 and 1916 — men like Hoover and Morris L. Cooke, his well-known progressive colleague.

For Hoover and Cooke and the progressive minority of engineers like them there was, in this instance, a fortunate convergence between their altruism, their sense of social responsibility and their self-interest. In Hoover's case, the progressive activism he supported while an engineer became an integral part of his later philosophy of cooperative individualism. He insisted that engineers could justify greater prestige for themselves only if they accepted collective responsibility for the well-being of the public in their attempt to organize a more efficient society. And he believed that their professional training in impartial logic uniquely qualified engineers for this responsibility; they occupied a "position of disinterested service," and "want[ed] nothing . . . from Congress [except] . . . efficiency in government." Their objectivity and selflessness were seen as fundamental to the task of moving America forward toward efficiency and justice. Hoover characterized the engineer in his *Memoirs* as "an economic and social force. Every time he discovers a new application of science, thereby creating a new industry, providing new jobs, adding to the standards of living, he also disturbs everything that is. . . . He is also the person who really corrects monopolies and redistributes national wealth."

But not even the small group of progressive engineers who agreed with Hoover were united before the war on the best way to pursue social responsibility collectively. Differences between the two types of progressive engineers and reformers — the scientific urbanites and the rural moralists — fostered confusion and uncertainty. In practice, most engineers and reformers represented blends of both approaches. This was surely true of Herbert Hoover on the eve of World War I.

It was important that both these basic types of prewar American Progressives ultimately reflected the unspoken desire of a new middle class of Americans (like the engineers) to achieve material satisfaction without losing a sense of spiritual and individual worth. In their attempt to achieve peace of mind and to maintain their newfound status and wealth, they urged a new socioeconomic order based largely on bureaucratic, organizational techniques. Their search for a new order was subconscious at best; they could not know that the United States, like all industrialized nations at the turn of the century, was caught up in the need for greater rationalization of its political economy.

In the last quarter of the nineteenth century, government officials, businessmen, and reformers searched agonizingly for a new system of human values and for more efficient organizational and industrial techniques. In the United States, what followed can only be called a vague corporatist philosophy.

Early in the twentieth century an amorphous set of reformist ideas evolved in response to the growing fears of American leaders about "destructive competition" and "social anarchy." This emerging corporatism was thought to be a viable political and economic compromise between state socialism and monopoly capitalism and, before and after World War I, was advocated by the progressive scientists and moralists alike.

Ideally, corporatist ideology projects a view of society as organized into functionally independent economic units including labor, agriculture, and management, that are supposed to remain voluntarily decentralized and simultaneously self-governing and self-regulating. In theory, these industry-wide units work efficiently together in the public interest through a sense of community and social responsibility. A blend of democratic liberalism and capitalism, this ideal of corporatism was proffered by men like Herbert Hoover as an ideological and economic means of preserving individual initiative while taking advantage of the latest technological advances. Hoover wanted it to become the cornerstone of New Era economics in the 1920s.

Progressive reformers seeking a corporatist economic order could take two courses — confusingly represented in the 1912 election by the "New Freedom" of Woodrow Wilson and the "New Nationalism" of Theodore Roosevelt. One stressed completely cooperative economic organization and regulation along neoguildist and voluntary associational lines. The other advocated federally directed and enforced organization along rigidly bureaucratic and statist lines. The American corporatism that first grew out of these different approaches was an ambiguous and often contradictory structure of federal regulatory agencies and antitrust procedures, purporting to preserve liberal democratic concepts about private property, individualism, voluntary effort, and local control. Concurrently, there was a significant increase in monopolistic or oligarchic economic practices; large-scale national economic organizations at all levels of society often dominated and utilized the federal regulatory apparatus in their own interests.

Hoover's principle of associational, decentralized corporatism, which involved an informal cooperation and delicate balance between private and public segments of the political economy, was thus significantly undermined in the course of the 1920s as the distinctions between and responsibilities of the private and public sectors became increasingly blurred. This neoguildist brand of corporatism was repudiated and finally abandoned in the panic of the Great Depression for an equally ambiguous, pluralist brand of liberal welfare statism. Neither version has yet established an economic and political order compatible with the proclaimed humanitarian, democratic and rural ideals of the nineteenth century.

One group of American engineers caught up in the Progressives' subconscious search for a new corporatist order was influenced by the scientific management ideas of Frederick Winslow Taylor. An engineer who specialized in developing industrial efficiency techniques applicable to all social activities and institutions, Taylor particularly emphasized analysis of statistical data and cause-and-effect relationships. On the theoretical level, Hoover agreed with Taylor that employer and employee had mutual interests that were rapidly being eroded by monopoly growth, and that could be restored only by a structural revolution led by scientifically oriented engineers. This social-control progressivism was statist in orientation. Its advocates were dedicated to reorganizing and coordinating governmental and economic functions through federal centralization, simplification, and statistical research.

Such a change would require a basic value change in American society, and the restructuring of capitalism. This in turn would require the formulation of a comprehensive, modern ideology for America. Hoover was one of the few social-control Progressives who understood the magnitude of the task and the dangers inherent in such an increase in national

power. Most efficiency engineers simply favored the development of some kind of technocracy, and therefore tended to
oppose those conservative elements of American society found
in the top echelon of business executives, who were suspicious
of national planning. Such engineers found a welcome among
the scientific-management Progressives who shared their conviction that people were often victimized by social and economic forces beyond their control. Both believed that society
could be turned into "an efficiently functioning unit."

A second group of engineers approached social responsibility from a moralistic point of view. They also believed in
progress through technology, but wanted to make sure that
free enterprise, individual initiative, and equality of opportunity survived in any reorganized society of the future.
Placing greater stress on *a priori* ethical judgments about
individualism and success through hard work, they also tried
to remain in the center of the political spectrum. In practice,
however, they usually defended traditional American capitalism against attacks from the left, especially from organized
labor. While believing that moral and technological progress
were "written into the laws of the universe," they did not
want to sacrifice the idealized view of an American way of life
that was based on the agrarian liberalism of Jefferson.

In times of crisis like war or depression, therefore, these
morally oriented engineers usually defended the status quo
and so were often viewed as rural reactionaries, especially by
later generations of New Deal urban reformers. They advocated only minor legislative modifications of economic and
political institutions, recognizing the engineers' special ability
to make society function more smoothly. Moral right would
prevail, they believed, because success depended on the individual's will and skill, regardless of societal problems. This
group of engineers could identify with the business-oriented
Progressives in the prewar reform movement (who initially
advocated guildist corporatism as opposed to statism) and
with the various social reformers who were simplistically try-

ing to impose nineteenth-century rural morality on twentieth-century urban sinners.

Both schools were implicitly elitist and scientifically oriented. Committed to individualistic values, both believed in absolute laws of either scientific or moral progress which were "immutable but knowable," and in the education of the public. Most important, while both saw the need for greater rationalization of the political economy, they ostensibly opposed any form of coercive collectivism — the urban Taylorites because it was inherently inefficient, and the rural moralists because it was evil. So although subtle shifts in emphasis placed an engineer in one camp or the other, all were corporatists. The degree to which an individual believed in a centralized or decentralized political economy could change periodically throughout his career, however. Such was the case with Hoover.

When he returned to the United States in 1919 to take up permanent residence for the first time in thirteen years, the Chief had for some time been well within the progressive wing of his profession, and was welcomed by remnants of the domestic Progressive movement. Warning against both the reactionary and radical tendencies which surfaced during the Red Scare of 1919–1920, Hoover said the nation had more to fear from the right than from the left. "Radicalism is blatant and displays itself in the open," he said, while "reaction too often fools the people through subtle channels of obstruction and progressive platitudes." Nonetheless, the Bolshevik Revolution of 1917 turned Herbert Hoover into an avowed ideologue, although he did not consider communism a threat in America. Communism thrived, he wrote to President Wilson in March 1919, "where the gulf between the middle classes and lower classes is large, and where the lower classes have been kept in ignorance and distress."

In the postwar hysteria that followed the Red Scare of 1919, therefore, Hoover protested against government violations of civil liberties. He saw the Red Scare as the outgrowth of an

economic problem caused by postwar unemployment, inequitable distribution of corporate profits, and low production due
to wasteful industrial methods. Bolshevism is not to blame for
American unrest, he claimed; "we shall never remedy justifi-
able discontent until we eradicate the misery which ruthless
individualism has imposed upon a minority." He admonished
Attorney General A. Mitchell Palmer that his "policemen
could not overtake an economic force allowed to run riot in
the country."

Not only did Hoover oppose repression of the civil liberties
of striking workers and political radicals after he returned to
the United States in 1919, he also took a stand in favor of
collective bargaining and peaceful picketing. Furthermore, he
wanted industrial profits more equitably distributed. He had
become convinced in his years abroad that economic inequity
fed the fires of domestic discontent and could lead to the
greatest conflagration of all — socialism.

The immediate postwar problem facing the nation, according to Hoover, was not foreign ideology but low production,
brought on by wasteful industrial methods. This industrial
inefficiency could not be solved by the unorganized actions of
individual businessmen, but required "national guidance and
a national plan for its solution," as did such problems as rail
and water transportation, irrigation and conservation, fuel
and electric-power development. This would require the cooperation of all the interests involved, not more legislation or
more bureaucratic red tape. Labor and management had to
appreciate their mutual economic self-interest; no national
plan, however scientific, could maximize production and efficiency if there were irrevocable antagonisms between classes.

It came as no surprise, therefore, when as head of the newly
created American Engineering Council Hoover called for
the "abandonment of the unrestricted capitalism of Adam
Smith . . . , for a new economic system based neither on the
capitalism of Adam Smith nor upon the socialism of Karl
Marx," but on the cooperation of all economic groups. Hoover

was so convinced that postwar economic conditions had de-
parted from the notions of the classical economists that he
later insisted in *American Individualism* and *The Challenge
to Liberty* that laissez faire had been "dead in America for
generations," except in the recalcitrant hearts of "some reactionary souls." It had died, he claimed, when "we adopted
the ideal of equality of opportunity." Between 1919 and 1920
Hoover repeatedly struck out in public addresses against
"vicious speculators" and the unrestricted accumulation of
wealth, and supported the existing inheritance, income, and
excess profit taxes in order to control corporations. Social-
control progressives like Hoover were not in basic conflict with
capitalist concepts of private property, but their emphasis was
on cooperative capitalism — on use rather than ownership, on
maximum production rather than maximum profit. This was
the ideal of associational or guildist corporatism — to make
capitalism more equitable and efficient — just as some medieval
guilds were based on mutual aid and craftsmanship.

Both Hoover's scientific orientation and his economic attitudes were undisputedly liberal by 1920 progressive standards
in the United States. He was the "engineering profession
personified," exclaimed progressive engineer M. L. Cooke in
January 1917. Yet Hoover also appealed to the more conservative engineers, because of his elitist professionalism and his
respect for the values of nineteenth-century rural American
communities: classlessness, initiative, frontier neighborliness,
hard work, voluntary cooperation, honesty, and self-discipline.
It was this uniquely personal and pragmatic blend of liberal
and conservative progressive characteristics that appealed so to
different segments of Hoover's profession. By the end of the
war, his progressive philosophy had earned him respect outside
his circle of colleagues as well; lay admirers began to believe,
as Will Irwin asserted in a 1928 campaign biography, that he
had "lifted engineering to its highest level."

But it was not until Hoover's World War I relief work
received international acclaim that nonengineering Progres-

sives at home began to pay much attention to him. And it was only after he returned from his long absence from the United States to serve as the federal Food Administrator that he paid much attention to the highly developed, if fragmented, progressive movement which had emerged in the United States since 1900. This coincidence was to be of inestimable value in laying the foundations for his political popularity after the war.

Despite his previously acknowledged personal desire for a public service career, the Great Engineer's public debut was a lucky accident. When the war broke out in 1914, Hoover happened to be in England promoting the Panama-Pacific Exposition for a group of San Francisco businessmen. As a well-known American in London and as a personal friend of Robert F. Skinner, the United States consul-general there, Hoover was asked to aid about a thousand stranded American tourists. Because English banks were temporarily closed by the war, these travelers could not exchange their letters of credit, travelers checks, or American money for British currency. Quietly and methodically Hoover set up an exchange service, drawing on the cash reserves of his London office. He even loaned money directly to some Americans who had none to exchange. As thousands of frightened American tourists streamed into London from Europe, Lou Hoover stepped in and arranged hotel accommodations, food, and clothing for them until ship reservations could be arranged by her husband's volunteer staff. In six weeks the American Relief Committee, under Hoover's direction, handled over $1.5 million in exchange transactions and loans for approximately 120,000 Americans in England and Europe. Defaults from the entire effort came to a nominal three hundred dollars, and the efficiency of Hoover's self-effacing efforts prompted United States Ambassador Walter Hines Page to write to President Wilson: "Life is worth more, too, knowing Hoover. . . . He's a simple, modest, energetic man who began his career in California and will end it in Heaven."

While engaged in this first relief project of the war, Hoover learned that the British government would not allow shipments of food for famine relief to German-occupied Brussels. He talked to Ambassador Page and Foreign Minister Edward Grey about the blockade and was asked to direct a private operation to ease the impending starvation, with the unofficial endorsement of the American government.

Hoover deliberated only a day. He had worked out the logistics of feeding hungry people hundreds of times in the past — at every isolated mining camp he had headed and at Tientsin during the Boxer Rebellion. But the unprecedented scale of the proposed task would test all his organizational talents. Raising enormous amounts of money and buying food were the least of the problems facing a relief operation. Enemy lines would have to be crossed to negotiate safe passage, and the food, once delivered, would have to be kept out of German hands. This was a tempting challenge, and the successful, retiring "Californian in London," as Hoover referred to himself, did aspire to the gratitude and esteem of his fellow Americans.

According to one historian, Hoover imagined himself acting as a "hidden catalyst 'stimulating others to action,'" by his sacrifice of the opportunity to make a fortune as a wartime engineer. There is some evidence, however, that his decision was not so completely altruistic. In an undated autobiographical fragment Hoover wrote: "Altogether by June 1st, 1914, I was in a position apparently to [amass] a fortune of some $30,000,000 at least and perhaps more . . .," had he sold out then. Insisting that war taxes "crushed this fortune down by 95 percent . . . [to] under $1,000,000," he nonetheless thought it sufficient "not only to live upon but to further diminish by the necessities of charity."

In contrast to a 1932 *Fortune* magazine account, which estimated his wealth to exceed $4,000,000 in 1914, Hoover privately explained that he had "invested every penny I could save or earn and borrow [in the Burma Mines] until I owned

18 percent . . . but the earning stage was not entered until just as the war broke out . . . [then] war taxes piled up. . . ." This personal, handwritten account of his financial situation clearly suggests that the war had destroyed 92.5 percent of the worth of this single investment, and he concluded: "I was glad to sell my interest to a group who were willing to speculate on a short war and a reduction of taxes. . . ." His decision to head the relief effort, then, seems not entirely unrelated to financial considerations based on the uncertain and inflationary wartime condition of the mineral and metal market. Whether or not he suffered financially from his decision to undertake wartime relief work, Hoover did genuinely want to begin public service. And this was his opportunity.

He quickly delegated his professional obligations to his associates and gathered a group of American engineering, business, and newspaper friends to create the Commission for the Relief of Belgium (CRB) on October 20, 1914. When the war ended four years later, the CRB had transported five million tons of food and had spent $1 billion in loans and private donations, of which less than .5 percent was overhead. The postwar American Relief Administration (ARA), which Hoover also headed, distributed nineteen million tons of food, clothing, and other supplies, valued at $3.5 billion. In his *Memoirs* Hoover estimated that all of the food relief organizations he directed during and after the war shipped 33,841,307 tons of American food and supplies abroad, valued at $5.234 billion, not including the coordination of European supplies.

The lives saved and suffering alleviated through these complex relief operations were inestimable. Hoover had cajoled, bullied, and bluffed his way through another successful venture, and had squarely faced both allied and enemy resistance to relief. Interestingly, he never referred privately or publicly to the human suffering of any of the war victims. They all became statistics — by the same impersonal, scientific engineering approach and temperament that was to shock and dismay his fellow Americans during the Great Depression and erode his political credibility with them. As one friendly biographer sadly summed it up: "Herbert Hoover can do things more intensely personal with a more helpless and hopeless impersonality than almost anybody else."

Impersonal as it was, his war relief effort temporarily transformed Hoover's public image from that of the Great Engineer into that of the Great Humanitarian; nearly four million signatures appeared on the letters and scrolls he received from grateful Europeans. And a new verb appeared in the Finnish language, "to hoover," meaning to be kind, to help. Characteristically, Hoover refused to accept any decorations ("buttons," as he called them) or public honors for his CRB or ARA work. Part of this self-effacement stemmed from his diffident personal style; part from the unfamiliarity of such public adulation. Mostly, however, it reflected Hoover's uncertain transition from the private successful professional to the public servant hero. Not even his closest friends anticipated the phenomenal rate of this impressive transition from the Great Engineer to the Great Humanitarian during the war years.

Although adjusting to his new role took time, Hoover undoubtedly would have become prominent as a public figure even without the opportunities presented by the war. His energy, ambition, and organizational talents had been frustrated by the limitations of the engineering profession since at least 1907, when he had first confided his dissatisfaction to his friend David Starr Jordan. As well as accelerating his public career, the war hastened the formulation of Hoover's economic, political, and foreign policy views — his "American system." Convinced that the United States needed a new philosophical synthesis of traditional rural values and applied urban technology, Hoover must have been pleasantly surprised when, in 1917, he returned to the country as Wilson's Food Administrator and found that a number of Progressives had been moving toward the same position.

American progressivism before World War I encompassed almost every imaginable kind of social reformer, and all but the avowed Socialists or Communists were well within the scientific or moral bounds of corporatism. Moralists and scientists of every type struggled with the psychological and physical problems created by modern industrialization. A diverse and unlikely affinity group emerged — rural reactionaries, liberal urbanites, radical farmers, enlightened businessmen, church groups, professional people (doctors, economists, historians, and engineers), middle-class women, technocrats, prohibitionists, pacifists, suffragists, and even die-hard Social Darwinists.

Most of the problems Progressives foresaw are now commonplace in technological societies. Some groups, for example, were concerned with the social and industrial inefficiency that depleted human, as well as mineral, resources. Some deplored the political corruption that was particularly rampant in American cities at the turn of the century, or the increased concentration of economic power, or uncontrolled bureaucratic growth at all levels of government and industry. Some noted excessive individual selfishness, the absence of social responsibility and community pride, and the anonymity of large cities with its attendant social and economic unrest. Finally, the socioeconomic and cultural deprivation of most rural areas was obvious. How could all these problems be resolved and reconciled? How could America maintain the traditional values without inhibiting technological progress? What synthesis would set things right again, preventing both authoritarianism and anarchy? The country wanted sensible, practicable solutions; alternatives to the communism and socialism offered in other parts of the world.

It was the very absence of ideological and behavioral unity among prewar Progressives that attracted so many mainstream Americans to the movement. This same diversity, of course, has prompted a number of historians to characterize the reforms that grew out of the Progressive movement as ineffectual, naive, basically conservative, and, in some instances, actually reactionary. For example, some "progressive" reform did indeed include the legislation of morality through prohibition, immigration restriction, and imposed "Americanization" of aliens. Yet other Progressives advocated liberal social justice activities — settlement houses, urban housing projects, child labor laws, improved factory conditions, elimination of municipal political corruption, antitrust legislation, and other federal regulatory laws and agencies.

Underlying this melange of reform activity, increasingly serious cultural and class antagonisms were developing between urban and rural elements of American society. Moving to a city or gaining increased access to urban areas did not transform an individual into an urbanite, as Hoover himself demonstrated perfectly. Yet city-dwellers were not immune to fundamental racist and prohibitionist arguments. Compounding this basic cultural conflict was the uneven development of consumerism, which first arose in the early twentieth century and was an accepted economic variable by the 1920s. Urban, middle-class citizens began to associate status with buying power rather than with production capacity long before the urban or rural poor did.

But for a brief, idyllic period before World War I, the search for a new order assumed national, although often contradictory proportions. The byword was efficiency. All reformers, whether motivated by self-interest or altruism, by science or morality, by urban or rural prejudices, could respond to the call to eliminate waste and restore social order through efficient organization. So while Hoover was eliminating wasteful production methods through technological innovations and closely supervised work routines, many domestic Progressives were also captivated by the efficiency approach to reform. There was a new emphasis on research, on professional expertise, on simplification of processes and procedures, and above all on order. In practice, though, social-control Progressives often unwittingly employed progressive means that

subverted progressive ends. The demand for order seemed
all too often to encourage physically improved but depersonalized working and living conditions, and to be incompatible
with trust-busting and participatory democracy.

While many well-meaning municipal reformers hoped to
restore a sense of community and political power to increasingly isolated urban dwellers, their reforms often resulted in
government by an elite group of professional urban planners
and self-perpetuating, nonelective bureaucrats. Compassion
and community were often the victims of efficient city management. Likewise, at the national level, the incentive toward
greater rationalization of the political economy often left
monopolistic practices and the profit motive untouched. Sometimes this happened because businessmen, with little commitment to social responsibility, ended up directing federal
agencies that had been created to control their own economic
activities. It was most difficult for those like Hoover to find an
appropriate compromise between the elitism inherent in efficiency and their commitment to decentralized execution of
reforms. The reformers who most respected scientific expertise
and who put specialists in charge of bringing about change
had to face the possibility that their activities might prove
counterproductive to their basically humane, democratic im-
pulses.

Progressivism was a well-intentioned, if frantic, uncoordi-
nated, and sometimes counterproductive movement. It was
intended to produce both more democracy and more efficiency
while preserving individualism and increasing cooperation.
Despite its undeniable and unfortunate failures, it did signal
a new social consciousness among Americans, and few generations of social reformers have come closer to publicly recognizing and combating the inequities inherent in the modern
industrialized state. This was because most middle-class citizens remained convinced between 1900 and 1914 that they had
the power and the time to effect a new social order.

Only a few outstanding theorists of the day, far-sighted

pragmatists like Thorsten Veblen, Herbert Croly, and John Dewey anticipated conflicts between the centralized propensities of the capitalist's profit motive and the idealized cooperative forms of social and economic organizations. But most Progressives ignored the socioeconomic paradoxes of their reform movement until the antagonisms developing along rural-urban, moralistic-scientific lines finally surfaced during and after World War I. These internal divisions further undermined the already delicately balanced national conglomeration of progressive reform activity.

Just as progressivism was disintegrating as a national movement, Hoover returned to the United States with a special version of pragmatic idealism that for a time promised to unite the disparate postwar political and economic factions. He returned with diverse appeal, enjoying a public prominence which he found both unfamiliar and uncomfortable. "My ambition," he confided in several private letters in the fall of 1919, "is to get out of the limelight as fast as possible. . . . I am convinced that this country needs a few officials who will not be seeking public honors for having done their simple duty."

The Quaker who returned home was still a Jeffersonian agrarian, even a rural reactionary, at heart. But he was also more sophisticated, more intellectually mature, more internationally and philanthropically oriented, than the man who had achieved unprecedented professional success only a few years before. For a time it looked as though he would be able to at least symbolically unite the dying progressive movement; he had begun to distill from his varied experiences a cohesive philosophy for managing American domestic and foreign postwar economic policy, based on an unalterable belief in the scientific and moral laws of progress. Moreover, he seemed to have transcended the need to use his own professional expertise for personal gain. He had attained what Paul Goodman has described as an "authentic professionalism," the spirit of the master guildsman who, confident of his skills, could place in humble perspective the recognition which normally accrues to a successful specialist. Hoover had served his apprenticeship as a rugged individualist; it was now time to turn his scientific training and his faith in technology and efficiency exclusively to public service. But he recognized that he would have to serve unobtrusively, behind the scenes, being temperamentally unsuited to a public role.

Hoover's Quaker background had instilled in him not only a moral absolutism and a ruthless righteousness, but also a belief in the legitimacy of equal opportunity and cooperative individualism. His engineering days had convinced him first of the material rewards of hard work, and then of the need for using scientific expertise to improve socioeconomic conditions. Finally, the war had confirmed his humanitarian belief in voluntary decentralization and in the efficacy of public-relations techniques. Because the United States was looking for a leader who would maximize its technological progress in the twentieth century without perverting its best nineteenth-century ideals, Hoover appeared to many postwar Progressives to offer a last hope. Perhaps he could point the way to a rational control of economic expansion, to a viable noninterventionist foreign policy, to a system for ordering their individualism so they could live more humanely through cooperation, to a means of decentralizing an economy enormously expanded and centralized by the war effort, and to a restructuring of the anonymous, self-serving postwar bureaucracies in business and government.

Hoover's background and philosophy seemed quite compatible with the nation's immediate postwar needs, and he was deluged with offers to run for public office. But he had not yet made the final transition from a private, protected individual to an exposed public servant. First, he would have to synthesize the important lessons he had learned from the war, from his Quakerism, from his engineering career. He was quietly confident that this new self-knowledge and his international experience would enable him to devise a coordinated domestic and foreign policy, one which would end some of the dialectical tensions of American society in 1920.

Unfortunately, the odds and the times were against Hoover. In fact, the postwar Progressives who most enthusiastically supported his attempt to chart a new course for America were the first to forget the honest, if somewhat naive, effort he made between 1920 and 1929 to convince his fellow Americans of the lessons he had learned from the war.

I I I

The Progressive
in Transition

*"He is not dominantly a 'reformer.' He is more a
'former.'"*

WHILE IT WAS HASTENING his transformation from a private to
a public figure, World War I had taught Herbert Hoover some
significant lessons. The most important was the need for an
American ideology to counter both the radical and conservative
ideologies he had observed during his diplomatic and relief
activities in war-torn Europe between 1914 and 1919.

Although he did not believe that such foreign ideologies as
German imperialism or Russian communism would spread to
postwar America, Hoover did express his concern to President
Wilson in 1919 that the Bolsheviks might "undertake large
military crusades in an attempt to impose their doctrines on
. . . defenseless people" in Europe. He questioned the efficacy
of American military intervention were that to happen, because "we should probably be involved in years of police duty,
and our first act would probably, in the nature of things, make
us a party to establishing the reactionary classes in their
economic domination over the lower classes. This is against
our fundamental national spirit," he said privately to Wilson,
"and I doubt whether our soldiers under these circumstances

could resist infection with Bolshevik ideas." He also doubted whether Americans would stand for such a lengthy police action, one which he believed would only reinforce reactionary foreign regimes at the expense of the lower classes in these countries. Hoover emphatically and correctly predicted in 1919 that military intervention by the United States could not permanently stabilize nations suffering from internal social and economic problems or protect them from the spread of communism.

To the degree that Russian Bolsheviks, and later Communists, could capitalize upon legitimate social and economic grievances through propaganda techniques, the United States had to counter, according to Hoover, with its own brand of propaganda. He came out of the war convinced that it was futile to try to impose American ideals of freedom and peace upon other peoples by arms or treaties. Only publicity could be an effective major weapon against foreign ideologies, and so it was necessary to distill, package, and market the essence of American politics and economics. But it was not until Hoover returned to the United States permanently in 1919 that he began to articulate an American social philosophy in scattered articles and speeches.

When *American Individualism* was printed in 1922, a *New York Times* review hailed it as "among the few great formulations of American political theory. It bears much the same relation to the problems of the present and the future that the essays of Hamilton, Madison, Jay, and Noah Webster bore to the problems that occupied men's minds when the Constitution was framed."

Until the publication of this work, Hoover had usually linked progress with applied science, i.e., technological innovation, but now because of his wartime experiences he emphasized a more moralistic view of progress. Based largely on theories about racial instincts (by which he meant national characteristics), this new inclination led him to a more precise definition of the unique features of the American system. It depended, he proposed, upon a recognition of the divine in each human being, the stimulation of economic initiative through self-interest blended with a sense of service, government guidance and advice implemented through voluntary cooperation, and the leadership of those rare selfless professionals who could promote the widespread application of their discoveries.

The socioeconomic system it represented could not accurately be described by such words as progressivism, laissez-faire capitalism, communism, statism, socialism, corporatism, guildism, or syndicalism. The absolute laws of progress that he believed in required a new and superior synthesis that he simply called the American system. What he had in mind was a pragmatic utopianism that defied standard economic and political classifications and was, in truth, progressive in the broadest sense — it was forward looking. Perhaps it could best be characterized as an informal brand of liberal corporatism. Hoover unfortunately chose common terms — e.g., American system and American individualism — to describe his unusual combination of cooperation and a superior form of self-government.

Inspiring labels or slogans were noticeably absent throughout the work, and the title, *American Individualism,* was a gross misnomer as well. It left his contemporaries confused and uncertain; the term had long been familiar in another context. In fact, Hoover meant to describe Americans and their institutions as they ought to be, not as they actually were.

Hoover saw the world, and America in particular, as standing at a crossroads in history after World War I — one path leading to higher standards of living through decentralized techno-corporate organization and cooperative individualism; the other leading to socialism, fascism, syndicalism, or communism, through the establishment of authoritarian collectivism and the dehumanized collective personality that would destroy individual initiative and retard progress. It was imperative in such a transitional time that the country re-evaluate its past liberal-democratic heritage in light of present and future technological needs. In particular, Hoover looked to the past individualistic ideals of America to see how all forms of authoritarian collectivism could be avoided in the future. Ideals, he believed, were the most potent force in any society. Yet he realistically noted that no economic or social system could last if founded on altruism alone.

In *American Individualism* he insisted that idealism could be balanced with self-interest and technological innovation to counter the equally enervating systems of state socialism or monopoly capitalism. Socialism, Hoover wrote in 1922, neces-sitated a "bureaucracy of the entire population" and de-stroyed the economic initiative of each citizen. Likewise, he thought that capitalism often allowed a few men, through unrestrained control of property, to determine the welfare of great numbers, and made the individual "feel capital as [*sic*] an oppressor." While state socialism was based on the assump-tion that "human animals" could be motivated by altruism alone, monopoly capitalism posited the idea that materialism was an end in itself. Both concepts violated Hoover's defi-nition of American individualism, as he remembered it work-ing among Quakers during the last quarter of the nineteenth century. The problem was to find a way to make it function under modern, industrialized, postwar conditions.

The means that the Chief proposed for achieving this balance between state socialism and monopoly capitalism arose directly from his wartime experiences with the CRB and ARA. He had accomplished superb engineering feats, which had convinced him of the efficacy of two methods he also employed successfully as Wilson's wartime Food Adminis-trator — the use of publicity in molding a public philosophy, and the use of voluntarily decentralized groups for carrying out nationally coordinated programs — the heart of what Hoover insisted on calling American individualism. It was a misleading term, proposed as a solution to a central paradox of American society since colonial times: the attempt to reconcile individualism and cooperation through voluntarism. Had he been more precise, he might have called it cooperative individualism, or used the social historian's term collective individualism.

Despite his inaccurate and cumbersome terminology, Hoover's innovative publicity techniques appeared to have succeeded during World War I. He was one of the first American leaders in this century to understand that voluntary, uncoerced action depends in large measure on establishing public identification with an impersonal agency through a person who is not a demagogue. As head of the CRB, ARA, and the Food Administration, Hoover projected his image as the selfless personification of each organization and its humanitarian purposes. In addition, he realized that social philosophy can not be changed at the mass level unless it can be made to seem relevant and necessary to the daily lives of the people. New values would not evolve from the old ideals through the encouragement of materialism, the superimposition of legislation, or the development of an elaborate federal bureaucracy. Widespread value changes had to come from the bottom up; not from the top down.

Hoover was also only too well aware of the postwar trends that stood in the way of achieving cooperative individualism. Monopoly capitalism was inefficient; the machinery of government was too far removed from the American people to have any significant effect on their value system. In particular, Hoover realized that traditional concepts of private property and profit often produced efficiently coordinated production techniques within individual corporations, while they prevented even a moderate degree of efficiency and coordination at regional or national levels.

The problem was to preserve the necessary amount of competition and initiative in the daily economic lives and experiences of Americans, while preserving equality of opportunity and coordinating numerous individual efforts for the collective benefit. Hoover hoped to change values at the grass-roots level by propagating an ideology of cooperative individualism and playing down materialism. Massive education and propaganda campaigns could transform traditional attitudes about private property and profit into a new sense of social responsibility. Technology would bring the material benefits of modern society within the reach of all Americans, so that in small communities and through voluntary associations they could concentrate on higher spiritual pursuits in an atmosphere of cooperation rather than competition. Publicity would translate federal guidelines based on expert advice into everyday actions.

Hoover was not simply trying to "retraditionalize" American society in the 1920s according to some static set of old ideals. Instead, he deliberately set out to reconstruct America, not to patch things up temporarily. In the words of one 1928 biography by William Hard, he was more of a "former" than a "reformer," because he wanted to create a viable ideology based on the personal experiences of postwar citizens. New attitudes could be shaped to help them cope with the critical transition that was facing the nation — the transition from a chaotic, nineteenth-century semi-industrialized society to a fully rationalized twentieth-century one — without falling victim to some form of authoritarian collectivism. He did not propose to destroy capitalism. He hoped only to make it more humane and democratic. Later, as secretary of commerce, he would devise a publicity-conference method of keeping the American public informed and of making individuals feel a greater sense of participation in governmental decisions.

One reason for the simplicity of his terminology and methodology can be found in a 1917 interview in the *Saturday Evening Post*. The war had convinced him, he said, "that the world lived by phrases," Americans perhaps most of all. This was confirmed by the success of Hoover's Food Administration staff in creating dozens of successful slogans and symbols to influence American women as consumers. "Food Will Win the

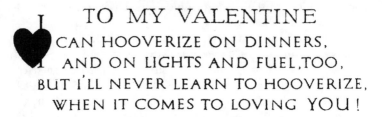

TO MY VALENTINE
I CAN HOOVERIZE ON DINNERS,
AND ON LIGHTS AND FUEL, TOO,
BUT I'LL NEVER LEARN TO HOOVERIZE,
WHEN IT COMES TO LOVING YOU!

War!" Window stickers identified households abiding by the
Food Administration's recommended wheatless and meatless
days, while parents exhorted children to "Clean up your
plate — think of the starving children in. . . ." Hoover methodically proceeded as Food Administrator to awaken the
national conscience and to "guide the public mind" about
food and fuel conservation. He was so successful that the practice of voluntary rationing came to be known as "Hooveriz-
ing." A "stamp of shame" was used by his office against those
who would not cooperate, especially trade groups that violated
recommended retail and wholesale prices. This wartime job
confirmed his hunch about the power of the press to educate,
to change habits and values, and to bring about voluntary
cooperation among disparate groups — all without rationing
or other coercive measures. It finally led him to conclude publicly in 1920 that only propaganda could educate the American public to the ideals of democracy.

The war also taught him that decentralization and local
committee structure in the administration of government gave
people a personal sense of participation — whether they were
donating money, reconsidering their values, or changing their
eating habits. As a consequence, while insisting on full authority for himself and his planning staff in efforts to overcome
foreign and domestic red tape, Hoover did not seek such
authority for personal aggrandizement nor did he bring this
centralized power to bear upon the American people. Instead,
he directed his influence against lethargic bureaucracies and
recalcitrant politicians and military officials, and relied upon
voluntary cooperation from the people. No event after World
War I, including the Great Depression, ever weakened the
private belief he first expressed in 1915 to Lindon W. Bates,
head of the CRB's New York office, that strong decentralized
community organization was capable of "elevat[ing] the
efforts of the individuals in these communities to as high a
point as possible in order to give them a stimulating interest
. . . a personal interest . . ." in the task at hand.

Correspondingly, no event after the war ever mitigated his belief in the ineffectiveness of legislative solutions for national problems, and he scorned suggestions that he become a more adept politician himself. Senator William E. Borah once prophetically noted that while Hoover had been a virtual dictator during the war, "you cannot run the Presidency the way you run a Food Administration." And even his friends sadly admitted that his enormous skill as an administrator was never fully translated into traditional political ability. In fact, the war only confirmed Hoover's worst suspicions as an engineer about European diplomats and politicians. To Hoover, they appeared to lack not only efficiency and expertise, but also any altruistic commitment to the guildist type of professionalism that had led him and a number of other progressive reformers towards associational solutions to socioeconomic problems, instead of electoral or Congressional politics.

Voluntary organizations, decentralization at all levels of society, and administrative reorganization were the keys to Hoover's American system. They alone, he believed, could avoid the smug paternalism on the part of experts and reformers, preserve participatory democracy, and prevent the spread of both inefficient federal bureaucracies and demagogic appeals to selfish foreign or domestic interest groups. He came out of the war firmly believing, as do so many social critics today, that an excessively bureaucratic America is no democracy, and a truly democratic America would inhibit the growth of bureaucracy.

Hoover's disdain for electoral and Congressional politics did not restrict his effectiveness during the war (nor did it before he became a depression president in 1929) due to his successful use of nontraditional administrative policies and tactics. In this sense, Hoover can be described as apolitical, for he refused to practice traditional power politics and insisted on a non-coercive role for government. Thus, during the war he was able to deal summarily and bluntly with politicians and diplomats, because he was a private citizen working behind the scenes. He would tell representatives of the German government in 1918 to "go to hell with my compliments" when they continued to oppose his Belgian relief operations as readily as he would berate the British Admiral, Sir Rosslyn Wemyss, after the war when the English were still enforcing a food blockade against the defeated Germans. He could afford to use the coarse language and tactics of a mining camp chief while still a private citizen working voluntarily for the war effort, but was to find that even as an apolitical public figure he could not be so abrupt with diplomats and politicians. Never again did he have the instant personal command he had enjoyed in his wartime assignments.

The personal autonomy with which Hoover operated during the war years certainly deluded him about the need for tact and sociability and the limited privacy that would be his lot as a public figure — apolitical or not. He succeeded in meeting these demands to a surprising degree while secretary of commerce and even during his first two years as president, despite the Great Depression. Inevitably, however, his temperament and noncoercive approach failed in a sustained domestic crisis demanding more personalized, charismatic leadership and enforced public policy than he was able or willing to utilize. The immediate importance, however, of the apolitical administrative lessons and tactics that he learned from the war was the efficacy of enlightened mass propaganda, decentralized organization and American voluntarism. The question was whether they would work in time of peace. Hoover thought so.

It was natural that, if Hoover's wartime experiences hastened his transformation into a pragmatic idealist with a general social philosophy based on American individualism, this in turn would affect his specific views and actions concerning United States foreign and domestic policy after 1919. Although he did not start his official career as a diplomatist until he became a member of President Wilson's War Council in March 1918, he had unofficially assumed diplomatic respon-

sibilities since 1912, when he had served as promotional agent
for the Panama-Pacific Exposition. His war-related duties
catapulted him into the international spotlight. Besides organizing with the Commission for the Relief of Belgium, he also
served as United States Food Administrator (1917–1919), as a
member of the War Trade Council (1917–1920), as chairman
of the United States Grain Corporation (1917–1918), as chairman of the Sugar Equalization Board (1918–1919), as secretary of the Supreme Economic Council (1919), as chairman of
the European Coal Council (1919), and as Director-General
of the American Relief Administration in Europe (1919–
1920).

In all of these positions Hoover began to piece together
interlocking foreign and domestic theories. Both stressed
apolitical means of achieving voluntary cooperation at home
and abroad. "Independent internationalism" was the foreign
policy parallel to his domestic philosophy of cooperative individualism, what he called American individualism. His brand
of postwar diplomacy did not stress permanent alliances between nations, nor centralized state-directed foreign military
or economic policies. Instead, according to Hoover, voluntary
associationalism between nations that engaged in peaceful
economic competition would obviate the need of governments
to dictate foreign trade policy to their private import-export
interests, or to use military force in carrying out their political
objectives.

The implicit assumption of independent internationalism
was that the United States should cooperate in world affairs
when it could not or did not want to solve a particular problem through unilateral actions. Just as he believed that the
war had promoted domestic economic and political cooperation, similarly it had promoted unprecedented international
economic interdependence. Business practices could never be
as competitive at home or abroad as they had been before the
war. He was confident that the United States must adjust to

this dramatically changed world by assuming a well-defined political and economic leadership in world affairs.

Hoover came back from Europe in 1919 committed more strongly than ever to the uniqueness of an American system, which he attributed to the moral, political, and economic superiority of his countrymen. Convinced as he was that the economic strength of the United States was vital to the economic health of the entire world, he frankly recommended "Americanism" to Europeans as the solution to their postwar problems. This meant the practice of the traditional virtues of thrift, frontier neighborliness, public service tempered by self-interest, efficiency, and the "maximum exertion of every individual within his physical ability."

If indeed it was axiomatic that international recovery would follow naturally from American prosperity, then American economic development had to be carefully guided. Hoover believed that the country was destined for almost unlimited economic growth, if it could maintain a high degree of economic self-sufficiency. To Hoover this meant *not* allowing U.S. industry to become too dependent on foreign markets. He was proud that the United States exported only 6 to 10 percent of its total productivity and was confident that even this level of self-sufficiency could be improved by increasing domestic consumption. But the immediate postwar problem was maintaining world peace. So in the 1920s his nationalistic concern for preserving and increasing economic self-sufficiency did not outweigh his desire to bring about international economic cooperation for the reconstruction of war-torn Europe.

Many things were different in this postwar world. The unusual prosperity of the war years had turned the United States into a creditor nation for the first time in its history. No single individual in business or government circles completely understood the complex ramifications of this dramatic and rapid change in the world economic position of the United States, or of the general economic maladjustments between nations in the postwar period. Hoover at least saw that economic reform at home, in addition to reconstruction of foreign economic systems, was necessary for future world stability.

His comprehensive postwar economic plan called for energetic management and innovation at all levels. America required a more equitable balance of trade, and to achieve this Hoover believed it had to increase imports of nonstrategic goods and become less dependent upon both agricultural and manufacturing exports through a more judicious and scientific tariff policy. Foreign loan supervision had to include controls not only to insure that private American loans would constructively contribute to world productivity and prosperity, but also to counter the attractiveness of high foreign interest rates and thereby preserve American capital for needed internal development. National policy had to stimulate economic "associationalism" and self-regulating corporatism based on voluntary decentralization and cooperation, which would preserve both a sense of social responsibility and individualism. Domestic monetary guidelines had to be designed to stabilize prices and wages through the actions of the Federal Reserve Board and through indirect government regulation of business cycles. These policies, in turn, had to be coordinated with international attempts to stabilize currency by a return to the gold standard. And finally he thought that the United States had to actively participate in the creation of a world community of industrial nations under American leadership, based on voluntary cooperation among commercial and financial interests involved in international business.

Hoover insisted that this new world community or "commercial league of nations" be based on the principle of equal economic opportunity. This Open Door policy paralleled the equal opportunity he wanted to insure for Americans at home, and was consistent with his desire to see the country maximize its economic independence. In neither instance would he ever resort to traditional, coercive institutional means to enforce equal opportunity at home or abroad, and in retrospect this produced unsolvable problems in his domestic and foreign policies.

At the time, however, from Hoover's perspective, the Open Door policy presented just the right blend of nationalist self-interest with internationalist altruism — in theory it would stimulate a harmonious world economy where peaceful cooperative economic expansion substituted for political and military confrontations; in practice, equal economic opportunity in world trade and finance would benefit the strongest competitor. Naturally, Hoover knew that the United States would have a distinct advantage if granted the same opportunities as all other nations to buy, sell, and invest. This realization prevented him from endorsing any limitless, open-ended concept of expansion abroad based on the Open Door policy because in the long run such expansion would decrease American self-sufficiency by vastly increasing foreign market dependency. Thus, to a greater degree than most postwar diplomatists or later generations of American policy-makers, Hoover based his advocacy of the Open Door policy on its controlled and cooperative, rather than its unregulated and competitive, aspects.

This emphasis on achieving domestic economic self-sufficiency demanded comprehensive coordination of domestic and foreign policies to insure that one did not work to further internal development while the other retarded it. It also inclined him toward a noninterventionist or noncoercive military policy, a position reinforced by his Quaker background and by the associational approach to world affairs he had developed in his earlier experiences. While he was no pacifist, he did believe that no new economic or political world community could be achieved through the use of force, and that military action abroad usually created more domestic problems than it solved. So, in his foreign policy, Hoover assumed a public relations administrative role, committed to shaping public opinion through the use of educational publicity and voluntary organizations based on a combination of altruism and self-interest. When these tactics failed, however, he almost always remained true to his own beliefs regardless of public opinion.

His domestic policy reflected the same associational, cooperative approach. Convinced that the country was entering a new economic and social era in the wake of the war, Hoover repeatedly predicted the emergence of a new economic system in the United States based on voluntary organizations that would mitigate the worst excesses of competition. This was not only his goal but the direction in which he thought the American economy and society were evolving. Hence, the term "New Era" is often used to describe the economics of the 1920s, and Hoover was no advocate of any "return to normalcy."

Where the classical economists like Adam Smith had argued for uncontrolled competition between independent economic units guided only by the invisible hand of supply and demand, he talked about voluntary national economic planning arising from cooperation between business interests and the government. The aim was to eliminate waste, through greater production efficiency, lowering prices, raising wages, and controlling business cycles. Instead of negative governmental action in time of depression, he advocated the expansion of public works, avoidance of wage cuts, increased rather than decreased production — measures which would expand rather than contract purchasing power. Finally Hoover was convinced that postwar America was, "almost unnoticed, in the midst of a great revolution — or perhaps a better word, a transformation in the whole super-organization of our economic life. We are passing," he told the United States Chamber of Commerce in 1924, "from a period of extreme individualistic action into a period of associational activities." Part of this belief was a reflection of his own professional guildism; part of it came from knowledge of how technology and the war had changed America's political economy.

The immediate postwar domestic problem, Hoover wrote in *American Individualism,* was "to curb the forces in business which would destroy equality of opportunity and yet maintain the initiative and creative faculties of our people." It was a question of devising a plan of individualism and associational activities that would also allow the nation to synchronize socially and economically the gigantic machine that had been built with applied science. His solution was to encourage trade associations to regulate themselves by developing and adhering to socially responsible ethical and business codes which the government would periodically review and promulgate as a standard of fair practice.

This delicate balance could only be achieved and maintained if the federal government stayed out of the production and distribution of commodities and services. Government should act as a source of information, coordination, and national guidance, but there was no need for it to become a coercive force if individuals were properly educated to willingly assume social and economic responsibilities at the local and state levels, through voluntary organizations like trade and farmer's associations and civic groups. Such decentralized administration of national policy was to be achieved by convincing the American people that their own self-interest lay in responsible cooperation with each other. This enlightened point of view would, in turn, produce communities that literally governed themselves on the basis of tempered or cooperative individualism, rather than on the basis of unlimited individual material acquisition or a morass of legislation. "National character," he insisted, "cannot be built by law," for laws implied compulsion and inflexibility.

"Self-government," Hoover would finally proclaim in 1929, "does not and should not imply the use of political agencies alone. Progress is born of cooperation in the community — not from governmental restraints. . . . The Government should assist and encourage these movements of collective self-help by itself cooperating with them . . . [for] there is an equally important field of cooperation by the Federal Government with the multitude of agencies, state, municipal, and private in the systematic development of those processes which directly affect public health, recreation, education, and the home. We have need further to perfect the means by which the Government can be adapted to human service."

The difference between Hoover's progressive ideas on business-government relations in the 1920s and the standard Republican view can be summed up by comparing Harding's famous 1920 dictum, "What this country needs is less government in business and more business in government," to Hoover's analysis, "It is just as important that business keep out of government as that government keep out of business." This 1928 public statement by Hoover climaxed almost a decade of effort in which he tried to reshape the role of the federal government through the development of cooperative individualism and associationalism. Had he succeeded, his ideas would have drastically altered the traditional capitalist concept of private property to the point where ownership would no longer be an object in itself, as he said in *American Individualism,* but rather an opportunity to serve the community. The economic interests of the United States needed a lifting purpose greater than the struggle of materialism, he told businessmen attending the national Electric Light Association conference in 1924, if they were to organize "the great tools in our economic life" to "produce happier individual lives, more secure employment, wider possibilities of comfort and enjoyment, [and] larger possibilities of intellectual life."

What Hoover was describing in these very general terms was significant, nonetheless, because it was a non-Marxist plan for expanding and sharing national wealth cooperatively. Specifically, he wanted poor subsistence farmers to leave the land for the smaller towns in the United States, and prosperous businessmen to decentralize their operations by developing industry in such towns. "The very best results of all the forces in

American life," he said to an agricultural convention in 1927, "are in towns from one thousand up to one hundred and fifty thousand." Decentralized economic expansion, the use of advanced technological methods in farming and manufacturing, increased efficiency through conscious planning and cooperative coordinated group action — these were the keys to a healthy expanding economy based on a "higher individualism."

All of these specific remarks were anticipated in 1922 when he predicted that if Americans acted on his definition of individualism they would have "increasing quantities to share" and "time and leisure and taxes with which to fight out proper sharing of the 'surplus.'" The sharing, according to Hoover, was to be based on "the wider gains to all of us through cheapening the costs of production and distribution through the eliminating of their wastes, [and] from increasing the volume of products by each and every one doing his utmost." Such sharing would not work, however, if there were large numbers of shirkers or people devoted to "the selfish snatching and hoarding of the common product." And here Hoover's dream for America, like that of so many other postwar Progressives, paradoxically rested on his faith in the average citizen to rise above individual acquisition and yet to preserve a sense of private initiative and a commitment to capitalism.

To the degree that Hoover's pragmatic idealism was even minimally materialistic, it was apt to be misunderstood and misused by most Americans. Their values were still largely based on the uncontrolled, individual acquisitiveness and open-ended national expansion so characteristic of the late nineteenth century. They were not altruistic professionals who now believed, as Hoover did, in a cooperative system based on sharing abundance to improve the quality of twentieth-century life and meet the demands of a modern technological society. They were not going to be easy to convince that

tempered or cooperative individualism was essential to survival in the increasingly interdependent world, and in an
industrialized, urban society.

As right as Hoover was about the organizational revolution
that was taking place along corporatist lines, and as representative as he was of the campaign to decentralize that
reorganization, he himself was creating power based simply on
a new bureaucratic structure, despite its voluntary nature.
Two things were absolutely essential for this private power to
work in the public interest: commitment to a scientific elimination of wasteful organizational and production methods,
and a value change on the part of the American people away
from the crass materialism of their past.

The one prerequisite totally absent from Hoover's associational dream for America was the use of public power to keep
recalcitrant businessmen and their trade associations in line
during this period of transition. Consequently, if his voluntary
organizational methods failed to downgrade materialism or to
instill cooperative activities in the public interest, then there
was no traditional institutionalized means to force compliance
with his new socioeconomic system. By trying to eliminate
coercion from public policy Hoover invited private interest-
group domination and the charge that associationalism was
simply an administrative vehicle for furthering the growth of
monopoly capitalism — the last thing he wanted for America.

Thus in his consistent attempt to avoid the coercive tendencies of the federal bureaucracy, he closed his eyes to the
fact that regional and local bureaucrats could also impose
conformity, create self-serving provincial elitism, and lose sight
of broad public interests. His ideas about cooperative individualism and associationalism never adequately came to
terms with the specific problem of public versus private power
and the relative merits and deficiencies of each, because of his
abiding faith in the efficacy of voluntarism.

Hoover also failed to anticipate the difficult distinction
between the systematic education of public opinion to volun-

tary action, and outright manipulation of the mass mind for the purposes of state. If, as Hoover once said, "the most dangerous animal in the United States is the man with an emotion and a desire to pass a new law," it is equally true that governmental power restricted by federal legislation might be preferable to pseudo grass-roots pressure groups who have in fact been created by government propaganda. Such massive federal publicity efforts in the future, after all, might not always be directed by an honorable Quaker like Herbert Hoover. It is indeed unfortunate, though typical of reformers at the time, that he did not foresee that promotional activity in the name of voluntarism and associationalism could lead first to no public control of private interests and then to the demand that big government step in and set things right.

This lack of foresight was a direct result of the unfamiliarity of most Americans with the immense power of a then still nascent, managerial corporate state. In the early twentieth century it was most difficult to anticipate that both extreme types of corporatism would contribute to the development of a socioeconomic system in which the functions of public and private interest groups would become hopelessly blurred, and in which public and private bureaucracies would create their own anonymous justification for existence, so that no person or group could be held responsible for any specific policy. If progressive reformers of this postwar decade appear naively hopeful or superficial, it is because they were the original participants in a rationalization process — a search for a new corporate order — which did not reveal its most negative features until several generations later.

So in 1920 it was possible for Progressives to support Hoover for the presidency for a wide variety of reasons. Some concentrated on his pro–League of Nations stand as an indication of his internationalism in foreign affairs; others looked to his democratic ideas about decentralization and administration of government from the bottom up rather than the top down. Still others took up his emphasis on national planning or his interest in the welfare of children, his insistence on economical, efficient, impersonal public service, his commitment to scientific expertise as a means of achieving social and economic reform, or his reliance on publicity to educate Americans and mobilize them voluntarily behind worthwhile projects. And his disdain for traditional politics surely endeared him to many.

The more conservative Progressives liked Hoover's obvious professional elitism and his faith in individualism. They saw a reflection of their own commitment to the work ethic, and were encouraged by the possibility of mediating political differences from an apolitical position. The more liberal reformers remembered that in 1917 he had said that "civilization spells the protection of the helpless. . . . The survival of the strong, the development of the individual, must be tempered, or else we return two thousand years in our civilization." And, certainly, the few union-oriented Progressives were impressed with Hoover's stand on labor. Quite clearly, he was a man who could represent the diverse progressive movement after the war, and many Progressives wanted to see him elected president.

Reluctantly, Hoover let himself become a presidential contender in 1920. He at least did nothing to suppress the many Hoover-for-President committees, especially in his adopted home state of California. But the attempt was short-lived. It had been primarily a nonpartisan effort, financed mostly by men who had worked for him during the war years, and run by amateurs. Once Hiram Johnson decisively defeated him in the May 1920 primary in California, Hoover's threat to party regulars quickly diminished. Political power would remain with men like Warren G. Harding, Frank O. Lowden, and General Leonard Wood. Nonetheless, he remained personally popular with the American public, and next to Woodrow Wilson, was perhaps the most familiar national figure, largely because of his work as Food Administrator during the war.

For a time his progressive support was impressive, including social worker Jane Addams, lawyer Louis Brandeis, reform economist Frank W. Taussig, sociologist Edward A. Ross, progressive engineer Morris L. Cooke, science professor and ARA official Vernon L. Kellogg. In addition, prewar muckrakers like Ray Stannard Baker, Ida Tarbell, Dr. Frank Crane, Will Irwin, Mark Sullivan, William Hard, and William Allen White endorsed him. So did Herbert Croly and Walter Lippmann, editors on the *New Republic* staff, George Lorimer of the *Saturday Evening Post,* Norman Hapgood of *Hearst's International Magazine,* French Strother of *World's Work,* Hartford Powell of *Colliers,* Frank Cobb of the *New York World,* and Edward Bok, editor of the *Ladies Home Journal.* Even Democratic Progressives such as Franklin Roosevelt, businessman Edward A. Filene, Wilson's personal adviser Col. Edward M. House, Senator James D. Phelan, and former secretary of the Democratic National Committee Robert Jackson pushed Hoover for president until he cleared up the matter of his party affiliation.

In addition to Hoover's progressivism, his admiration for Wilson, and his pro-League stand, some Democrats believed that he might become their presidential candidate simply because a *Literary Digest* poll for April 1920 showed him more popular than any of the established party leaders. Others presumed he was a Democrat, primarily because he had allegedly written a public letter in 1918 calling for the support of Woodrow Wilson in the president's efforts to resolve the nation's postwar problems. But what had been intended as a nonpartisan gesture of support for the national leadership was in fact written by his young assistant Lewis L. Strauss. Moreover, the statement did not specifically refer to the impending congressional elections; instead, it called for united support of the president because he alone had the "confidence of the great mass of people in Europe," and because on the important postwar issues facing the country "it is vital that we have a solid front and sustained leadership." Hoover took complete responsibility for the letter, however, because he sincerely believed at the time that there could "be no party policies" associated with the peacemaking process. Later he said he was shocked to learn that Wilson had made such a partisan appeal in the 1918 congressional elections.

In fact, his limited political activity had always been Republican, probably because of his Quaker background and Stanford education. He had registered Republican as early as 1896, had joined the National Republican Club in 1909, and had financially supported Theodore Roosevelt in 1912. However, Hoover had yet to vote in any presidential election because he had always been out of the country. Then between 1914 and 1920 he had no time for domestic political activities because of his wartime public-service jobs. As the country gradually turned away from an ailing Wilson during the fight over ratification of the peace treaty, Democratic leaders desperately looked to Hoover as the only national figure who might insure them the progressive, pro-League, and woman vote.

During the early stages of his presidential "boom" in 1919, Hoover viewed himself essentially as his contemporary supporters did — an independent Progressive who thought that the postwar issues before the country transcended partisanship. In a public letter dated March 8, 1920, he said he would continue to speak out on the issues and to "engage in team play with any organization and leadership that has for its objective the consummation and maintenance of great issues in the form that I believe are to the public interest and benefit." While he believed that like any other citizen he should always be ready for service when called upon, to campaign for such a call was contrary to his every instinct.

So it came as quite a surprise to members of both parties when Hoover suddenly announced on March 30 that while he would not actively seek the Republican nomination, he would accept it if the party adopted a "forward looking, liberal constructive platform on the Treaty and our economic issues and . . . proposed measures for sound business administration of the country, and is neither reactionary or radical in its approach to our great domestic questions." This statement quickly terminated both the broad nonpartisan support he had accrued and any opportunity he might have had for the Democratic nomination. But his refusal to actively campaign for the nomination, even in California, where Hiram Johnson was maintaining his anti-League position, made it easy for the Old Guard Republicans to ignore his candidacy at the GOP convention in June.

Perhaps Hoover had taken a calculated risk. First by cultivating a nonpartisan image and then by making an ill-timed, nominal commitment to the Republicans, he had made himself an attractive contender for a cabinet post under either party's leadership. Such a position, outside the limelight and the demands for condescension and ceremony incumbent upon the average politician, would suit him well. While he clearly wanted to remain in public service after the war he knew that he should avoid electoral politics at all costs. "I do not believe," he wrote in one private letter on April 12, 1919, "that I have the mental attitude or the politician's manner . . . and above all I am too sensitive to political mud," to seek public office. In still another private letter on September 29, 1919, he lamented that he did not have the "politician's skill needed to arrive at such a job" as the presidency of the United States.

Given this realistic assessment of his political disabilities, his short-lived candidacy appears all the more to have been a calculated means to a quite different end. He had already received several attractive offers from private business. Financier Paul Warburg invited him to join the International Bank of Acceptance in 1920, and in 1921 Daniel Guggenheim proposed a partnership in one of the world's largest mining and metallurgical firms, with a guaranteed annual income of $500,000. He declined them all. Instead, he accepted an appointment to President Harding's cabinet — a position better suited to his temperament and administrative techniques.

Hoover's transition from private citizen to public servant was at last complete.

I V

The Progressive
as Domestic Dynamo

"I felt, looking at him, that he has never known failure."

As THE GREAT ENGINEER-HUMANITARIAN, and popular, if unsuccessful, presidential contender in 1920, Herbert Hoover agreed
to be Harding's secretary of commerce only after the president-
elect had promised to give him a voice on all important economic policies of the administration. By such policies, Hoover's
Memoirs said, he meant "business, agriculture, labor, finance,
and foreign affairs" insofar as they affected commercial matters.
His subsequent activities in all of these fields led S. Parker
Gilbert, an international banker and Treasury official, to remark that Hoover was trying to be "Under-Secretary of all
other departments." Another contemporary said he "served for
seven years as handy man to the administration," words
graphically illustrated by a 1928 cartoon depicting a "View of
Washington" in which the secretary of commerce was seen to
be everywhere at once. His conversion to public servant was not
only complete, but became so all-consuming that it appeared to
obliterate his existence as a private individual.

Hoover's record as secretary of commerce is all the more impressive if one remembers that he was appointed over the
objections not only of Old Guard Republicans like Sena-

tors Philander C. Knox, Charles Curtis, and Reed Smoot, but also of insurgents like Hiram Johnson and William E. Borah, as well as of the Hearst press, and of Progressives such as Raymond Robins, Gifford Pinchot, and George W. Norris. To these men Hoover appeared either too apolitical, too progressive, too internationally minded, too popular, or simply too ambitious. But Warren G. Harding was determined to have Hoover in his cabinet and held firm against all complaints, finally appeasing at least some members of the Old Guard with the appointment of Andrew W. Mellon as secretary of the treasury.

Despite this GOP resistance, Hoover immediately set about trying to make the heretofore insignificant Department of Commerce post into one of the most important in the cabinet. In the process he became one of Harding's closest advisers, and the president insisted on his frank advice on a wide variety of subjects. The Commerce Department represented the greatest *engineering* challenge in the Chief's career — one that allowed him to test all of his socioeconomic, moral, and scientific principles simultaneously. This time, however, the immediate objective was the virtual elimination of poverty in the United States rather than the reorganization of a sick mining company for a share of the profits, or distribution of food to disaster victims. Characteristically, Hoover wasted no time setting about his task and integrating it into his long-range dream for the country — no less than the transformation of American society.

He began in typically methodical fashion by surrounding himself with some of the best public-relations men and the ablest professional experts in the country. It was through administrative reorganization and mass media dissemination of expert information that he hoped to avoid the worst paternalistic features of professional elitism and to encourage informed grass-roots participation in the 1920s. He predicted that this decade would mark the country's official entrance into the twentieth century.

Some of the reporters and editors who came to his aid were friends who had worked with Hoover during the war; others simply came out of admiration for his ideas. The first category included such men as George Akerson, Frederick M. Feiker, and Arch W. Shaw — who would remain with him in various capacities for most of the decade. The second category included such well-known postwar reporters and editors as Ida Tarbell, David Lawrence, William Allen White and Mark Sullivan — most of whom would desert Hoover by the end of the decade. From the social sciences, business, and engineering professions his list of consultants reads like a condensation of *Who's Who* for the 1920s, including several reformed socialists like Edward Eyre Hunt and John Spargo. Probably the most respected of the experts who advised Hoover were economists Edwin F. Gay and Wesley Clair Mitchell.

While Hoover tended to hire "yes men" in public-relations positions, this was not true of most of his other appointments as either secretary of commerce or as president. (It is said by people of considerably differing political views that his only questionable recommendations were J. Edgar Hoover as FBI director and a young man named Kenneth G. Ormiston, whom he sent to manage Aimee Semple McPherson's radio station and who ended up running off with the evangelist to Mexico in one of the most publicized love trysts of the decade.) But unfortunately those closest to him did cater to his ideas and to his personal sensitivities, either out of a sense of awe, blind loyalty, or fear of arousing his temper. In the depression, when he most needed new ideas and novel public-relations techniques to restore confidence among the American people, his publicity staff was suffering from tired blood — many of them having worked with him almost a decade. This was particularly true of George Akerson, Hoover's chief press agent, and of Lawrence Richey, his overly protective private correspondence secretary.

Because Hoover looked upon public relations as an "exact science" indispensable to government administration, his approach reflected his own lack of emotional appeal and human warmth. He not only continued his "memo mania" to communicate with his public-relations staff, but as secretary of commerce he also devised other impersonal means of communication, like the well-organized publicity conferences and factfinding commissions.

Each conference or commission was a publicity tool, designed to dramatize cooperative individualism and associationalism and to disseminate educational information throughout the country. Both as secretary of commerce and later as president Hoover planned more than 3,000 well-publicized conferences to bring specific problems and solutions to the attention of as many Americans as possible. The purpose of the conferences was not to discover or devise answers — these were usually thought out in advance by professional experts in the appropriate Commerce Department division. The success of such conferences ultimately depended, instead, on how much voluntary collective effort they generated at the local and state levels. It was through this conference method that Hoover hoped to perfect a cooperative system tied to the needs and energies of the people it served, guided by advice and direction from national experts — all *without* greatly expanding the federal legislative power or bureaucratic structure. Success was measured by the degree to which federally sponsored conferences and propaganda changed values enough to produce voluntary reform or state and local legislation.

In calling such conferences and in making press releases, Hoover left nothing to chance. He carefully avoided destructive criticism in favor of what he deemed constructive ideas. Destructive criticism, to Hoover, was anything not firmly rooted in statistical data. But facts alone do not make an effective ideologue, as he was later to discover. Charisma and effective oratory also played important roles in ideological propaganda. Not personally adept at using symbolic phrases, slogans, metaphors, and other rhetorical devices to persuade his fellow Americans of the wisdom of his ideas, Hoover appears to have somewhat inhibited his publicity staff from using them as well. While his writing was unclear, theirs was uninspiring.

But this defect in his publicity-conference approach was not immediately evident as the secretary of commerce began his career by trying to restructure the entire executive branch of government – a goal of many Progressives since 1900. He started by reorganizing the Department of Commerce and other departments by attempting to use his influence with Presidents Harding and Coolidge to transfer some of their functions to his jurisdiction. In a 1924 summary of the achievements of his department he asserted that his ultimate goal was to eliminate wasteful overlapping and "to change the attitude of government relations with business from that of interference to that of cooperation," so the Commerce Department might "be effective in service to the producers, manufacturers, and distributors of commodities, able to give economic interpretation of importance to the American public generally, and to stimulate American trade."

With the advice of the noted economic historian and first dean of Harvard's Business School, Edwin F. Gay, Hoover originally tried to restructure his whole department by dividing it into three large sections representing industry, trade, and transportation. This comprehensive reorganization required that the Interior Department's Bureau of Mines and Patent Office be transferred to the new industrial division, which was to include a new Bureau of Federal Statistics as well. The trade division called for an enlarged Bureau of Foreign and Domestic Commerce (BFDC) and would have incorporated the Bureau of Markets from the Agricultural Department, the foreign trade activities (including economic consulates) from the State Department, the Inter-American High Commission from the Treasury Department, and the data-gathering functions of the Federal Trade Commission. Finally, the third division, encompassing transportation, was to have received all government property in merchant shipping, wharves, and supplies from the Shipping Board to the Emergency Fleet Corporation and would include a new Division of Merchant Marine headed by an undersecretary of commerce. This new division would thus consolidate twelve different bureaus scattered through four departments and would extend Commerce Department jurisdiction to the Panama Canal, the Inland Waterways, the Shipping Subsidies, and a new Bureau of Aeronautics.

In addition to restructuring and expanding his own department, Hoover also had plans for a general reorganization of the executive branch of government. As he would later recommend to Presidents Truman and Eisenhower, Hoover wanted new cabinet positions created along functional lines, like health, education, and welfare; or defense. The reorganization of older departments like Interior, a new budget system, and reevaluation of executive regulatory agencies were also in Hoover's restructuring program. His determination not to practice power politics based on government coercion of private interests led him to believe that administrative and executive functions should not be carried out by boards whose primary duty was semijudicial, regulatory, or advisory. As a result, his reorganization plans left most regulatory functions regarding business practices outside of the federal bureaucracy, where he did *not* think they belonged.

Hoover's plans for comprehensive governmental restructuring, although strongly supported by Harding, met with determined opposition from all of the other strong cabinet members, like Secretary of State Charles Evans Hughes, Secretary of the Treasury Andrew W. Mellon, and especially Secretary of Agriculture Henry C. Wallace, who was backed by the farm bloc in Congress. Hoover bitterly complained about the emotionalism of some of his opponents, calling them "vested officials" and "paid propagandists." Nevertheless, he was forced to back down. Even his modified reorganization proposals after 1922 failed to receive complete congressional approval, despite President Coolidge's endorsement.

In the long run Hoover had to confine his reorganizational efforts largely to his own department. He succeeded in transferring from the Treasury to his jurisdiction the Inter-American High Commission in 1921 and the Bureau of Customs Statistics in 1923; the Bureau of Mines, the Patent Office, and that portion of the Geological Survey dealing with mineral statistics were all transferred from the Interior Department in 1925. Otherwise his department acquired only the Seismology Division of the Weather Bureau, and, from the Agricultural Department, responsibility for gathering statistics and setting standards for grades of lumber, wool, naval stores, meat packing, and farm machinery. Secretary Wallace steadfastly refused to turn the Bureau of Markets over to the Commerce Department, or to give Hoover jurisdiction over the marketing of farm products.

Disappointed over this limited transfer of power, Hoover employed other means to extend his influence within the federal government. He created new agencies and bureaus with his men in charge, provided instant leadership when other department heads or the president himself hesitated to act, and made certain functions extradepartmental or cooperative so that he could indirectly control them. He also saw to it that cabinet vacancies were filled by men who either agreed with his philosophy or could be easily dominated. It was no accident that Hubert Work followed Albert Fall as secretary of interior in 1923, nor that William Jardine succeeded Henry C. Wallace as secretary of agriculture in 1925. Both were Hoover protegés, who received their appointments after the Chief had refused the positions himself. While James J. Davis, secretary of labor, openly deferred to Hoover's leadership, even the two strongest cabinet members, Secretary of the Treasury Andrew Mellon and Secretary of State Charles Evans Hughes were not able to withstand completely the commerce secretary's aggrandizement of his department between 1921 and 1928.

Ultimately, however, Hoover's most impressive extension of

his administrative power and political ability was reflected in the overall growth of his own department and most notably, the Bureau of Foreign and Domestic Commerce (BFDC). From the very economy-minded Congress of the 1920s he obtained a substantial increase in appropriations, from $24.5 million to $37.6 million, and hired over 3,000 new commerce employees. The BFDC expanded into 37 divisions representing the same major commodity lines used by American companies trading abroad. It increased its personnel fivefold while nearly doubling both its foreign and domestic branch offices until there were 42 overseas and 46 at home.

With this expansion of the BFDC and older departmental units such as the Bureau of Fisheries, Standards, and the Census, plus the creation of new ones for supervising the aviation and radio industries, Hoover thought he had created a decentralized model for organizing business into harmoniously functioning units. It consisted of a complex cooperative system with the Department of Commerce acting as the central "transforming station" for a network of self-regulating component parts, the most important of which were "outside of the government" in the form of state and local coordinating committees and boards, and national trade associations. This was not the inflexible, initiative-stifling bureaucracy of socialism or decaying European capitalism, according to Hoover and his band of Commerce Department publicists. This was the "constructive self-government of industry," based on a responsive, decentralized structure of service and efficiency that simultaneously honored individual initiative and grassroots responsibility. Hoover's newly organized Department of Commerce was a microcosmic version of his dream of informal, associational corporatism for America — a middle way between individualism and collectivism, between monopoly capitalism and state socialism — his answer to the twentieth-century search for order on the part of industrialized nations.

Nonetheless, it remained a bureaucratic structure based largely on traditional administrative hierarchy with the secretary of commerce at its apex. Yet Hoover supporters insisted that this bureaucracy was not like others in personnel or purpose. Where typical bureaucracies at home and abroad were characterized by duplication of effort, red tape, and incompetent meddlers, Hoover's associational bureaucratic structure would consist of experts who understood the postwar needs of modern America and who would efficiently guide the nation during this crucial time of transition. In fact, defenders of Hooverian governmental reorganization even argued that because associationalism functioned without coercion, it would ultimately reduce the need for big government and federal control. Associationalism was purely a temporary agent for change until such time when the activity of state was reduced to that of umpire or caretaker for harmoniously functioning, self-regulating economic units.

In the meantime, however, Hoover's reorganization was necessary because conditions in the United States were far from this ideal of the "associative state." There was too much lawlessness, destructive competition, and economic waste, too much unemployment, and repetitiveness in factory work; the twelve-hour day was too long; labor lacked the guarantee of collective bargaining; child labor still existed despite prewar progressive legislation; education was inadequate in most states; some people were making too much money — "far beyond the needs of stimulation to initiative" — and religious intolerance prevailed as did political debauchery and inefficient structural defects at all levels of government. But local communities, regional commissions, or individual industries could handle most of these problems, Hoover believed. National legislation or federal interference were at best temporary expedients and secondary to advisory and mediation roles of government.

Far more important than these defects, according to Hoover, were signs in America of greater cooperation and less materialism. For example, he thought that prohibition, which had liquidated the liquor industry during World War I without compensation to individual brewers, showed that private property was no longer the fetish in America that it once had been. The financial sacrifice of the "dollar-a-year man," who had worked during the war for government without compensation, was another encouraging sign away from materialism and in the direction of public service; so was the war-stimulated trend toward uniform standards within individual industries. Finally, in *American Individualism* he asserted that economic domination by individual ownership was disappearing: the "works of today are steadily growing more and more beyond the resources of any one individual, and steadily taxation will reduce relatively excessive accumulations." This trend toward division of ownership through an increasing number of stockholders, Hoover believed, would make the administration of large corporations more efficient and "more sensitive to the moral opinions of the people in order to attract their support," and as a result the directors of such firms would begin to reflect a spirit of community responsibility, a sense of "mutuality with the prosperity of the community."

Later in the decade, at the 1926 convention of the United States Chamber of Commerce, Hoover described this trend as the "mutualization" of the postwar American economy, and said that it was transforming the old relationship between the separate interests of owner, customer, and laborer. Hoover used the term mutualization to mean the "diffusion of stock into multitudes of inert holders and governmental limitations of profits in certain industries." He saw mutualization developing in three major segments of the economy: financial institutions, the public utilities, and a group of certain older established manufacturing and distribution organizations. In the first category, which included mutual insurance institutions, the mutual savings banks, fraternal and benefit organizations, the buildings and loan associations, and the farmers' and other cooperative commodity organizations, as well as the endowments of private educational and charitable institutions, leadership was passing from the original owners to professional managers with "little participation in ownership," so that there was "no longer so dominant a pressure for profits" and a possibility of larger shares to workers and customers. In the second mutualized category he put the public utility companies, the profits of which were indirectly limited by governmental regulation. Hoover saw in these companies the same wide dispersion of ownership and shift away from pure profit motivation. Finally, in the third category of older and larger manufacturing or distributing establishments, Hoover said the same conditions applied. He estimated that these three mutualized groupings held from 40 to 50 percent of all the corporate wealth of the nation.

To Hoover such figures confirmed postwar trends not only toward mutualization, but also toward greater cooperation, less materialism, and more sense of community responsibility, obligation, and service. Unlimited capital accumulation and excessive materialism were not part of his economic philosophy, any more than unlimited individualism was a part of his social philosophy. He realized that cooperative individualism could only survive in a system where a sense of personal participation and civic responsibility was not a meaningless shibboleth, but a practical part of the political, economic, and social activities of average citizens. Later in his book *Challenge to Liberty* he said that in the 1920s he saw "tens of thousands of associations meeting in village and city for the advancement of economic, scientific, moral and social professional and governmental ideas. Through their exchange of ideas, their coordination of action, their lift in standards and ideals, we had greatly developed in the highest area of government — that is, self-government outside of formal government."

The development of this informal, decentralized "functional self-government," in the words of one historian, was to "meet the needs of industrial democracy without the interference of governmental bureaucrats." To accomplish this

Hoover relied excessively on the belief that enlightened businessmen would act voluntarily in the public interest once they were made fully aware of the value of cooperative individualism, associationalism, and the elimination of waste. (In a 1925 address to a National Distribution Conference he defined waste as the "natural outgrowth of a competitive system." Accordingly in a number of speeches he said: "I do not mean the waste that any single individual can correct by his own initiative, but the waste that can only find remedy in collective action." Then he usually went on to list the thirteen different varieties of collective economic waste which could be eliminated by cooperative self-regulation.)

The problem of postwar unemployment provides an excellent illustration of Hoover's goals and tactics. He became secretary of commerce in the midst of the 1920–1921 depression, when four to six million Americans were out of work. Unemployment on this scale meant one thing to Hoover — waste and inefficiency. As president of the Federated American Engineering Societies, he had already initiated a study of waste in industry under the direction of progressive engineers, most of whom were adherents of Frederick W. Taylor's school of scientific management. These engineers had concluded that management was responsible for over half of all industrial waste, while labor accounted for only a quarter of it. These conclusions reinforced Hoover's long-held belief that unemployment was essentially a technical problem that could be solved by socially responsible efficiency engineers, but they were not well received by either conservative engineers or the business community.

Nonetheless, on the basis of this report and the knowledge he had gained from presiding over an industrial conference called by President Wilson between December 1919 and March 1920, Hoover urged President Harding to establish the President's Conference on Unemployment. This conference convened on September 26, 1921, and became the prototype of all such Hoover-sponsored conferences for the rest of the decade. Like the other 250 major conferences he organized as secretary of commerce, this one was well planned in advance. And though he publicly denied that he had preconceived ideas about the results of any given conference or investigatory commission, his private correspondence and Commerce Department reports indicate the contrary. Every recommendation and action resulting from this 1921 Conference on Unemployment could have been derived either from Hoover's previous speeches on the topic or from his general philosophical concern for decentralized cooperation and avoidance of federal coercion in solving national economic problems.

For example, the findings of the Economic Advisory Committee, a select group of academic economists and engineers, reformers and industrialists, which Hoover had appointed before the first plenary session of the conference, could subsequently be found in the report of the official delegates to the President's Conference on Unemployment. Dividing its recommendations into the three categories of relief, recovery and long-term reform, the Economic Advisory Committee (EAC) said that local governments had to assume the bulk of the responsibility of relieving postwar unemployment. Although they felt these local efforts had to be supplemented by federal appropriations for public works, members of the EAC agreed with Hoover that the primary role of the national government was to disseminate information, to educate the public so that unemployment could be relieved voluntarily by individual communities. As a result, a flood of propaganda — press releases, informational pamphlets, "pep" letters to local and state officials, and special publicity campaigns designed to appeal to women, professional groups, and even the unemployed themselves — poured forth from the Department of Commerce.

It was through this kind of massive government educational activity that Hoover hoped to pass on to a relatively uninformed public the expertise of his advisers. His American corporate system depended in the last analysis upon voluntary, decentralized implementation of diverse and individual local programs conforming to the general guidelines set by federal experts.

Hoover viewed the 1921 Conference on Unemployment as a gigantic educational device. Since it had not been conceived as a policy-making body, he thought it almost completely successful in arousing local and state cooperative actions for ending unemployment. As the conference was ending he told the assembled delegates that their work was a "milestone in the progress of social thought." However, both its educational and practical effects left much to be desired — a fact Hoover conveniently ignored.

For example, the conference produced little cooperative spirit among the nation's large cities like New York, Chicago, and Detroit. The programs begun with so much fanfare in the smaller cities soon waned. Furthermore, with one exception, none of the recommendations for federal legislation ever passed Congress. And that exception — higher tariff rates — would have materialized under GOP rule without the President's Conference on Unemployment. Indeed, the entire experience confirmed Hoover's suspicions of Congress as an ineffective body for dealing with national recovery programs, and accounts in part for his attempt to ignore that branch of government during the early stages of the depression of 1929. But it also left him overconfident about the publicity conference as an effective approach to economic problems.

At the same time that Congress was refusing most requests for appropriations, Hoover's colleagues within the executive branch were proving reluctant to initiate remedial measures over which their respective departments had jurisdiction. Treasury Secretary Andrew Mellon and Director of the Budget Charles G. Dawes sided with parsimonious Congressmen of the early 1920s on the need for federal retrenchment. Attorney General Harry M. Daugherty was openly antagonistic to any action favoring organized labor. And while Secretary of Labor James J. Davis was nominally in favor of an accelerated program of public works to aid the unemployed, he proved incapable of strong leadership. Even President Harding, after having supported Hoover's suggestion for the conference, did not help get its relief and recovery measures through Congress.

In the area of permanent economic reform the results were no more concrete. The most progressive recommendation of the unemployment conference called for providing employment during depression periods by a planned program of public works. Money for this purpose was to come from a federal reserve fund built up during prosperous years. Various forms of this proposal died in Congress between 1921 and 1928, despite Hoover's strong endorsement.

As progressive and impressive as the President's Conference on Unemployment appeared on the surface, it contributed little to the upswing in the economy which occurred in 1922. It did, however, temporarily attract national attention to the problem of unemployment and to the possibility of using statistical analysis to counter or control fluctuating business cycles — quite an advanced economic concept for the time. It was also responsible for four other national surveys. One in 1922–1923 on Business Cycles and Unemployment and another in 1923–1924 on Seasonal Operations in the Construction Industry were direct results of the conference. In addition, it later gave rise to a preliminary study in 1928–1929 of the United States economy (this later became President Hoover's Committee on Recent Economic Changes), and to the 1929–1930 study on the Planning and Control of Public Works. Most important, this first national unemployment conference symbolized a change in the role of the executive branch of government, if not Congress, in time of economic distress. Harding did not, after all, have to call such a conference to deal with the postwar depression; nor did the Economic Advisory Committee have to make the recommendations it did. Both unprecedented actions were taken at Hoover's insistence and were clearly in keeping with his prewar progressive reputation.

Hoover's concern for employment did not end with this conference. His most effective labor action came in 1923 when he finally succeeded in converting the steel industry to an eight-hour day without resorting to federal legislation. Asserting his leadership over that of Labor Secretary Davis, Hoover literally prosecuted leading steel executives like Judge Elbert Gary in a court of public opinion by keeping the inequities and inefficiency of the twelve-hour day "boiling in the press." It took him two years to "persuade" management to institute an eight-hour day. The fact that the success of his publicity tactics and private conferences in this case depended upon a number of unusually favorable circumstances, such as church support and the extremely weak arguments of management, did not deter Hoover from proclaiming an unqualified victory for voluntarism. He also ignored the fact that individual steel companies partly nullified the financial significance of the eight-hour day victory by hiring greater numbers of black and chicano workers at below average wages.

The heart of labor's problems in the postwar decade was how to obtain effective representation in disputes with management and in decisions leading to greater productivity and efficiency. In 1920, before becoming secretary of commerce, Hoover had strongly supported participation of democratically elected shop-level committees of workers in settling labor disputes. But for the rest of the decade, as secretary of commerce, his pubic statements about such representation were few and never precise in terms of the exact nature of these shop committees and their relationship to trade unionism.

Instead, Hoover became the chief initiator of labor policy under both Harding and Coolidge, concentrating on exposing the problems of production and efficiency and recommending voluntary means for their solution, rather than advocating federal legislation that would have insured labor unions the right of collective bargaining. Such legislation was beyond the limits of his voluntary philosophy. Nonetheless he did counter in a limited and progressive fashion the antilabor attitudes of Attorney General Daugherty and Budget Director Dawes. He also continued, at least in theory, to support the principle of noncoercive collective bargaining. Later he recalled in his *Memoirs* that he opposed the sweeping federal labor injunction against striking railroad workers in 1922 as an "obvious transgression of the most rudimentary rights of the men." He also tried to convince private insurance companies that they should provide unemployment programs for workers, and asserted at numerous business conventions the traditional right of labor to strike except when it interfered with what he called the "superior right" of the public. He placed the same restraint of public interest on the right of management to use the tactical weapons of lockout and open shop.

At the same time Hoover also insisted that to maintain the high American standard of living each worker had to produce at a maximum rate in return for high wages and low prices. His entire American system relied upon increasing domestic consumption in order to make the country less dependent upon foreign markets. One way to accomplish this was to maintain the purchasing power of labor through high real wages. Above all else, he told the United States Chamber of Commerce in 1926, both employer and employee had to realize that their mutual advantage lay in increased production and consumption. This could only be accomplished through the "constant growth of national efficiency."

Hoover-sponsored conferences and educational publicity based on these economic assumptions ultimately led to the 1926 Railway Labor Act, which explicitly endorsed collective bargaining and set up mediation procedures for railroad unions and carriers to follow in future disputes. These tactics had earlier led to both the Baltimore Agreement of 1922 which provided a fair settlement for many striking railroad workers, and the Jacksonville Agreement of 1924 between management and labor in the soft coal industry. Violations of the latter quickly prompted Hoover to deny that the government was in any way responsible for making either side live up to its terms. John L. Lewis, as head of the United Mine Workers (UMW), disputed this claim, arguing that since the Departments of Commerce, Justice, and Labor had made the Jacksonville Agreement possible in the first place, the federal government should take action against coal companies who ignored it. This difference of opinion is indicative of the serious limitations of the labor policy that Hoover developed for the GOP in the 1920s. In this instance, Hoover apparently decided that the UMW was not essential to the health and stability of the bituminous coal industry, so he refused pleas from Lewis for government enforcement of the Jacksonville Agreement.

It was clear by 1927 that his repeated calls for the coal industry to solve its own problems through internal cooperation had not ended the senseless overproduction and competition for markets among mine owners; instead, this hands-off policy effectively undermined the UMW bargaining position. Membership had declined drastically by that year, and nonunion mines paying the lowest wages were producing enough to satisfy the shrinking national demand for soft coal. Moreover, the wage reductions that UMW members had to settle for after the unsuccessful strikes of 1927 and 1928 were in direct contradiction of Hoover's contention that high wages were necessary for continued American prosperity.

Although Hoover had encouraged leading industrialists to "establish liaison" with the AFL in 1919, had supported a highly qualified version of the closed shop in 1921, and had worked closely as secretary of commerce with moderate individual labor leaders like Samuel Gompers, William Green, William Doaks, and even the more volatile John L. Lewis, such labor policies could not prevent a crippling drop in union membership — from around 5 million in 1921 to 3,442,600 in 1929. This occurred for a number of reasons: the capitulation of certain labor leaders to the corporate ideology of big business (and the government) in return for a nominal increase in wages and living standards, the eight-hour day in the steel industry, restricted immigration, the Railway Act of 1926. Also, employers drew laborers away from radical union-ism with such enticements as profit-sharing plans, company-sponsored unions, and minimal pension plans.

These developments along with the superficial prosperity of the decade, including easy credit which artificially increased the purchasing power of workers, accounted in large measure for the overall decline in union membership. They also obvi-ated the necessity for Republicans (or Democrats) to question the welfare-capitalism propaganda of big corporations. There was in essence no national labor reform policy in the 1920s, with the exception of Hoover's attempt to improve working conditions and wages through the voluntary cooperation of individual workers at the local plant level, and through national union demands backed by the force of public opin-ion, rather than by strikes. Under his leadership, however, successive Republican administrations never developed a prac-tical policy for creating effective representation for workers in shop committees or combating representation schemes by em-ployers that weakened trade unionism. In large measure this was because Hoover and other Republicans deluded them-selves that conditions of the average workers were appreciably better than they were.

"One of the most astonishing transformations in economic history," Hoover exclaimed in the *Annual Report* of the Commerce Department for 1926, "lies in . . . the parallel increase of wages with decreasing prices." To prove this point he often favorably compared union wages and average whole-sale prices in the United States with those in England since 1920. We now know, however, that while real wages for all categories of workers rose only slightly between 1923 and 1928, there was a disproportionate 62 percent increase in corporate profits. Instead of being used for developing more efficient means of production, lowering prices, or increasing wages (as Hoover advocated), most of these profits went into higher corporate dividends and speculative ventures. By 1929 fewer than two thousand individuals directed the two hundred largest corporations in America, whiie more than 40 percent of the population earned less than $1,500 — the established minimum poverty level of the time. Overall, some 60 percent had annual incomes of less than $2,000. The uneven prosperity of the New Era in fact meant that the rich became richer and the poor barely held their own; the "mutualization" of the American economy that Hoover had anticipated did not take place; and union membership dropped to the point where organized labor could not function as a countervailing force in the economy.

Nonetheless, Hoover continued to include labor unions in his list of beneficial economic associations through which the United States was slowly moving in the direction of "industrial democracy" based on "associational activities." (Other such groups were mutual insurance and savings institutions, professional organizations, farmers' cooperatives, chambers of commerce, and trade associations.) However, his opinion of the role of labor unions in attaining economic stability through collective action was never as clearly developed as his view of the role of trade associations. Although Hoover thought collective bargaining was an obvious means for avoiding the instability caused by strikes, he placed greater hope for controlling business cycles in the development of trade associations. Because these were made up of employers or producers rather than workers, they might succeed in curbing the excessive competition that led to economic waste especially in such natural-resource industries as agriculture, soft coal, oil and timber or cotton textiles.

These trade associations represented the cornerstone of Hoover's economic "associationalism," for they were the major means by which he hoped to achieve both price stabilization and general economic stability — all without coercive federal action. The idea of trade associationalism or "cooperative competition," as it has been called, had gained considerable ground during World War I. It was a way to stabilize war production by eliminating wasteful competition and still preserve national antitrust laws to protect against informal price-fixing cartels. Hoover viewed associationalism as the means for stabilizing economic activity and increasing industrial efficiency — without sacrificing the principle of competition within functional economic units or interest groups. This was the essential component of his brand of neoguildist American corporatism. It provided the voluntary means for *integrating* rather than *regimenting* the political economy of the nation.

This was not to be accomplished simply through the exchange of information about prices, production standardization, and improved cost-accounting techniques within a single industry, although some businessmen and later critics of associationalism assumed this to be the case. When the Commerce Department began to publish the monthly *Survey of Current Business* in 1921, it was only part of a multifaceted program for informing, reeducating and bringing extralegal pressure to bear on businessmen to solve the problems of industrial waste, business cycles, inadequate housing, sick industries, unemployment, foreign trade, and even the perennial farm problem. To Hoover trade associationalism was a comprehensive attempt to institutionalize those aspects of the wartime economy that had relied on voluntary cooperation and collective action.

As early as 1922, however, Hoover realized that it would be easy for individual businessmen and industries to think of trade associationalism exclusively in terms of the private exchange of statistics and to misuse such information to control prices and markets. He condemned as not "in the public interest" the extremist "open price" policies, which advocated the exchange of data to fix prices. Not only did the Department of Commerce discourage domestic price-fixing through such statistical exchanges, it also opposed revision of the Sherman Antitrust Act to legalize such actions. But because of Hoover's strong endorsement in the 1920s of trade associationalism and his earlier endorsement of the Edge Act of 1919, which permitted bankers to combine (without fear of prosecution under the existing antitrust laws) in order to provide private financing for postwar trade abroad, the impression was created that he was personally in favor of drastic antitrust revision. Nothing could have been further from the truth. Price-fixing (as opposed to price stabilization) was anathema to Hoover because of his wartime experiences as Food Administrator. "I have done more of it than any other man who lives," he once stated, "and I would not propose price-fixing in any form short of again reentering the trenches in another World War."

Nonetheless his position remained somewhat ambiguous. It became a likely target for criticism in the early 1920s, when both the Justice Department and the Federal Trade Commission (FTC) began to challenge even the most innocuous types of statistical exchanges. This campaign, triggered by the high cost of living resulting from postwar inflation, ruined Hoover's hopes for obtaining quick approval from Justice or FTC officials for those associational activities that did not lend themselves to price-fixing or to violations of the antitrust laws. Because it rapidly turned into an attack on trade associationalism in general, the backlash forced Hoover to clarify his stand on both statistical exchanges and antitrust revision. At one point in the fall of 1921 he stated that price reporting should be given up entirely by the trade associations, and he finally recommended that only averages be reported.

Also, it is clear from his support of the 1919 Edge Act that he was more favorably disposed toward antitrust revision immediately following the war, to promote the sale of manufactured products abroad, than he was later in the 1920s when he defended trade associations in the name of efficient production and increased domestic consumption. He continued throughout the decade to give stronger support to export-import trade associations, including those which led to informal buying pools for the procurement of scarce raw materials like rubber, because he believed there was a greater foreign market for manufactured goods than for agricultural products. On the one hand he was concerned that Americans be able to compete for overseas trade; on the other he wanted the nation to be economically self-sufficient, by consuming most of its own gross national product. There was bound to be some confusion, if not outright contradiction, between these two goals.

After the Supreme Court finally upheld Hoover's typically middle-of-the road position on trade associationalism in 1925, he was automatically seen as the unofficial champion of all kinds of trade associationalism, when in fact he represented only the most moderate segment of the movement. His later presidential antitrust activity against domestic cartels clearly confirms this. Although some businessmen continued to abuse their statistical and cooperative programs, while still others wanted to repeal all antitrust laws, especially after the 1929 depression began, Hoover continued to oppose actions by trade associations advocating any amendment of the Sherman Antitrust law that would create monopoly, price-fixing, or any type of collective action "incompatible with the maintenance of a competitive economy."

While he can be criticized for not using the power of the Commerce Department or for not obtaining federal legislation to prevent extremists within trade associations from abusing their statistical exchanges, Hoover never gave free reign or wholehearted endorsement to the associations, except possibly to those engaged *exclusively* in the export of manufactured products or in the import of scarce raw materials. It cannot be overemphasized, however, that trade associationalism remained more important to his economic plans for the nation than militant unionism. Like most Progressives, both before and after World War I, if given the choice between oligopolistic development in the name of economic stability and production efficiency, and prolonged disruptive actions by organized labor, he unhesitatingly chose the former.

The three "sickest" industries (soft coal, textiles, and agriculture) and others whose profits were below average throughout the decade because of contracting markets wanted revision of the antitrust laws and refused to respond to Hoover's appeals for associational activity. These were the most disorganized industries from a cooperative point of view, and Hoover liked to think that given time even these atomistic, recalcitrant ones would fall into line with his voluntarism. In retrospect we can see that his economic theories failed in the face of serious economic dislocation and contracting markets, such as existed in these three key American industries in the relatively prosperous times before 1929. As this contraction became widespread with the Great Depression, violations of cooperative individualism increased perceptibly, as did lack of faith in the presumed mutual self-interest of labor and management.

In summary, Hoover's economic philosophy before the depression of 1929 in certain unstable sectors of the economy had failed for several reasons. Associationalism did not prove a viable alternative for the most cut-throat industries; it was instead most useful to cartel-oriented groups within such industries, and it ended up fostering oligopoly rather than providing an alternative to it. In overestimating his own ability to convince business leaders that it was in their own interest to practice voluntary cooperative individualism and eschew the temptation of monopoly profits, Hoover contributed to the decline of his reputation as a Progressive and to confusion over his position on antitrust revisionism. To succeed without federal coercion, associationalism required the kind of socially responsible professionals that were all too scarce in the business community of the 1920s.

Agriculture, more than any other "sick" industry, seemed to defy Hoover's New Era economic theories. In 1927 he regretfully admitted to an agricultural conference that it was proving next to impossible to integrate the agricultural industry into his comprehensive plans for eliminating the contradictions between the domestic and foreign policies of the United States. The extreme individualism of the American farmer had persistently kept individuals competing with the farmers' cooperatives, and the farmers themselves were unable to provide large sums of working capital to build more cooperative associations. Other obstacles to the growth of marketing cooperatives and to increased domestic consumption through diversification of production, he had told the United States Chamber of Commerce the year before, were the lack of initiative and leadership among farmers and the discouragement brought about by years of failure without "skilled direction."

Hoover also thought that the farm problem was aggravated by what he called the socialist ideas of the secretary of agriculture in Harding's cabinet, Henry Cantwell Wallace — ideas which in retrospect are clearly the views of statist corporatism. Before his death in 1924, Wallace and his farm bloc friends did more than any other single group to thwart Hoover's plans for expanding the powers of the Department of Commerce at the expense of the Department of Agriculture, to hamper the creation of the marketing cooperatives that Hoover regarded as the equivalent of trade associations for farmers, and to tarnish the Great Humanitarian's image as a Progressive.

Hoover and Wallace had clashed earlier during the war over some of the prices set by the Food Administration for agricultural products. Convinced that Hoover was not only stuffy and bloodless, but also an "exceptionally big-brained business man" who did not understand the unique problems of the farmer during or after the war, Wallace opposed the presidential boom for Hoover, throwing his support at the GOP convention of 1920 to Illinois Governor Frank O. Lowden. Nonetheless, Hoover recognized that Wallace was "admirably fitted for the work" of secretary of agriculture, and he refused to oppose the nomination of the fiery farm editor when he learned that Harding was considering him.

These two Iowa-born cabinet members first disagreed about which department should control foreign and domestic agricultural marketing. Their major confrontation, however, occurred over the best way to bring the American farm industry out of its postwar decline. The secretary of agriculture favored direct government intervention in the form of a federal export corporation that would purchase surplus agricultural commodities and sell them abroad. Variations of this idea appeared in various congressional bills throughout the decade, most notably in McNary-Haugen legislation, which embodied the so-called two-price system — a high domestic price and a low export price. The former would be arbitrarily determined by the United States government without relation to actual domestic supply and demand, while the latter would automatically be determined by the current world price. (Based on the "parity" principle, the high domestic prices were designed to give farmers the purchasing power they had in the years before 1914.)

In contrast, the secretary of commerce opposed any federal tampering with domestic prices and the laws of supply and demand. He also feared foreign retaliation against such large American agricultural exports, in the form of trade embargoes or prohibitive tariffs. Hoover urged instead that the government develop a system of voluntary marketing cooperatives to reduce "waste of materials and motion between the farmer and the consumer . . . and thus give a larger part of the consumer's dollar to the farmer." These cooperatives, according to his address to the American Dairy Federation on October 1, 1924, should also encourage the greater diversification of crops among farmers who found themselves suffering from continuous overproduction, the conversion of occasional seasonal surpluses into alternative by-products, and the standardization of quality by government certification. "Generally," he said later in the same year at the President's Agriculture Conference, "the fundamental need is the balancing of agricultural production to our home demand."

These ideas constituted the underlying philosophy of both the Cooperative Marketing Act of 1926 and the Federal Farm

Board created when Hoover was president. He remained unalterably opposed to price-fixing on the basis of his wartime experiences. He personally thought that most farm prices had been fixed too high during the war, encouraging the very overproduction that would plague farmers in the 1920s. Although this position was very unpopular among farmers, he remained absolutely certain from his Food Administration days that even greater surpluses from overproduction would result if the government established artificially high domestic prices for a select group of agricultural commodities.

In addition to possibly disrupting harmonious economic relations with certain foreign nations, Hoover argued, the McNary-Haugen legislation would: 1) create uncontrolled inflation in food prices and correspondingly inflationary demands for increased wages by organized labor; 2) encourage the same type of overproduction in agriculture that the war had; 3) benefit primarily the large agricultural producers rather than the small, traditionally independent farmers and thus possibly produce oligopolistic control of the industry; and 4) prompt other industries to request similar direct government aid. This, of course, would mean the politicizing of the American economy with extensive lobbying in Congress by major interest groups.

"I hesitate to contemplate the future of our institutions, of our government, and of our country," Hoover once remarked, "if the preoccupation of its officials is to be no longer the promotion of justice and equal opportunity but is to be devoted to barter in the markets." To Hoover, McNary-Haugenism meant the ultimate destruction of the American system as he envisaged it based on informal guildist corporatism. And he was correct; it became one of the first steps in the direction of statist corporatism taken by New Deal agricultural reformers under the leadership of Wallace's son, Henry Agard Wallace.

Ironically, it was under the leadership of George N. Peek, a successful midwestern farm-implement executive and presi-

dent of the American Council of Agriculture, a powerful
lobbying organization, that hostile relations between the
country's agrarian interests and the secretary of commerce
temporarily escalated after Wallace's unexpected death in
October 1924. Peek could scarcely qualify as an unselfish
spokesman for the common "dirt" farmer, yet that is exactly
how he was portrayed at the time. At the end of 1924 and well
into 1925 Hoover privately accused Peek, who was the chief
architect of the two-price system, of distributing a memorandum containing "gross misrepresentations" about the
Department of Commerce. It included the charges that Commerce officials were "invading the functions of the Department
of Agriculture in foreign trade," and that Hoover personally
was "endeavoring to secure the transfer of the Bureau of
Markets from the Department of Agriculture." Hoover cate-
gorically, but unconvincingly, denied both charges. This personal squabble dragged on through the summer of 1926,
ending inconclusively and unsatisfactorily for all concerned.

Hoover's frankness in some off-the-record remarks at the
Business Man's Conference on Agriculture of 1927 simply
reaffirmed that the Commerce Department under his leadership generally recommended solutions for agricultural problems similar to those for other "sick" industries; that is, tariff
protection combined with more efficient production and
marketing systems, resulting in lower costs and higher wages.
The major difference between Hoover's economic policies for
agriculture and for the mining or manufacturing industries
was that he did not anticipate a growing foreign market for
American staples, as he did for American manufactured
products. Hence, he placed more emphasis on providing short-
term agricultural credit and on crop diversification than on
staple production or refined food products for export, in the
mistaken belief that population growth in the United States
would expand the domestic market until it absorbed the bulk
of farm crops.

The degree to which Hoover believed that international

relations affected American agriculture cannot be overestimated. But he was never able to convince opponents of his farm policies that the United States had to consider the production capabilities and import needs of foreign nations as well as its own. He was perfectly willing to export food products for famine relief abroad, especially if the American market was suffering from a surplus as was the case in the early 1920s. Under his direction the American Relief Administration in Russia did just this between 1921 and 1923, and even sold a certain percentage of the 1922 United States wheat crop to the Bolsheviks, whom Hoover would not deal with under any other circumstances. He also deliberately expanded the foreign offices of the Bureau of Foreign and Domestic Commerce (BFDC) not only to aid the sales of manufactured goods abroad, but to gather data on possible foreign agricultural markets as well. Nonetheless, he refused to view the farm problem as an isolated domestic issue and always dealt with it in terms of tariff policy, international loans, balance of payments, and the rate of postwar reconstruction taking place in Europe. In particular, he refused to operate under the illusion of Wallace, Peek, Senator George W. Norris, and others that the United States could simply replace Russia as the grain supplier of Europe.

Above all else, Hoover feared making farm profits dependent upon any extensive foreign marketing schemes (illusory or otherwise) because of his desire that the United States economy be as self-sufficient as possible. He already thought that manufacturing profits were becoming too dependent upon overseas sales. But he worried *more* about how foreign debtor nations which produced the same agricultural surpluses for export as the United States would be able to meet their balance of payments if they had to compete with American farmers, than he worried about those debtor nations which were trying to sell manufactured goods in direct competition with the United States. This seeming inconsistency possibly reflects what Wallace and Peek (and later historians) thought was Hoover's unconscious businessman's bias against farmers. But Hoover insisted that agricultural markets would be much more limited in the future than those for American manufactured products, and that manufactured exports would not obtain the same degree of dependence on foreign markets as would agricultural exports.

His critics notwithstanding, during his eight years as secretary of commerce Hoover did greatly influence the agricultural administrative policy, if not popular agricultural attitudes. Despite the less than successful President's Conferences on Agriculture in 1922 and 1924, and the Business Man's Conference on Agriculture in 1927, the business community in general endorsed Hoover's cooperative marketing approach rather than subsidy plans based on a two-price system or export debenture corporations. (However, the annual National Agricultural Conferences called by the Wallace-Peek forces during the decade invariably supported plans for subsidizing farm production.) Hoover's greatest influence over agricultural policy was exercised directly when, largely upon his advice, President Coolidge vetoed two consecutive McNary-Haugen bills passed by Congress in 1927 and 1928.

Hoover's agricultural policies also significantly influenced some of his other domestic programs, most especially in the area of transportation. The distribution problems so many farmers faced, he believed, could be solved by eliminating waste — in this case inefficient or inadequate transportation systems. So his railway, waterway, highway, subsidized shipbuilding, and even airway projects were all related directly or indirectly to the agricultural problem. The same is true of his activities in the field of conservation. But little credit has been given to the comprehensive view that he took of the farm crisis, or to the general services that his department rendered to the agricultural industry.

Despite Hoover's running battle with Peek and his less than positive reputation among organized farm interest groups,

President Coolidge offered him the position of secretary of agriculture upon Wallace's death. Hoover refused without hesitation, as he had the year before declined to become secretary of the interior, because he believed he was in the process of creating a Department of Commerce that could best serve all the major economic needs of the country. It is possible, however, that one of the unstated reasons for refusing to replace Wallace was the fact that he could see no sure way of solving the complex problems of American agriculture.

Hoover's relations with the Department of Agriculture (if not with the agricultural industry as a whole) improved perceptibly when William M. Jardine was appointed to succeed Wallace. Like the secretary of commerce, Jardine supported cooperative marketing and voluntarily controlled agricultural output. Hoover continued to make proposals along these lines, but large producers and processors, as well as average farmers, stubbornly defied his recommendations (albeit for different reasons). However, most of his public statements after 1925 on the farm crisis revealed an uncertainty that cannot be found in his pronouncements about the economic problems of other sick industries.

Hoover's agricultural policy was only one part of a comprehensive economic plan for the United States that he thought would also indirectly aid the American farmer. It involved combating waste, unemployment, and widely fluctuating business cycles through cooperative and scientific methods, developing waterways, and generally promoting a high standard of living for all Americans through tariff protection and expanded foreign exports. His was the only agricultural policy of the 1920s to call for changing the negative attitude of farmers about cooperative production control, which was at the root of the surplus problem. From the beginning of the decade Wallace and Peek insisted that it was impossible to reeducate farmers along the lines of cooperative individualism because they were too insulated from normal publicity tactics and public pressure. In taking this position, however, they were ignoring both their own successful public-relations campaigns among farmers and recent developments in mass communication. Instead they made self-fulfilling prophecies by refusing to participate in any long-term educational program aimed at changing the values of farmers. Hoover was also one of the few public figures in the 1920s who saw that unlimited agricultural production would perpetuate international marketing problems regardless of high tariffs, debenture export plans, domestic price-fixing, or subsidies. Finally, he correctly predicted that surplus production and overdependence on foreign markets would remain major farm problems despite all the government controls instituted after 1933.

Central to all of Hoover's activities during his eight years as secretary of commerce were his efforts to eliminate waste in industry in order to lower production costs and broaden domestic consumption. To aid him in this mammoth task he created the Division of Simplified Practice within the Bureau of Standards. Between 1921 and 1928, in cooperation with almost 900 trade associations and over 7,000 individual firms, eighty-six major simplifications involving the standardization of specifications and scientific testing were effected and over 1,200 conferences were held on the elimination of waste in design, production, and distribution. Unnecessary varieties of everything from the sizes of cans and bottles, automobile tires, paving bricks, electrical fixtures, and bedsprings to toilet paper, blackboards, and all kinds of bolts, nuts, and pipes were reduced in number. The way was cleared for mass production on a much larger scale, and for the concept of interchangeable parts which made American manufactured goods so popular abroad in the course of the 1920s.

Standardization in the field of private housing also interested Hoover. In the early 1920s he instituted a widely publicized campaign for reform and expansion through the Division of Building and Housing and a voluntary national organization known as Better Homes in America. This group of approximately 30,000 members consisted largely of women

who by 1926 had formed more than 1,800 volnutary committees. Each one had a public-relations staff for disseminating
information from the Department of Commerce on how to
build low-cost dwellings. The Division of Building and Housing successfully promoted the adoption of uniform building
codes and zoning laws in 37 states, and in general reflected
Hoover's own personal commitment to preserving the American family as a physical as well as spiritual unit.

Hoover's standardization and simplification programs led
some to speculate that he was trying to create a "whole nation
riding in the same kind of cars, wearing the same kind of
clothes, thinking the same thoughts." Hoover's supporters
vehemently denied that simplification meant a drab, uniform
way of life for Americans of the future. However, given his
personality and almost total indifference to his physical surroundings when concentrating on a particular task, his minimal concern about the sameness in dress styles, modes of
transportation, or other physical necessities of life is not surprising. "When I go to ride in an automobile," he dourly
informed author Sherwood Anderson, who asked him whether
standardization posed a threat to civilization, "it does not
matter to me that there are a million automobiles on the road
just like mine. I am going somewhere and I want to get there
in what comfort I can and at the lowest cost."

Long interested in the welfare of children, Hoover headed
the Child Health Association from 1923 until 1935. During
that time some $5 million was raised for increasing community
services to children, especially to remedy nutritional deficiencies
in urban areas. When speaking about proper diets for children
after World War I, Hoover came closer to expressing personal
emotion than on any other public topic. He was also extremely influential in the field of education, championing the
cause of free, publicly supported schools at all levels because of
his belief in equality of opportunity and his conviction that
successful associationalism requires an intelligent citizenry.
"Our education . . . is the central power-house of our whole

system," he said in a 1928 interview with William Hard. "To-day our leaders must be experts; they must be specialists." He was instrumental as well in initiating several national research funds and enlarging the scientific research facilities of many universities through money raised from private donations.

Outside the field of social welfare Hoover turned to more uncharted waters: the development of new industries. When chaos within the fledgling radio industry demanded federal action in 1921, Hoover stepped in without hesitation. Even though his department had only limited authority to license stations and operators, he quickly developed guidelines for the new industry with the help of four national radio conferences. As might be expected, Hoover originally advocated self-regulation. But the four conferences held between 1922 and 1925 were far from successful, because there was no effective federal legislation to enforce their recommendations. Some of the confusion within the industry was due to Hoover's own hesitation and vacillation over how to define and regulate radio advertising and over how to control the growth of monopoly control by large pioneering broadcasters like RCA, AT&T, General Electric, and Westinghouse.

For example, Hoover first opposed the airing of all "advertising chatter" and then switched to trying to distinguish between "unobtrusive publicity" and "unobtrusive advertising." Thus he never advocated a federal ban on all radio advertising but rather helped to open the door for the unlimited proliferation of radio commercials. During these same formative years in the history of radio he also officially favored the big station operators by assigning them preferred broadcast frequencies, by consulting them about pending legislation in Congress, and by opposing the European method of taxing individual radio receivers as a means of financing station operations. Such a federal tax would have eased the financial burden of small stations and placed more of it on large broadcasters, who also sold radio receivers. As usual in dealing with industry, Hoover was more willing to risk the development of private monopoly or oligopoly than federal control. In part the favoritism Hoover showed for large broadcasters in the 1920s was natural, because he relied extensively on their expertise for his own information. Radio was a new industry and from a technical standpoint the big companies were essential to its rapid development. But however logical his reasons were for relying upon this select group of broadcasters, in doing so he fostered monopolistic trends. Despite his promotion of the radio industry, though, he remained suspicious of its use; as he later said in his *Memoirs,* "there is little adequate answer to a lying microphone" and so "propaganda over the air raises emotion at the expense of reason far more than the printed word."

Another new industry over which Hoover exercised decided influence during its formative years was commercial aviation. Aided by expert advice from the usual well-publicized educational conferences that Hoover called, Congress finally passed legislation in 1926 for Hoover to organize the Bureau of Aeronautics within the Department of Commerce. He also recognized the inequities which had arisen during the Coolidge administration, when the Post Office contracted with private transfer companies to carry the United States mail on a commercial basis. Subsequently, under his Postmaster General Walter Brown, rates for flying the mail were reduced from as much as three dollars per mile in 1929 to twenty-six cents per mile in 1933. Between 1922 and 1926 only 369 miles of regular commercial air service had been developed and only 3,000 miles of mail lines under the jurisdiction of the Post Office. Then from 1926 to 1929 there appeared 25,000 miles of government-improved airways, 1,000 privately funded airports, and 6,400 planes licensed and in regular flights of over 25 million miles annually. "I felt a personal triumph with every mile of service we added," Hoover later recalled.

His other all-consuming activities as secretary of commerce included conferences and recommendations for legislation aimed at the conservation of fish, wild life, and domestic oil

reserves; regional waterway and electrical development all
under coordinated state, not federal regulation; control of
water and air pollution; and development of highway safety
standards. Hoover's views on conservation and environmental
problems in general were advanced for the period; he did not
believe in the traditional, prewar, "cold storage" interpretation of conservation of national resources. Instead, he advocated "use for public interest, not prevention of use."
Although most of his conservation and ecological plans were
not directly implemented until he became president, he did
do much to combat oil pollution of the American coastline by
offshore dumping. Largely unnoticed by the public at the
time, his efforts nonetheless resulted in the passage of the Oil
Pollution Act of 1924 and the 1926 Preliminary International
Conference to control oil pollution in cooperation with other
nations. Hoover was again ahead of his times in realizing the
seriousness of the problem for both the United States and the
world, but after 1926 he became discouraged by opposition
from oil lobbies and public indifference.

Probably the most dramatic application of Hoover's various
economic and political theories while secretary of commerce
came during the 1927 Mississippi flood. As chairman of the
Special Mississippi Food Committee appointed by President
Coolidge, he first created a decentralized promotional campaign that raised approximately $17 million in cash gifts from
the American people; some $15 million of which came from a
national Red Cross radio appeal — the first of its kind. In
addition, he obtained $10 million in federal funds and with
this combined working capital he concentrated on providing
immediate relief to 1.5 million homeless people in inundated
areas covering portions of seven states. Most of this private
and federal money was used to repair dikes as the flood waters
retreated, to rescue stranded individuals, and to establish
more than 150 "great towns of tents." At each location, technical information and equipment was provided by Hoover's

committee, but the work was carried out by grass-roots leaders and local committees.

Although much of this first stage of his flood operations could technically be called charity, it bolstered his conviction that Americans also "expected to take care of one another in time of disaster." Proof of this, he said in a 1928 interview, was the fact that only one of these local committees "failed morally in the handlng of its financial trust." This record marked the great difference between American citizens and those of foreign countries. Unlike his experience with famine-stricken Europeans during World War I, Hoover now saw no lack of "sufficient intelligence, organizational ability and leadership . . . to carry on the local work" in the Mississippi flood area, and proudly concluded: "We rescued Main Street with Main Street."

Once the camps had provided immediate shelter, food, and clothing, and the flood victims were given some basic furniture, seed, farm implements, and even a few farm animals with which to return to their land, the purely charitable activities of the Special Mississippi Flood Committee ended. Then it began the second phase of its operations, for flood damage to the 2 million acres of crops and buildings approached $300 million, a figure far beyond what could be collected from private sources. At this point Hoover decided extensive credit facilities must be established so that those stricken could complete their own rehabilitation. He first organized grass-roots credit facilities in the form of local banks and then integrated them into various private regional systems, such as the Arkansas Farm Credit Company, the Mississippi Rehabilitation Corporation, and the Louisiana Farm Credit Company. Through the United States Chamber of Commerce he established a nonprofit organization that provided an additional $10 million in low-interest loans. The Federal Intermediate Credit Corporation, an adjunct of the Federal Farm Board, opened up another $5 million in low-interest loans. Clearly, under crisis circumstances of such financial magnitude Hoover did not hesitate to turn to federal as well as private sources for credit.

Moreover, the flood offered him a chance to introduce basic land reform into a region long plagued by subsistence-level tenant farming and sharecropping. In a memorandum dated May 12, 1927, Hoover outlined a comprehensive plan for the area whereby a "land resettlement corporation" would use private and government credit to buy and subdivide large plantations into family-sized plots. Stocked with rudimentary housing, equipment, and animals, these would be resold to the "great numbers of buyers amongst both black and whites," in the formerly inundated regions. In this final stage of his Mississippi operation, Hoover attempted to capitalize on the crisis to break up large southern plantations and to achieve a total revision of the government's flood control measures. He succeeded only in his second objective.

Since long-term flood control was beyond the financial and administrative capabilities of local communities, Hoover converted economy-minded congressmen as well as President Coolidge to a comprehensive plan for controlling the Mississippi River from Cairo to New Orleans. His other long-range waterway projects — for the Columbia River basin, the Central Valley of California, the Great Lakes and St. Lawrence seaway, and Muscle Shoals in the Tennessee Valley — all fell victim to the parsimonious and parochial attitudes within the White House and Congress. He did, however, have the satisfaction of seeing his plans for the development of the Colorado River basin, which ultimately led to the building of Boulder Dam, and Mississippi flood control begun while he was secretary of commerce and continued almost to completion while he was president. In terms of Hoover's own ideology, his flood relief activity represented an almost ideal balance between decentralized and central authority, between government and private funds, and between charity and self-help. Also, the experience seemed to offer conclusive proof that his American system based on cooperative individualism could operate effectively in crises not generated by war. Hoover came out of the Mississippi valley a hero, with his reputation as the Great Humanitarian enhanced, and personally more popular than ever before. People were beginning to look at him in a new light. One flood victim remarked: "We think Hoover is the most useful American of his day. Why, he'd make a fine President." To Will Rogers and many others in the country it became common to think that the only rest "Bert" got was between calamities.

Hoover's increasing popularity in the decade of the 1920s did not rest on his work in the Mississippi valley alone. In retrospect, however, given the cold, impersonal exterior which Hoover projected in all of his activities, even in his humanitarian work, it is somewhat difficult to believe he was as popular as the mass media reported. This is especially true when Hoover is placed next to notables of the Jazz Age such as Paul Whiteman, Louis Armstrong, Charles Lindbergh, Amelia Earhart, F. Scott Fitzgerald, Ernest Hemingway, Mary Pickford, Rudolf Valentino, Gloria Swanson, Clara Bow, Douglas Fairbanks, Mae West, Aimee Semple McPherson, Paul Robeson, Will Rogers, Rudy Vallee, Charlie Chaplin, Al Capone, and Izzy and Moe — the two best-known prohibition agents. That Hoover should capture the political limelight in such a bizarre and colorful period seems unusual. But in fact the New Era was a curiously lackluster political decade, and by any criteria Hoover was obviously the most active, the most vocal, and hence, perhaps by default, the most popular political leader. Americans were, after all, weary of the crusading, charismatic leaders that the war had produced at home and abroad.

Contrary to what his critics later claimed, Hoover's popularity did not arise from a personal promotion effort by his well-organized publicity staff; in fact, just as he had asked the press during the war years "not to personalize the Food Administration," he shunned the limelight as secretary of commerce. Writing to the editor of the *Journal of Commerce* in 1921, for example, Hoover said: "I would much prefer to have my name omitted — emphasis being placed on the Department of Commerce as the source of the information rather than myself. It seems to me that constantly improving permanent service of government agencies must be built around the agencies themselves and not the temporary individual who happens on the job."

But Hoover's unceasing activities as secretary of commerce were so farflung, so impressive in their own right, and so well publicized, that his fame was inevitable. The one political figure most out of tune with the flamboyant aspects of the Roaring Twenties became its best known Washington official. Movie stars, literary figures, gangsters, and flappers were immortalized through sensationalism between 1921 and 1929. On the other hand, Herbert Hoover, portrayed by one Washington reporter as "sedate, laconic, undramatic, berating nobody, asserting nothing that his laboriously gathered facts and figures" would not sustain, presented a picture that everybody understood. He was "the despair and wonder of fame-famished Washington," a calming, welcome relief from the standard array of Jazz Age figures.

He projected an image of service, efficiency, morality, and prosperity, blending the apolitical with politics, the urban with the rural and traditional. It was an image which would serve Hoover well in the presidential campaign of 1928, poorly in 1932. In Hoover, American politics had a self-effacing ideologue who had perfected the systematic administrative use of publicity and then used it to popularize the progressive ideal of the nonpartisan manager of government. Small wonder that Walter S. Gifford, president of AT&T, chose to speak with Hoover in the first publicized test of a televised phone conversation between New York and Washington on April 7, 1927.

There were, however, overwhelming obligations associated with such an image, as Hoover knew only too well and over which he privately despaired. In particular, he was not com-

The traffic problem in Washington, D. C.

pletely satisfied with his performance as secretary of commerce. He felt frustrated by the persistent economic problems in agriculture and other depressed industries; by the continued wasteful practices and duplication of equipment within the oil industry, electric utilities, the merchant marine, and commercial aviation; and by his inability to effect a reorganization of the entire executive branch of government. Congress had refused to appropriate enough money for comprehensive statistical studies of business cycles and unemployment, for the flood control, power development, and waterway projects he had proposed, and for a public reserve fund to finance public works. Despite his department's impressive record, Hoover felt that much remained to be done, especially in the way of reshaping ideas and values.

During most of the decade he had thought that through new organizational policies and massive publicity campaigns to educate the public and influence Congress, he would achieve his dream of a permanently decentralized, prosperous, efficient America. To facilitate this indirect form of national economic planning based on voluntarily coordinated individual efforts, Hoover arranged one educative, ritualistic conference or commission of experts or trade association meeting after another, until the public came to look upon them as his standard escape device. As commonplace as bootleg liquor, they unfortunately were not as much in popular demand and lacked the "kick" or impact Hoover desired. And so the transformation of the country's economic and value systems continued to elude him. It is also conceivable that Hoover had simply spread himself too thin as secretary of commerce in his superhuman effort to achieve this comprehensive goal.

Given his ability to delude himself, Hoover probably had not consciously come to this conclusion on the eve of President Coolidge's unexpected withdrawal from the 1928 presidential campaign. But no doubt he sensed a good deal of frustration over not having hit upon the combination of administrative leadership and educational publicity he needed to realize all his comprehensive goals and ideals. Only the presidency could provide him with more direct influence and power. Yet this was the very position in government for which his dour temperament and reticent personality were least suited. In addition, he was sure that Coolidge would win a bid for a second term in office in 1928.

It is possible that while Hoover was relaxing at Bohemian Grove in California at the end of July 1927 some of these thoughts occurred to him, as he pondered how to revitalize his long-term plans for the country. He had become a human dynamo as secretary of commerce, apparently almost totally at the expense of a normal life. With the help of his publicity staff he conveyed the public impression, according to author Sherwood Anderson, that he had "never known failure." But as a cabinet member under Harding and Coolidge he had not known complete personal success either. His synthesis of a number of contradictory experiences and values for himself and his country was far from completed. There was no way he could know that at noon on August 2, 1927, President Coolidge would enter his White House office and hand each of the newspapermen there a slip of paper which read: "I do not choose to run for President in nineteen twenty-eight."

Shortly after hearing this announcement Hoover left California for Washington amidst a flood of telegrams "demanding that I announce my candidacy." The Coolidge statement had been made just as he was seriously questioning his current position within government. His last and only unsuccessful career decision was close at hand.

V

The Progressive
in Time of Depression

"Here is tragedy . . . a brave man fighting valiantly, futilely to the end."

HERBERT HOOVER decided he wanted to be president of the United States, after much cautious soul-searching and statistical analysis, sometime between August 2, 1927 (when Coolidge said he did "not choose to run"), and February 12, 1928 (when Hoover entered his first primary race). A month after President Coolidge's puzzling statement, Hoover asked him point-blank what it meant and received no direct reply. As a result of this inconclusive meeting Hoover announced to the press that in all likelihood Coolidge would be renominated and reelected.

On two subsequent occasions in February and May 1928 Coolidge again refused to explain his intentions to Hoover. Moreover, the president neither publicly endorsed nor privately encouraged the Chief's political ambitions; unlike Harding, who looked upon his secretary of commerce as "the smartest 'gink' I know," Coolidge resented what he called the "Wonder Boy's" spendthrift programs and finally in 1928 said: "That man has offered me unsolicited advice for six years, all of it bad." Meanwhile Hoover's staff continued to stimulate and then sample public opinion. Remembering the amateurish presidential boom in 1920, this time his public-relations men operated in a very professional and efficient fashion.

In fact, Hoover had tacitly begun to promote himself for the 1928 Republican presidential nomination years before with the hiring of George E. Akerson as press secretary in 1925 and the subsequent appointment of the able Ohio politician Walter F. Brown as assistant secretary of commerce. In October 1927 Akerson officially organized a group of journalists and editor friends to mold public sentiment behind "the Secretary." The group included Will Irwin, William Hard, George Barr Baker, Henry Sell, Frederick Feiker, Bruce Barton, and Merle Thorpe. Baker, for example, used Hoover's ARA and American Child Health Association offices in New York to distribute copies of his past public statements, and under Feiker's direction the Associated Business Editors organized a group that sent out campaign material to business editors across the country. Others such as Irwin and Hard wrote articles and prepared campaign biographies of Hoover, while Barton answered specific attacks by H. L. Mencken. Finally Sell, a Hearst newspaperman, conducted a private poll to determine public sentiment.

Hoover-for-President clubs sprang up under the leadership of old friends from Stanford and the war relief days who had supported their Chief in 1920. By January 1928, they had been coordinated into a national association by Hoover's professional aides. But many former Progressives were missing from his list of supporters. Hoover had, after all, opposed Robert La Follette's advocacy of government ownership of railroads and public utilities when the senator ran as a progressive candidate in 1924. He had alienated farm leaders in Congress like George Norris by his stand against McNary-Haugenism. And he had acquired two new, unprogressive-sounding appellations in the course of the 1920s: that of Superbusinessman and Supersalesman.

While Hoover had not changed his brand of "independent

progressivism" since 1920, many other Progressives had either joined the Socialist party, succumbed to postwar disillusionment and political cynicism, or become involved in obtaining benefits for specific interest groups. No presidential candidate from either major party could have enlisted the support of the entire fragmented progressive movement by 1928. Many Senate Progressives, for example, who continued to favor rural over urban values — like William E. Borah, Hiram Johnson, and Gerald P. Nye — stayed with Hoover, but so did urban-oriented social workers like Jane Addams who could not accept Smith's opposition to prohibition. Most liberal intellectuals and editors, however, deserted Hoover, including those associated with *The Nation* and *The New Republic,* as did John Dewey, Felix Frankfurter, and Clarence Darrow.

Despite the feverish activity of his personal staff and the encouragement of friends and supporters across the country, Hoover refused to rush into a public decision. So his staff did what was necessary to convince him with statistical data that he should declare his candidacy. In addition to sampling public opinion, they investigated Coolidge's eleven-word pronouncement with scientific care to discover its true meaning. One of his economic advisers, Arch W. Shaw, personally pored over lexicons and interviewed people who specialized in New England phraseology to find out what the president had really meant.

Perhaps they should have simply consulted Mrs. Coolidge. According to *Time* she had knitted a prophetic bedspread a full year before her husband made his ambiguous statement. On one side it read: "Lincoln, 1861–65"; on the other it unequivocally proclaimed: "Calvin Coolidge, 1923–1929." When a friend questioned her back in 1926 about these dates, *Time* reported on December 26, 1927, she had replied: "I know what I am doing."

Though Hoover did not appoint a campaign manager or make a political speech or partisan statement before his nomination at the GOP convention in August 1928, he was pursuing the nomination in earnest by the end of 1927. He worked as usual through informal, decentralized, grass-roots activity, accompanied by an organized publicity campaign under the direction of close friends. Typically, the Great Humanitarian had to be convinced that he was being drafted for further service to his country before he would run for public office. Although widespread popular support already existed for Hoover by the end of his flood relief work in 1927, this support did not remain totally spontaneous, unorganized or unsupervised by Hoover's Washington staff.

The best indication that Hoover was running a high-powered political campaign for the nomination was his opposition by certain Republican politicians and Wall Street financiers by the end of 1927. The former consisted largely of old guard senators, who wanted to end the decade as they had begun it with a chief executive who would not try to be president too much of the time. Harding's card games and Coolidge's long naps were fine, but they rightly suspected that Hoover's penchant for fly fishing would not interfere with his White House duties. Eastern financial opposition came mainly from bankers whom Hoover had alienated as commerce secretary with his attempts to control American loans abroad and with his attacks on easy credit, unrestrained speculation and the Federal Reserve Board.

Initially Hoover's Senate opponents either supported a "draft Coolidge" movement, or rallied behind well-known favorite-son candidates like Vice-President Charles G. Dawes, and such relatively obscure senators as James E. Watson, Charles Curtis, and Frank B. Willis. Their arguments against Hoover ranged from the old 1920 ones — his prolonged absences from the country before 1917, his unimpressive party loyalty, and his general political inexperience — to scarcely less up-to-date objections to his business deals in China before the Boxer Rebellion, and his elitist-royalist tendencies. "Sir Herbert," they dubbed him. They also charged him, to no avail, with being a Quaker pacifist, a desegregationist, and an

Anglophile. Other Republicans implied, with greater substance but no more success, that they feared his unorthodox economics and his internationalist reputation in foreign affairs, particularly the possibility that he would take the United States into the World Court.

Hoover officially became a candidate in February 1928 in order to run against Willis in the Ohio primary, saying that while he would "not strive for the nomination," if elected he would "carry' forward the princples of the Republican party and the great objectives of President Coolidge's policies — all of which have brought to our country such a high degree of happiness, progress and security." Safely identifying with the party and Coolidge despite the fact that the president had yet to endorse him, Hoover entered this first primary knowing that 502 of the 1,089 delegates to the 1928 GOP convention would be chosen by direct election. Even though his political organization raised $380,151 for these presidential primaries (more than the rest of his Republican opponents together), Hoover lost to Willis in Ohio and to all other favorite sons in their home states.

However, by May when he asked Coolidge for the last time if he wanted the nomination, Hoover had 400 convention delegates pledged to him on the first ballot. His strongest opponent at the June convention was a man he had unsuccessfully faced in 1920, Governor Frank O. Lowden of Illinois, still the farmers' choice. In an exceedingly dull gathering, Hoover won easily on the first ballot with a resounding 837 votes. This was later "made unanimous amid great enthusiasm" by Republicans who had heard him described as an "engineer, practical scientist, minister of mercy to the hungry and the poor, administrator, executive, statesman, beneficent American, kindly neighbor and wholesome human being." On July 14 he resigned as secretary of commerce to devote all his time to capturing the presidency.

The presidential campaign of this taciturn Quaker, who had never run for public office before and who intensely disliked the ballyhoo of politics, consisted of seven major radio addresses. All seven he laboriously wrote himself in his convoluted and uninspiring style. While they were intended to educate the American people about the advantages of cooperative individualism, in essence Hoover composed only one speech — his nomination acceptance address, delivered in a monotone on August 11, 1928, from the Stanford stadium in Palo Alto before 70,000 spectators and a radio audience of millions. The occasion, one day after his fifty-fourth birthday, was a testimonial to a public career that had risen as meteorically after 1914 as his private one had before.

In his address Hoover reiterated the comprehensive program he had been trying to implement since 1921: farm relief through cooperative marketing, adequate tariff protection, greater cooperation between government and business through self-governing associations, better conditions for labor, development of regional water and electrical systems, conservation of natural resources, enforcement of prohibition, avoidance of government regulation except to guarantee equal opportunity for all citizens, simplification in government and business operations to avoid waste and corruption, concern for the welfare of youth, support of international cooperation and arms limitation in the interest of peace, and promotion of religious tolerance. This last reference had been but an implicit part of Hoover's dream for America until this speech. Anticipating that Al Smith, the Catholic governor of New York, would be nominated by the Democrats, he now specifically included religious tolerance as an important American ideal.

Hoover used statistical data to prove the existence of unprecedented material progress in the United States since the end of World War I, uttering words that his enemies were to take out of context and use against him for the rest of his life: "We in America today are nearer to the final triumph over poverty than ever before in the history of any land. The poorhouse is vanishing from among us. We have not yet reached the goal, but, *given a chance to go forward with the policies of the last eight years,* we shall soon with the help of God be in sight of the day when poverty will be banished from this nation." (Emphasis added.) He concluded his acceptance address with a summary of his political philosophy: "Our purpose is to build in this nation a human society, not an economic system. . . . No one believes these aspirations and hopes can be realized in a day. Progress or remedy lie often enough in the hands of state and local government. But the awakening of the national conscience and the stimulation of every remedial agency is indeed a function of the national government."

Turning to a friend near him after it was all over, Hoover said: "I wonder if this speech will help me to live down my reputation as an engineer." He was apparently apprehensive that his managerial image had been exaggerated out of all proportion by the time the presidential campaign officially began. Later as president-elect he was more explicitly pessimistic about his greatly inflated reputation. "My friends have made the American people think me a sort of superman, able to cope successfully with the most difficult and complicated problems," he confided to Willis J. Abbot, the editor of the *Christian Science Monitor.* "They expect the impossible of me and should there arise in the land conditions with which the political machinery is unable to cope, I will be the one to suffer." It was as though Hoover's administrative machinery for publicizing his activities had acquired an independent existence over the years that was beyond his control by 1928. He feared a negative reaction, a backlash of resentment against him even before the depression occurred. In 1932, during the worst economic crisis the country had ever experienced, he was all the more convinced that he had "been absurdly oversold." As he told Senator George Moses of New Hampshire, "No man can live up to it."

But to the majority of Americans in 1928, Hoover was the immensely successful "super expert," a practical man of action who could be counted on to solve any problem with his facts and figures. During the campaign his publicity staff did little to qualify this image, although they did try to humanize it somewhat. His smashing victory further enhanced his reputation and heightened public expectations. Hoover carried all but eight states, and won 444 electoral votes to Smith's 87, accumulating 58 percent of the popular vote. This was at the time the second highest percentage of a popular presidential vote, and remains the fourth highest to date. In 1932 the figures were nearly the reverse of those of 1928, with Franklin Delano Roosevelt receiving 57 percent of the popular vote and 472 electoral votes while Hoover retained 39 percent and 59 electoral votes.

The 1928 presidential campaign between Al Smith and Herbert Hoover brought out the intellectual best in the two men and the worst in their supporters. Their most publicized differences centered on the emotionally charged issue of religion and prohibition. Neither candidate directly attacked the other, largely because Hoover refused to conduct his campaign through debate, or to mention Smith's name in public. But at the state and local levels vicious battles were waged between Protestant "drys" and Catholic "wets." Racism also entered the campaign scene in the South, with the Democrats circulating a picture purportedly of Hoover dancing (a social grace he never mastered) with Mary Booze, a black Republican committeewoman, along with rumors about the secretary's relationships with black women during his Mississippi flood work. They also exploited the fact that the former secretary of commerce had abolished segregation in his department. Southern Republicans in turn tried to connect Smith with the rising expectations of black people in New York, distributing a picture of a Harlem politician dictating to a white stenographer.

The few important substantive differences which did exist between the two men paled beside these dirty and bigoted campaign tactics, as their supporters tried to convince the

public that their respective candidates were the exact oppo-
sites of one another. In truth, the platforms of both parties
exhibited more similarities than differences as each tried to
capitalize on the pervasive underlying theme of the campaign:
prosperity. Nonetheless, Hoover and Smith were assigned
"packaged" images by friend and foe alike. The selling of
political contenders through advertising techniques having
little to do with political principles, now so common, was
effective for the first time in 1928 because of two new means of
national communication — radio and films.

Although Smith had a reputation in New York as an effective public speaker, he made no better use of the radio than
the inarticulate Hoover. Outside of New York State his East
Side accent irritated more Americans than it persuaded, and
Smith stubbornly refused to try to speak in a different manner. Hoover had a discernible midwestern accent and a
monotonous delivery, but the combination proved less grating
on the ears of the listening public in the last prosperous year
of the New Era than Smith's more dramatically delivered
speeches.

Despite these speech pattern difficulties, both candidates
made conscious use of the radio as a campaign device. In May
1928 Alan Fox, Hoover's New York campaign manager, announced that if Hoover were nominated his campaign would
consist almost exclusively of radio broadcasts and films. Obviously Hoover's technical knowledge and association with the
radio industry as secretary of commerce had made him very
aware of its potential political value. Without any such inside
connections, Smith had used radio broadcasts as early as 1924
in New York to force Republican leaders to lower state income
taxes. Although he later said he found radio "a cold affair,"
Smith actually delivered more radio addresses than Hoover in
the course of the 1928 campaign. Unfortunately the radio
campaigns of their supporters increased emotional reactions to
the religious and drinking questions, instead of clarifying

their different positions on public power, farm policy and foreign affairs.

Despite basic disagreements and their contrasting religions and imbibitions, there were many similarities between the two candidates. Both were self-made men — Smith was the urban counterpart to Hoover's rural rag-to-riches image. Both had reputations as efficient, progressive administrators (Hoover's governmental reorganization was at the national level, Smith's at the state level) ; both had the support of labor (Hoover had consistently opposed "excessive use of injunctions in labor disputes" throughout the decade, while Smith worked to improve the conditions of city workers in his home state) ; both made a conscious effort to appeal to women voters in 1928 (although it was Hoover and not Smith who captured the militant Woman's Party endorsement) ; both surrounded themselves with experts for advice when dealing with economic and social reform matters; both refused to succumb to postwar Red Scare hysteria and other examples of reactionary and nativist trends in the 1920s such as the revival of the Ku Klux Klan; finally, both defended capitalism, businessmen, and the prosperity of the period and could count numerous millionaires among their supporters.

In one area, however, there was no comparison. Hoover was considered apolitical, having never run for public office; while Smith had an undisputed reputation as a professional politician by 1928; a "miracle worker in electioneering," having lost only one political contest in twenty-five years. Smith's deserved progressive record as governor of New York in the 1920s, despite his Tammany connections, was based on his administrative reforms; on social welfare legislation aimed at improving working conditions, housing, and recreational facilities; on support not simply for state regulation of public power but for government ownership of power facilities in direct competition with private enterprise; and on his strong civil liberties record, especially with respect to protecting the rights of Socialists. But Smith was no Bryan or La Follette nor even a neo-Populist, much to the disappointment of the most progressive elements within the Democratic party. Ostensibly committed to McNary-Haugenism, the New York governor had serious reservations about executing it and no alternative program to offer farmers. Even this did not stop George Peek from trying to deliver the traditionally Republican farm vote into Smith's camp. Yet he naturally frightened many Democratic conservatives, and Smith is usually described as the liberal candidate in 1928 because he represented the urban masses — especially second-generation immigrants who abided neither by the laws against drinking nor by traditional American social and religious values. His domestic socioeconomic and political views, however, were more traditionally conservative than Hoover's, if only because they were more provincial in light of changing postwar conditions. And the same is true of Smith's foreign policy — a subject he almost entirely ignored in the postwar decade.

Voters in this election assumed that "rum and romanism" played an important role in Smith's defeat. But in fact, neither prohibition nor Catholicism appears in retrospect to have been a significant factor. Despite these liabilities Smith ran better than two previous Democratic candidates of the decade, netting the first Democratic plurality in the nation's twelve largest cities. His greatest strength lay in his attractiveness to city voters of foreign white stock; his greatest weaknesses in his stubborn refusal to mitigate his own urban provinciality with a broadly based progressive campaign, and in his insistence on contradicting his own party's plank on prohibition. Next to New Era prosperity, Smith was his own worst enemy in 1928.

Just as Smith was not as liberal as his partisans would have us believe, neither was Hoover as narrowly Waspish as they claimed. His support *did not* rest exclusively on Anglo-Saxon, small-town, middle-class citizens who were clinging to Protestantism and prohibition. On the contrary, one historian has recently noted that "his public image represented a highly successful blend of modern and traditional themes." He was the farm boy as well as the businessman; the engineer as well as the humanitarian; a Progressive without the taint of socialism; a champion of America and yet an internationalist and man of the world; a "square dealer" with labor as well as management; a successful administrator and yet not a politician; an orphan and millionaire all rolled into one. Finally, he stood for individualism as well as cooperation. He was thus "ten candidates in one," offering something to everyone; and what he offered appeared to be the best of the 1920s.

Probably no Democrat could have beaten this postwar Superman, let alone an Irish Catholic "wet" from the slums of New York. Even so, the Chief took no chances. Once he obtained Coolidge's lukewarm endorsement after the nominating convention Hoover ran an almost flawless campaign, making a conscious effort to minimize factionalism within the party since he could not automatically rely upon either GOP Progressives or the old guard for support. For its time it was the best financed campaign in history, and by refusing to debate with Smith directly over the most controversial and emotional issues Hoover united behind him such disparate Republicans as Senator William E. Borah and Charles Evans Hughes. In the long run, however, Hoover's victory proved less impressive than Smith's defeat; the Democratic vote was clear indication of a new partisan realignment that had been building gradually over the decade among the northern urban masses.

During the interregnum after his election Hoover skillfully continued to avoid alienating Coolidge and other powerful members of his party. The first thing he did was to leave the country for a goodwill tour of Latin America. This removed him from immediate domestic political pressures between the president and various Republican members of Congress, who personally had urged him to come back and consult with them. His cabinet appointments reflect the same ability to mollify the very elements in the GOP that distrusted him most: eastern businessmen and the old guard. While he chose cabinet members on the basis of administrative and executive ability rather than past service to the party, he made two very distinct types of appointments. Many of his top cabinet positions went to basically conservative, wealthy businessmen — the exceptions being Interior Secretary Ray Lyman Wilbur, Navy Secretary Charles Francis Adams, Jr., Attorney General William D. Mitchell and Secretary of State Henry L. Stimson. His subcabinet appointees, on the other hand — those undersecretaries who actually held policy-making positions — constituted an "inner cabinet" in accord with his progressive views on major questions, like William R. Castle, Jr., undersecretary of state, and Ogden L. Mills, assistant secretary of the treasury. In this fashion, Hoover placated old guard Republicans and members of the business community without compromising his long-held principles.

Immediately upon assuming the presidency, Hoover took up the "uncompleted tasks in government" that remained from his cabinet days. Convinced that it was only a matter of time before he could achieve his progressive dream for America, he called a special session of Congress to consider the chronic agricultural problem. It was the first and last special session he called.

Although Congress passed his Agricultural Marketing Act during this special session on June 15, 1929, Hoover had to fight to prevent the farm bloc from attaching an export debenture plan to it. Ultimately the Federal Farm Board created by this act lost approximately $345 million, trying to support farm prices between 1929 and 1931 with loans to cooperatives and stabilization corporations for the purchase of basic crops. The loss, due largely to the depression which began less than six months after the act was passed, was nonetheless a bitter disappointment for Hoover. It meant the failure of an "almost perfect illustration" of his faith in cooperative associations to regulate economic behavior without, in this case, entirely eliminating rural individualism. His other emergency session objective — a revision of the 1922 tariff to benefit farmers — met a similarly dismal fate. It took fourteen months to obtain passage on June 17, 1931, of the Hawley-Smoot Tariff, which pleased no one, including the president.

Despite the rancor and the disillusioning results of this special session of Congress, Hoover dramatically succeeded in making "forgotten progress" with his other uncompleted goals during the eight months he was in office before the onset of the Great Depression. Eight days after his inauguration, for example, he abruptly terminated further oil leasing on the public domain, ordered a review of all existing oil leases because the system had been so abused in the 1920s, and called a regulatory conference of all the major oil-producing states, which ultimately led to the Oil States Advisory Commission in 1931. Two days later, when Hoover ordered the publication of all large government refunds of income, estate, and gift taxes (over the objections of Treasury Secretary Andrew Mellon), he fulfilled a long-sought-after goal of congressional Progressives. Within a month after taking office he had also taken action against corrupt patronage practices, especially in the South, by publicly exposing partisan judicial appointments; had successfully prevented a strike on the Texas and Pacific Railroad; and had announced a graduated plan for reducing income taxes up to 20 percent on high incomes and as much as 67 percent on low incomes (once again forcing a progressive change against the wishes of Mellon, a conservative big businessman who was an unavoidable carryover from Coolidge's administration).

Clearly the new president was not wasting any time in implementing his progressive ideals on immediate, individual issues, particularly in the field of civil liberties. During the summer months of 1929 he refused to give any government backing to proposed "red hunts" against suspected communists, and later in the year he refused to take action against peaceful communist picketing of the White House. Then he investigated the issue of political prisoners, including the case of labor leader Thomas J. Mooney, and forced the resignation of Mabel Walker Willebrandt, the assistant attorney general most associated with religious bigotry and fanatical enforcement of prohibition during the 1928 campaign. Ignoring the racist protests of southerners, he supported his wife's right to entertain a black woman in the White House, demanded an increased budget for Howard University, commuted the sentence of a black man convicted of murder without due process, and recommended that the new federal parole board proportionately represent the number of blacks and women in prison.

The same sense of progressive urgency characterized his activity on long-range projects in the areas of labor legislation, leading finally to his signing in 1932 of the Norris-La Guardia Anti-Injunction Act — a landmark in labor legislation for that time. Other projects involved child welfare, conservation, public power systems, and public education (including the suggestion for a separate Department of Health, Education and Welfare, which was years ahead of its time). Perhaps the most forgotten of the foresighted tasks Hoover tried to complete as president was in the field of human rights for native Americans. According to one recent account, "by March 1933, the basic changes needed in Indian policy had been formulated by the Indians and their friends," aided in large measure by presidential appointments replacing racists like Hubert Work on the Indian Commission with Charles Rhoads and J. Henry Scattergood. Interior Secretary Wilbur was also a recognized proponent of Indian culture, a fact which contributed between 1928 and 1933 to the increase in appropriations for the Indian Bureau from $15 million to $28 million, despite the depression. Accomplished with Hoover's backing, this funding resulted in significant gains in Indian educational and health services. Hoover's sensitivity to minorities and women was generally more publicly evident while he was president than it had been during his commerce years, despite his liberal hiring practices. Ironically, Hoover's personal attempts as president to counter racial injustices were contradicted by an early version of the lily white "southern strategy" developed by his own party in the late 1920s.

All of Hoover's other long-range programs suffered from severe financial cutbacks after the Depression of 1929 began with the stock market crash in October. What had started out as a "dazzling" eight months in foreign as well as domestic affairs ended almost before it began, dashing Hoover's hopes for transforming America. But his methods remained essentially what they had been throughout the previous decade of prosperity: reliance on persuasion to raise private funds voluntarily, educational conferences, fact-finding commissions, and decentralized voluntary implementation of decisions reached by a centralized administrative source. In fact, Hoover expanded his cooperative programs during the crucial depression years of 1930–1931 and the early months of 1932. He attempted to revitalize trade associationalism with a decentralized national planning program through the Emergency Committee for Employment; encouraged the Cotton Textile Institute's attempts to end destructive competition; and appointed a privately financed Timber Conservation Board and the Federal Oil Conservation Board. In addition, he created a number of agencies to obtain constructive, cooperative action without resorting to government coercion or business cartels, such as the Federal Drought Relief Committee, the President's Organization for Unemployment Relief, the National Credit Corporation, the Citizens' Reconstruction Organization, the Federal Employment Stabilization Board, the Federal Power Commission, and a new network of Business and Industrial Committees. Far from losing faith in his associationalism, Hoover expanded it in the face of economic adversity.

Aside from the Wickersham Commission that he appointed to investigate crime and prohibition, the best known and most prestigious of all the commissions Hoover appointed was the 1929 President's Research Committee on Recent Social

Trends, instructed to study the national social resources and to report back in three years. Hoover hoped to use its findings to abolish poverty and to establish at long last what some were already calling the "Great Society." Instead, the Great Depression intervened, destroying in short order both Hoover's private plans "for ushering in the new order painlessly" and the immediate relevance of the 1932 committee report. Nonetheless, its analysis of recent social trends provided subtle insights into such problems as race, unemployment, income leveling, education, medical care, and urban sprawl. It remains the "single most comprehensive self-study of any era of American social history" and a turning point in the intellectual relationship between the academic community and the government. Another blue ribbon presidential committee was appointed to study recent economic trends. Although its findings were generally too optimistic in light of the depression, its report also remains one of the most authoritative economic sources for the 1920s.

Government reliance upon social scientists certainly did not originate in the 1920s. But under Herbert Hoover's tutelage, professionals did come to believe more confidently in the possibility that scientific research could be transformed into comprehensive social and economic reforms, without undue interference from politicians or popular sentiment. Like Hoover, they wanted to combine progressive humanitarianism, statistical data, and scientific management to insure that socioeconomic and political institutions did not fall too far behind technological development.

There was one element in Hoover's typically methodical, cooperative, expertise approach that only gradually revealed itself as the depression worsened. As verbal attacks upon his antidepression policies mounted, his publicity apparatus became increasingly ineffective. Always overly sensitive to criticism, the president responded not with direct counterattacks but rather with a stoic withdrawal, refusing to openly discuss crucial economic issues or to provide even as much information to reporters as he had when secretary of commerce. Part of the problem stemmed from the unfulfilled promises he had made to the press upon assuming office. He said then that he would hold personal meetings with reporters twice a week and that Akerson would meet with them daily, and he also indicated that he would allow more direct quoting than Coolidge had. Having stimulated the expectations of newsmen, Hoover did not deliver. Moreover, certain negative aspects of his public-relations approach, tolerable in the prosperous New Era days, were exacerbated by the tension of the depression.

As secretary of commerce, for example, he had quietly let it be known when news stories displeased him, and had personally reviewed all material originating in his department that contained major "economic interpretation, forecasting, or advice." While there had been some grumbling from the press corps about this type of individual censorship, Hoover had developed into one of the best Washington news sources in the 1920s and reporters expected him to remain so in the White House. When he failed them in this, any attempt to regulate news flow created more bitterness and suspicion than before, as did his continued refusal to permit "hokum" to be reported about his personal affairs. Hoover's first significant troubles with the press started on his Latin American tour when he was still president-elect. He intended this journey to be not only an escape from domestic political pressures, but also a foreign policy lesson for the American people: the "good neighbor" policy was initiated in the course of it. So George Barr Baker personally monitored all the radio dispatches of the eighteen correspondents traveling with the president-elect's party, much to their dismay, to insure that the proper educational information was conveyed.

Once the depression began, friends warned Hoover about the deterioration in his press relations, but he simply retreated behind increasingly antiquated publicity tactics and military rhetoric left over from World War I. He refused to update the old method of supplying "canned" information or to make regular radio broadcasts, or to appear more affable, empathetic, or available as far as average depression victims were concerned. His rejection of the radio as a means of effectively reaching out to frightened Americans was particularly shortsighted. According to an April 1929 report in the *Brooklyn Standard Union,* the 1928 campaign had convinced Hoover that the radio was revolutionizing political debates by making "us literally one people upon all occasions." Yet at the height of his communication problems during the depression he refused the suggestion to speak nationally for ten minutes a week, saying privately to Wallace Alexander that it was "very difficult to deal with anything over the radio except generalities."

Nonetheless, he did make ninety-five broadcasts between 1929 and 1933 — only nine fewer than FDR made during his first administration. Unfortunately, most of Hoover's were "glorified greetings" rather than policy addresses, and their impact was insignificant compared to Roosevelt's. After he left office in 1933, Hoover also refused offers from both Henry Ford and General Motors to make weekly broadcasts. He was simply unable to feel comfortable with the new media that he probably understood better than most politicians, and this speeded the disintegration of his formerly effective public-relations system.

This inability to relate in person or via radio to the plight of those stricken by economic disaster was not a new Hooverian characteristic, but previously it had not been so glaringly apparent. During the war he had assiduously avoided coming into personal contact with famine victims (this had always been Lou Henry Hoover's job) and now he could not stand to look at, let alone greet, those Americans who stood on street corners selling apples or who patiently waited in breadlines. These personal inhibitions became political liabilities in the depression years as they never had been before. No longer able to operate anonymously behind the scenes, Hoover relied more and more on secrecy and aloofness — and then petulantly blamed the press for wrecking his attempt to build up public confidence through stilted, stuffy platitudes about how things were not as bad as they seemed. Endlessly comparing the depression to the crisis created by World War I, he used a military vocabulary in an attempt to generate national unity and patriotism. But words like "attack," "enemy," and "fronts" did not rally people to make war on the Great Depression. 1929 was obviously not 1917.

To make matters worse, his publicity staff began to reflect the increased pressure and tension under which they worked to maintain a positive image of an increasingly isolated figure. Akerson, long the darling of Washington reporters because of his convivial drinking habits and back-slapping personality, became more defensive and inaccessible. Akerson finally left his position as press secretary under a cloud of innuendoes caused chiefly by antagonism between him and Hoover's confidential secretary Lawrence Richey, but also by a few inexcusable public-relations goofs, such as announcing the wrong name when Hoover nominated Charles Evans Hughes for chief justice of the Supreme Court. Replacing Akerson with Theodore G. Joslin, a man thoroughly disliked by the Washington press corps, did not improve Hoover's situation. His appointment was described by one reporter as the "first known instance of a rat joining a sinking ship."

The first of two major public-relations failures of the Hoover administration came when the White House released an evasive and misleading summary of the Wickersham Commission investigation of prohibition that distorted the divided opinions reflected in the report to fit the president's stand against repeal. The second occurred when the National Republican Committee unsuccessfully attempted to establish a newspaper called *Washington: A Journal of Information and Opinion Concerning the Operation of Our National Government*. Supposedly intended to positively present the administration's point of view independently of the regular White House reporters, its first issue dwelled on Hoover's personal handicaps as a political leader; the second was printed by a nonunion shop and subsequently destroyed before distribution for fear of repercussions from organized labor; and the third announced its demise due to a lack of subscriptions.

As a result of these and other public-relations faux pas, the Democratic press agent Charley Michelson did not have to go out of his way to ruin the president's rapidly declining prestige. His "smear Hoover" campaign received direct aid almost daily from the president and his personal staff. All Michelson did was to devise modern mass media techniques for capitalizing on the situation.

It was not, therefore, callousness or moral turpitude that prompted Hoover to say as conditions worsened that what the country needed was a good joke, a "big laugh," a song, or a "great poem" to make people "forget their troubles and the Depression." This was a desperate ideologue speaking; one who realized the power of words to restore confidence and to end hysteria, but who had lost his effectiveness as a propagandist. Instead of poems and jokes, the president heard people singing, "Brother, Can You Spare a Dime," talking about Hoovervilles (shanty towns outside of major cities where the poor and homeless lived), driving Hoovercarts (cars drawn by mules or horses because their owners could not afford gas), waving Hooverflags (empty pockets turned inside out), and marching, not from patriotism but in protest, as in the 1932 veterans' Bonus March. Worst of all, Hoover thought Americans in general were acting exactly like Europeans when faced with economic disaster — abandoning their individualism and voluntary associationalism and demanding direct government aid, that is, outright charity or the dreaded dole.

In the face of such a display of national weakness he remained true to his principles even if the American people did not. Hoover would not save the American system for them; they must do that for themselves. To act otherwise, he thought, would be not serving the people but ruling them. Trapped on the dialectical tightrope between individualism and collectivism, which he had been walking for so long, Hoover refused to fall off. He urged his fellow citizens to end their own depression in the only fashion he thought honorable — by emulating his delicate balancing act.

During the first phase of his antidepression activities, from October 1929 to the November midterm elections in 1930, Hoover essentially ignored Congress. As he told a farm audience in Iowa in 1925, since at least his Food Administration days he had realized that "every time we find solution outside of government we have not only strengthened character but we have preserved our sense of real self-government." Suspicious under normal conditions of Capitol Hill political machinations, he was convinced beyond any doubt of the Congress's inability to act quickly and effectively in times of crisis. His initial unilateral actions as chief executive prompted at least one Republican to remark that Hoover had "never really recognized the House and Senate as desirable factors in our government." In truth he was acting out of blind faith in the hardiness of the American character when faced with adversity, and in the basic soundness of the American economy.

On neither point was his confidence warranted. He had not succeeded in effecting any basic value change along the lines of cooperative individualism among Americans in general or corporation leaders in particular on the eve of the Great Depression. Characteristically, Hoover had deluded himself. The fact remained that the prosperity of the New Era, which he praised in such glowing terms, was manifestly uneven — based largely on easy credit, conspicuous consumption, and speculation. As early as 1924 Hoover had warned against such practices and the policies of the Federal Reserve Board (FRB) that fostered them. Nonetheless, he continued to believe that his policies as secretary of commerce had made substantial headway toward improving living standards and achieving "stable employment and profit." He also was convinced that the sick industries and inequitable distribution of wealth were marginal problems which could ultimately be worked out using associationalism, moderate fiscal reform, and the latest countercyclical theories of the noted economist Wesley Clair Mitchell.

But the false confidence and superficial prosperity of middle-class Americans in the first decade of transition following World War I made chances of reshaping their character or economy slight indeed. The materialistic success philosophy of businessmen and engineers had reached its zenith in the 1920s, limiting the response of most citizens to Hoover's educational propaganda. The postwar era was simply not receptive to any socioeconomic philosophy calling for a critical reevaluation of basic American values or improvement of their traditional capitalistic and democratic practices. It was more fun to attend a baseball game or prize fight, to drink illegal booze, to vicariously identify with glamorous criminals or movie stars of the Jazz Age, and to take for granted such technological innovations as the radio, electrification, and mass-produced automobiles.

It was against this background that Hoover entered his first or "offensive" phase as a depression president. He began by playing an extremely independent, active role, calling conferences of industrial and labor leaders and obtaining from them voluntary pledges to avoid strikes, hold to current employment, wage, and production levels, and in general expand their cooperative programs. At the same time, he asked the states and cities to speed up their public works in order to maintain employment and increase construction activity. Although Hoover had in mind large extensions of federal public works when he entered the White House, he did not ask for additional funds for this purpose in his 1929 budget message because he believed only in well-planned, long-term programs "for stabilizing prosperity." The $3 billion reserve fund he would have recommended had there not been a stock market crash was in theory, according to Herbert Stein, "Hoover's most daring venture in the use of public works as an antidepression device." But it was never intended as an emergency measure, and Hoover refused to propose his mammoth reserve fund plan after the depression set in and federal income began to decline. A committee he appointed in July 1929 to study the relationship between public works and unemployment confirmed the economic correctness of Hoover's refusal when it reported back in 1930. Large-scale public works would not be effective in relieving unemployment, it concluded, unless planned in advance in a period of relative stability. All the government could do if caught unexpectedly by a deflationary period was to expedite programs already in progress.

Having made this decision about public works, it is not surprising to find that Hoover's State of the Union address of December 4, 1929, confined the six-weeks-old stock market crash to one-and-a-half pages of very guarded language. Not wishing "to add alarm to the already rising fears," he simply recommended proceeding "expeditiously" with the current federal building program. On the basis of a federal surplus projected before the stock market collapsed, he also recommended a tax cut. By the end of 1929 he still thought the deflation following the stock market crash was merely an American recession (refusing yet to use the term depression) caused by "overspeculation in securities." Since it was American in origin and scope, Hoover reasoned that the solutions were also indigenous and probably were the same as those which had been suggested at the 1921 President's Conference on Unemployment.

While Hoover expressed some concern about the impact abroad of American deflation in 1929 and 1930, he concentrated on the domestic solutions. His initial decision to urge voluntary state and local expenditures over federal ones made sense: the national government played a relatively small role in the economy in the 1920s, and was not the source of expansion that it has since become. Hoover did, however, request from Congress in April 1930 an additional appropriation of $150 million for public buildings.

"I am convinced we have passed the worst," Hoover announced to the United States Chamber of Commerce in May 1930. "In remedial measures we have followed the recommendations of seven years ago as to the acceleration of construction work, the most practicable remedy for unemployment." A month later he proclaimed that his administration had already done more than any other in American history to combat deflation. Expansion of public works, he said, marked a "new experiment in our economic life" and an "advance in economic thought and in service to our people." Modern statistics partially confirm these statements. Through Hoover's numerous conferences and exhortations about voluntarism to state and local governments and to business and labor leaders, plus increased federal expenditures for public works, and the authorizing by Congress (over the president's veto) of payment up to 50 percent on veterans' certificates, the net stimulation of federal fiscal policy was larger in 1931 than in the next ten years except 1934, 1935, and 1936. Moreover, the total fiscal stimulation at all levels of governments — federal, state, and local — was larger in that year than in any other of the decade. From 1929 through 1930 beyond any doubt Hoover was the most active national leader dealing with the depression.

Despite increased federal, state, and local expenditures on public works, private construction fell off drastically in 1930 and so did government revenue at all levels. Hoover decided as a result that the 1 percent tax relief could not be continued for the fiscal year 1931. Ideas about economizing, preserving the gold standard, and balancing the budget also loomed large in his mind, and by the fall of 1930 the president was publicly admitting there was a worldwide depression, not simply an American recession.

On October 2 he told the American Bankers Association that this meant "its causes and its effects lie only partly in the United States." Yet he continued to think that America could go forward with its own remedial efforts, and did not have to "wait on the recovery of the rest of the world." He would brook no solution, however, that was based on lowering the American standard of living. Wages, prices, and production had to be maintained, he warned the bankers, or the country would "retreat into a perpetual unemployment and the acceptance of a cesspool of poverty for some large part of our people." In November Hoover lost the substantial Republican majority of the 71st Congress; in the 72nd Congress the Democrats controlled the House by five votes and a combination of some of his Republican enemies — old guard and insurgent — controlled the Senate by a nominal one vote. In addition, by the end of 1930 his unilateral antidepression leadership was increasingly challenged in and out of Congress by those who wanted more government spending.

"Why is it," he asked his political aide James H. MacLafferty, "that when a man is on this job as I am day and night, doing the best he can, that certain men . . . seek to oppose everything he does, just to oppose him?" With these words the president entered the second or "defensive" phase of his antidepression activities, extending from December 1930 to November 1932. No longer able to ignore Congress, he spent a good deal of time responding defensively and trying to keep its action within prescribed ideological bounds. Democratic and Republican leaders in either house were not seeking to usurp Hoover's leadership role. Both were uncertain of how to handle the worsening crisis, and both feared legislative responsibility. But there were enough Democratic activists proposing their own antidepression legislation to keep Hoover on his guard as he continued to propose cooperative solutions for the depression throughout 1931.

Partly to counter these congressional Democrats, partly because of foreign developments, but primarily because of his lifelong inability to admit to failure or mistakes, Hoover changed his mind about the origins of the Great Depression. Rather than confess publicly or privately that his cooperative policies based on the only true "laws of progress" were not

Of course we are all keeping our heads and doing all we can to help.

effective, he became firmly convinced of the foreign origins of the worldwide crisis and of the necessity of international cooperation for recovery abroad. His original views were thus reversed, making European recovery a prerequisite for permanent American recovery. When the European credit structure collapsed in the summer of 1931 and England abandoned the gold standard later that fall, Hoover turned to Congress for approval of several international agreements: the one-year moratorium on Allied debts and German reparations, and the London "standstill" agreement stabilizing short-term German credit. Both were necessary, he said, for world recovery from the depression. At the same time he took steps to try to insure that the United States would remain on the gold standard, obtaining an increase in the discount rate of the Federal Reserve Board and raising taxes to balance the budget.

These complex international and domestic actions did not solve the president's immediate domestic political problems with the 72nd Congress. Though both Democrats and Republicans almost killed him with kindness — passing all his major pieces of remedial legislation so that Hoover could be held responsible if they failed — the major bone of contention, direct relief, was never resolved to anyone's satisfaction.

Direct relief to Hoover meant the dole, while indirect relief meant public works projects. His memoirs distinguish between two kinds of public construction — nonproductive and reproductive. The former were those "public works, including roads, buildings, river and harbor improvements [which] involved a direct expenditure by the Federal Treasury and provided little subsequent employment." In contrast, the latter had some redeeming social value; they were financed "either by private enterprise or by government loans," and would ultimately pay for themselves at the same time and "furnish continued employment." In a February 3, 1931, press release, Hoover stated his position against the federal government's providing direct relief. He never changed his mind on this question, even though unemployment figures soared from over seven million in 1931 to over eleven million in 1933 when he left office. But Hoover's insistence that locally financed self-help programs were more worthy of Americans than direct federal aid eventually became monotonous and repulsive to the average citizen.

The simple fact was that as state and local funds disappeared the people wanted federal relief, and Congress responded for political if not humanitarian reasons. Most of the relief proposals from the 72nd Congress were in the form of public works bills, which Hoover rejected throughout 1931. He did not discourage all public building: from June 1930 through June 1933 his administration spent over $2 billion on nonproductive projects alone, and finally gave its approval to a $1.5 billion federal expenditure for reproductive public works in 1932. But he refused to approve those "pork barrel" proposals that he thought were largely for vote-getting purposes, such as the La Follette–Costigan and Garner-Wagner public works bills that he opposed in the spring and summer of 1932. His refusal to capitalize on the popularity of these grossly impractical programs cost him heavily in the 1932 election.

Although Hoover supported the Federal Employment Stabilization bill of 1931, which technically created a board with the power to control job fluctuation through public construction projects, he *did not encourage* such activity; he was personally convinced that the depression had made such controls impossible. However, in view of congressionally sponsored public works measures, he was forced to propose the Hoover-Robinson bills calling for reproductive public construction projects. He told Senator Arthur Vandenberg at the time that it was more important "to cut expenses and to give the country and the world an exhibit of a balanced budget" than it was to support further unproductive public works programs.

The Emergency and Relief Construction Act he signed on July 21, 1932, conformed, Hoover said, to his specifications; but he was only theoretically correct. The act appropriated

$2 billion for public works and $300 million for direct loans to the states "to be used in furnishing relief and work relief to needy and distressed people in relieving the hardships resulting from unemployment." While the act did call for reproductive public works, its passage was tacit admission that private and public works programs at the state and local levels had failed, that emergency rather than long-term public works programs had to be started, and that some direct federal relief was necessary.

The Emergency and Relief Construction Act pushed Hoover's principles on direct and indirect relief to their limits. Whether he could ever have been forced by Congress to approve the blatantly nonproductive direct relief projects such as those later endorsed by FDR's Works Progress Administration (WPA) remains highly doubtful, given all the restrictions he placed on the administration of this 1932 relief act. Moreover, in 1932 he privately (and ungrammatically) insisted to his friend John Callan O'Laughlin that all such emergency legislation had to be repealed to prevent the country from being "plunged into socialism and collectivism with its [sic] destruction of human liberty which pursuance of these measures are [sic] bringing."

While his refusal to endorse direct federal relief can easily be understood given his personal socioeconomic views, and while his reluctance to provide massive nonproductive construction projects can readily be explained by a consensus among his economic advisers, the reasons for his outright rejection of the Swope Plan for coordinating efforts of business and labor to end the depression are not immediately evident. A progressive Hooverian businessman, Gerard Swope was the president of General Electric who advocated compulsory economic and welfare planning beginning in September, 1931. The Swope Plan would have guaranteed labor such benefits as old-age, life, and unemployment insurance, and protected the public interest through federal supervision of certain business practices and through public representatives of all the trade association boards. Membership in these federally regulated trade associations would have been mandatory, but in return they would be allowed to rationalize the economy. Each group would have had the power to fix prices, control production, and regulate trade practices.

To understand Hoover's rejection of the Swope Plan and other "grandiose schemes" for controlling "destructive competition," it must be realized that it represented one of two extreme antidepression tactics that the president faced by the end of 1931. Both called for forms of corporatist coordination far beyond Hoover's decentralized approach. In particular Swope's ideas reflected a "statist" point of view, whereby the central power of the federal government would be used to force coordination through a vast bureaucratic system of syndicates representing the interests of management, labor, and the public. The other point of view was in essence Hoover's own informal corporate guildism, carried to its logical extreme by a committee of the United States Chamber of Commerce. Not surprisingly it was also espoused by a number of his friends and advisers like Julius Barnes, Mark Requa, and Julius Klein. It envisaged abandonment of antitrust restrictions to allow for legalized trade associational planning, accompanied by private rather than public unemployment insurance and coordinated through a national directorate representing the major private economic interest groups.

Confronted by a welfare state based on federal coercion on his left and a welfare state based on government-sanctioned cartels on his right, Hoover rejected both extremes as violations of voluntary associationalism and cooperative individualism. Characteristically holding to a middle course, he was charged with doing nothing by both sides. In the process he lost the support both of big business and of a substantial number of liberal intellectuals and academicians whose faith in scientific management had been awakened first by TR's New Nationalism and then by experiments with economic centralization during World War I. These groups now favored restoring economic order by compulsory federal regulation. At the same time Hoover also lost the support of groups like the United States Chamber of Commerce and the National Civic Federation, both of which included some of his closest friends and advisers, who now wanted to restore economic order through compulsory, private cartels.

Of these two groups of corporatists, the latter — the neo-guildists — probably felt the most frustrated and betrayed by the president when he directed his Antitrust Division Chief John Lord O'Brian to tighten up standards for any new cooperative programs proposed by trade associations and to take action against any semiformal cartels arising out of current associational programs. Although Hoover had championed the trade association movement in the 1920s and expressly favored some modification of the Sherman Antitrust Act as it applied to the chaotic national resource industries and to the American export trade, he had never advocated drastic antitrust revision. Always opposed to the misuse of cooperatively shared economic information, he deplored the lax enforcement of the antitrust laws by the Justice Department in the last years of the Coolidge administration under Col. William Donovan, the Antitrust Division chief. Convinced that Donovan had encouraged cartel behavior among trade associations, Hoover stepped up antitrust prosecutions and denounced price-fixing and other monopolistic practices of such industrial groups as the American Petroleum Institute and the Bolt, Nut and Rivet Manufacturers' Association.

While the quantitative record of the antitrust prosecutions of the Hoover administration is unimpressive, his personal encouragement of such actions and his continued criticisms of what he had always considered illegal, oligopolistic associationalism shocked and dismayed many large and small businessmen alike. Unfortunately his actions and words also did not satisfy those reform groups who wanted a return to Woodrow Wilson's New Freedom trustbusting approach. Having never been either a New Nationalist or a New Freedomite, Hoover was not about to become one now under pressure and in violation of his own cooperative version of corporatism.

Viewed from this middle position, his rejection of the best publicized of the two extreme corporatist plans for economic coordination, that is, the Swope Plan, made perfect sense. Hoover was convinced by the end of 1931 that external forces were detrimentally affecting American recovery and that the real solution to the depression lay in major international agreements, not in the minor domestic financial reforms that would create new credit facilities, and not in more drastic forms of national planning. He was also convinced that the Swope Plan, which became the basis for the National Recovery Act of the New Deal, was unconstitutional, would create a coercive, dehumanizing bureaucracy, and was in all probability inspired by the First Five Year Plan of the Soviet Union. To counter this type of subversive national planning Hoover actually proposed his own "Twenty Year Plan" in June 1931, arguing that at least this much time was necessary to give his American system a chance to prove itself.

Above all else, perhaps, acceptance of the Swope Plan would have been an admission of failure; "no President," he once told his old friend Julius Barnes, "must ever admit he has been wrong." What he was really refusing to admit to himself was that time had already run out on his American system, before it had ever been put into practice for any meaningful length of time between 1921 and 1929.

However, the widespread support in congressional and business circles for more federal action to rationalize the depressed economy did prompt Hoover to propose several other defensive pieces of legislation during the first session of the 72nd Congress in the spring of 1932. None of the bills in their final form technically violated the principles of the American system, according to Hoover, but the fact remains that he began to operate partially on an emergency basis rather than exclusively on the hallowed grounds of voluntary, long-term planning.

For example, the Federal Farm Board created during the special session of the 71st Congress began emergency operations when it launched a large wheat price stabilization effort through the purchase of surpluses. After it became evident during the summer of 1931 that the board was losing money on such purchases without achieving price stabilization, the question arose whether the price stabilization should be made a permanent money-losing proposition or should be abandoned. With Hoover's approval, the board chose the latter course and at the same time began recommending that farmers voluntarily destroy a portion of their staple crops. No monetary enticement was offered and no coercion was involved; Hoover viewed subsidies as tantamount to bribes and forced production control as "sheer Fascism." Without voluntary compliance, he correctly predicted, no amount of subsidies or federal legislation could prevent future surpluses. Once again he was unwilling to go beyond certain prescribed philosophical limits.

The same consistent adherence to principle marked the new legislation Hoover proposed during the 72nd Congress in 1932. All of it, except for the Emergency Relief and Construction Act, was exclusively designed to build confidence through cooperative action by bolstering the domestic credit structure weakened by foreign withdrawals of gold and private hoarding. Above all, Hoover hoped to avoid reviving an agency like the War Finance Corporation (WFC), which Eugene Meyer, Governor of the Federal Reserve Board, was urging. Instead he persuaded reluctant bankers and insurance executives on October 4, 1931, to form the National Credit Corporation (NCC) with a capital of $500 million. It represented Hoover's last attempt to save the country's credit structure through purely voluntary means. However, cautiousness of the bankers involved resulted in the NCC's failure as an effective credit pool by the end of November. The president was forced to fall back on the wartime model of the WFC by recommending the creation of the Reconstruction Finance Corporation (RFC) with Eugene Meyer, who had also headed the WFC, as its chairman. *Thus, the ill-fated Hoover administration became the first in American history to use the power of the federal government to intervene directly in the economy in time of peace.* Voluntarism had failed.

The RFC legislation became effective on January 22, 1932, with a $2 million appropriation from Congress earmarked for endangered financial institutions. Hoover hoped the RFC would increase confidence, stimulate employment, and aid foreign trade. Nonetheless, he looked upon it as he had on the WFC: as a temporary and emergency agency whose functions would end with the economic crisis and whose purpose was to liquefy the nation's frozen assets by loaning only to large businesses and financial institutions, rather than to average citizens. Not only did his personal philosophy and experiences with the WFC during World War I prevent him from allowing the RFC to make massive loans for direct relief of unemployment, but in creating the RFC he also indicated that his first concern remained the national credit structure.

Simultaneously and for the same reason, he pressed for passage of the Glass-Steagall Act of February 27, 1932, which made about $750 million of government gold available for industrial and business purposes. This legislation constituted Hoover's most revolutionary fiscal action, once again demonstrating his increasing dissatisfaction with the restrictive depression policies of the FRB. Together the RFC and the Glass-Steagall Act "helped the country get through 1932 without collapse," according to recent economic accounts of the period. With the signing of these two acts, the expansion of capital for Federal Land Banks, and the creation of Home Loan Banks, all economic indices temporarily shot up in the late summer of 1932, prompting Hoover to declare that the depression was being brought under control. But this brief respite had been achieved at enormous cost from the standpoint of Hoover's socioeconomic views, for it meant the temporary suspension of reliance on voluntarism and private sources of credit.

Hence, he became all the more determined not to compromise his principles any further on such issues as balancing the budget, remaining on the gold standard, and stabilizing international exchange rates through international agreements. This newfound determination led him to a logical, but extremely unpopular, decision at the end of the 1931 and another first in American history: a United States president asked for a tax increase in time of severe depression. Hoover could have juggled federal funds and made people believe the budget was balanced when it was not. Instead, he righteously announced a tax increase — because the Federal Reserve Board refused to expand the money supply; because he believed that an unbalanced budget would contribute to the international run on gold reserves; and because he feared a further erosion of public confidence if efforts were not made to balance the federal budget, then a symbol of governmental stability.

Instead of a popular and permissive nationalistic monetary policy based on an initial New Deal idea of a nonexpanding economy of scarcity, Hoover had chosen an austere yet controlled internationalist one based on limited economic expansion. His approach was too internationally oriented in this second phase of his antidepression activities; it remained too philosophically rigid to free American fiscal policy from the restraints imposed by genuine fear, a sense of diplomatic responsibility, and the balanced-budget syndrome of the New Era. Historians and economists now agree that it made more economic (albeit not political) sense to save the country's credit apparatus from further paralysis by extending RFC loans exclusively to leading financial institutions, than it did to use such loans to tackle the unemployment problem with direct relief measures. It also made ideological sense for the president to act in this fashion; Hoover's economic ideas had

never precluded *limited and temporary* government intervention into the economy when corporate (not individual)
conditions warranted it. But he continued to refuse to destroy
local self-government and personal initiative through the dole
or the creation of presumably benign federal bureaucracies to
administer direct relief for an undetermined length of time.

None of Hoover's depression actions, however, contributed
to the liberation of fiscal policy in the limitless way that FDR's
actions later did; that is, none of them freed fiscal policy from
foreign and domestic monetary restraints. Even the New
Deal's conversion to permissiveness in fiscal policy did not
occur overnight. It took years of depression and finally the
necessities of World War II to complete this conversion from
budget balancing to deficit financing. When this finally occurred it represented an evolution in American fiscal thought
that had taken decades — not a sudden repudiation of
Hoover's economic philosophy as of 1933. For partisan reasons
Hoover's innovative actions to relieve the Great Depression
have long been ignored, while those of the Roosevelt administrations have been exaggerated.

Nonetheless it is highly doubtful that there would have
been such experimentation in fiscal policy after 1932 if Hoover
had been reelected. Although Hoover always denied it, some
of his programs, such as those in agriculture, the RFC, and his
public works and relief appropriations, did open the door to
those who wanted to experiment in these fields. ("We didn't
admit it at the time," FDR's aide Rexford Tugwell finally
stated publicly in a 1974 interview, "but practically the whole
New Deal was extrapolated from programs that Hoover
started.") However, there is little evidence that Hoover could
have been persuaded to open that door any more than he
had on the eve of the 1932 presidential election — with the
possible exceptions of establishing a soil bank or other cooperative farm reforms, applying existing antitrust laws
less strictly against the most competitively destructive natural
resource industries, instituting government supervision of

banking practices, and *maybe* authorizing very limited social security benefits.

In general, however, his socioeconomic views had been stretched to their limit. He would take no further domestic action before the election, even though it would mean losing his progressive, humanitarian reputation along with the presidency. Ironically, it was neither congressional nor public opposition that prevented Hoover from experimenting in 1932 as the Democrats were to do in 1933 — only his own ideological limitations. He was the same progressive activist he had always been. He had never stopped trying to forge a new associational socioeconomic synthesis that would reconcile techno-corporate organization with America's rural, democratic heritage of individualism. But the times demanded more than a logical synthesis and philosophical consistency. Although his critics also failed to resolve the central organizational paradox of modern American society to which he addressed himself, it was Hoover who became the remembered reactionary and forgotten Progressive because he refused to follow the emotional dictates of mainstream America in time of depression.

This same self-imposed isolation was painfully evident when he dealt with prohibition and the Bonus March of 1932. Almost without exception, President Hoover's closest advisers and friends began urging him to modify his stand on prohibition in 1928 and 1929. These included his personal staff; William R. Castle, Jr., undersecretary of state; Ogden Mills, undersecretary of the treasury, Christian Herter, a former secretary from the Commerce Department days; and two old business associates, Jeremiah Milbank and Lewis L. Strauss. In the 1930 midterm elections prohibition as well as the depression played a prominent role in turning Republicans out of office, and these men once again urged the president to consider repeal of the Eighteenth Amendment. To all such suggestions Hoover usually replied that "our form of government . . . properly proscribes the Chief Executive from tampering with the Constitution under any circumstances," although he told his Washington political aide James H. Mac-Lafferty that he had no objection to Congress's placing a repeal amendment before state conventions. Under no circumstance did he want this done before the 1932 election; "it would beat us."

While Hoover's male advisers were trying to get him to change his stand on prohibition, the president found himself subjected to the opposite advice and pressure from a number of women. Lou Henry Hoover insisted they leave social gatherings if drinks were served, and the former Assistant Attorney General Mabel Willebrandt spoke for "millions of women . . . in the farming areas where overdrinking was a serious matter." Although a group of prominent eastern women had organized in favor of repeal of prohibition, it was apparently the midwestern and western women from rural areas who had Hoover's ear on this question. In addition to the positive influence of prohibition on rural women, Hoover's refusal to endorse repeal was based on his ingrained Quaker moralism and stubborn unwillingness to play the political game. Most important, however, was the economic significance he attached to prohibition.

Prohibition proved, he had proclaimed in *American Individualism,* that people could rise above materialism and destroy an entire industry without government compensation because it was the right thing to do. It symbolized for him the idea that property rights did not dominate the American spirit when the chips were down. Moreover, Hoover considered the liquor trade to be one of the nonproductive or least socially redeeming profitmaking industries, and for this reason he was not eager to see its legalized return. Finally, as secretary of commerce he had repeatedly tried to document with statistics the economic benefits of prohibition, insisting that it had especially increased agricultural production efficiency.

"There is no question, in my opinion," Hoover said in a 1925 *Christian Science Monitor* interview, "that prohibition is making America more productive . . . that it [is] putting money in the American family pocketbook." That organized criminals dealing in bootleg liquor might have been taking that same money right out of the family pocketbook, Hoover publicly ignored in the 1920s. Later as president he consistently refused to accept the argument that repeal would help alleviate depressed business conditions. Whatever the reasons behind his decision to defend prohibition in the 1932 election, he committed an error in judgment — one which he compounded by allowing his publicity staff to misrepresent the conclusions of the Wickersham report on prohibition.

Another error in judgment with tremendous political overtones that Hoover made in this defensive period leading up to the election of 1932 was his handling of the Bonus March. In 1931 Hoover had unsuccessfully vetoed the bill allowing ex-servicemen to borrow up to 50 percent of the value of their 1924 veteran certificates. The unpopularity of this veto (which Congress overrode) could not match the wrath he later incurred after authorizing military action against the veterans who had gathered in Washington to demand full and immediate redemption of their certificates. In this particular instance Hoover had won the battle with the Bonus Expeditionary Force (BEF) on Capitol Hill, when the Senate refused on June 17, 1932, to approve the request and all but 2,000 of the estimated 10,000 veterans accepted the offer of free railroad tickets home. Then he proceeded to lose it in the streets of Washington on July 28.

At the time Hoover publicly took full responsibility for the rout of the remaining veterans and their families from various Washington and surrounding area encampments. Actually he did not order the action taken by the army under the direction of General Douglas MacArthur on July 28, 1932. MacArthur, as Army Chief of Staff, deliberately ignored the president's orders to hold the veterans in check at their major camp site, Bonus City, in the Anacostia flats outside of Washington and not to drive them from it. Instead, using tanks, tear gas, and one thousand soldiers divided into infantry and cavalry units and a machine gun contingent, MacArthur personally commanded these federal troops and drove the BEF from the flats, leaving the encampment in flames.

Rather than publicly denounce MacArthur for disobeying orders, Hoover accepted the initial explanation offered by the general and endorsed by Secretary of War Patrick J. Hurley — that the veterans who had refused to leave Washington after the Senate defeated their bonus request were rioters and "insurrectionists" trying to overthrow the United States government. Accordingly, in defending the military action Hoover referred to "subversive influences" in control of the Bonus Army. Later in his *Memoirs* he stressed the criminal makeup more than the communist tinge of the BEF, and also claimed not to have ordered MacArthur's action. But he offered no proof in his own defense of this claim and so the public and historians have until recently continued to hold him solely responsible. The reasons why he did not charge the general with insubordination or attempt in some other way to exculpate himself before his death are complex. They are related to the breakdown of his public relations system, the forthcoming presidential election, his later admiration for MacArthur as a military commander during World War II, and, as always, personal ideological considerations.

By the summer of 1932 the depression had triggered untold frustrations, fears, doubts, and anxieties in Hoover. Byron Price, a newspaperman who saw him from time to time in this period later recalled: "He didn't look to me like the Hoover I had been seeing. His hair was rumpled. He was almost crouching behind his desk, and he burst out at me with a volley of angry words — not against me or against the press, but against the politicians and the foreign governments — with absolutely unbridled language and never hesitating to mention a name. . . . I've never heard anybody do a better or more vituperative job of laying out some of his political enemies than Mr.

Hoover did, in language that he must have learned in a mining camp." Following several visits to the White House in late 1931 and early 1932 Price recorded in his notebook that Hoover continually complained that he was being blamed for the depression when in fact he had done all he could as secretary of commerce and president "to avert the terrible situation in which we are today." But all his foreign and domestic efforts had been undermined, he continued: by European nations, by Republican party leaders like Senator James E. Watson and Speaker of the House John Nance Garner, and by the "stupidity and stubbornness" of Congress in general. "Is it my fault," he asked Price rhetorically, "that cheap politicians [and] selfish men over the whole world have refused to see the folly of their policies until it was too late?"

There is little doubt that Hoover was at his defensive worst by the summer of 1932. All his Quaker-bred belief in hard work and perseverance had failed. Confirmed by his engineering and wartime experiences, this idea that he would succeed if he just worked hard enough had always been both his greatest strength as a professional and his greatest liability as a human being. Now it took its final toll and turned the Great Depression into a personal tragedy. As William Allen White's father sadly commented in 1932: "Hoover will be known as the greatest innocent bystander in history . . . full of courage and patriotism, undaunted to the last . . . a brave man fighting valiantly, futilely to the end."

He had just spent several months in frantic negotiation with Congress over direct and indirect relief, finally signing the compromising Emergency Relief and Construction Act. Several months before, he had been forced to abandon the National Credit Corporation for the Reconstruction Finance Corporation, despite all his private meetings with bankers. Meanwhile he still found himself in an untenable "holding" position between the two extreme corporatist camps on national economic planning — the statists and the guildists —

even though he had supported all the significant legislation and cooperative programs within the limits of his socioeconomic views.

Yet Hoover knew that Congress and the country were still not satisfied, despite all his hard work. It must have both bewildered and disappointed him to see 10,000 veterans massing in Washington to demand a bonus, which to the president meant a degrading handout — a dole. He wanted to see them back in their communities practicing cooperative individualism, exhibiting self-reliance, and proving his unswerving faith in the natural "laws of progress." In sum, the veterans and all Americans should have been acting like earnest, altruistic professionals in the face of adversity.

Given this frame of reference, Hoover probably did delude himself into believing that the ragtag unemployed veterans were dangerous subversives out to destroy not simply the government, but the American dream — a dream which the Great Depression had already turned into a nightmare. Having blundered as a nervous, defensive ideologue in ordering federal troops against the BEF, he now compounded his error by insisting that many of the routed veterans were Communists or criminals. The latter charge came out of a Justice Department report for September 1932 after government investigatory agencies had been unable to substantiate the original Communist charge. This vague and poorly documented account was first presented to the annual American Legion convention to prevent delegates from censoring the president's anti-BEF action just before the November election.

The Justice Department report represented one of the worst public relations fiascoes of the Hoover administration. Before its issuance, newspaper editors across the country had generally supported the military action because they assumed that proof of a Communist plot would be forthcoming from the government. When it was not, Hoover's credibility with the press and the people was even more seriously damaged. By the 1932 election, rumors were rampant that Hoover had actually authorized "murdering veterans." In fact, none had been killed by MacArthur's troops; but the damage had been done and Michelson's forces were having a field day. With his publicity apparatus lying in shambles about him, Hoover stoically shouldered the blame for MacArthur's actions until his own death thirty-two years later.

The Bonus March incident was tragic for Hoover; it brought out all of his worst weaknesses at the very time when he so desperately wanted to instill confidence and trust. It confirmed not only the public image of his insensitivity to depression victims, but also his Russophobia, his excessive sensitivity to criticism, his inability to admit he had made a mistake, and his general limitations as a strictly managerial president.

After losing his bid for reelection Hoover became the last president to suffer through the longer "lame-duck" period, from November 1932 to March 1933. During this time he was much more active in combating the depression with diplomacy abroad than with new congressional legislation or more cooperative programs. It was in this period that he made a determined and futile effort to obtain Roosevelt's cooperation for a coordinated international economic settlement involving disarmament, sound currency and intergovernmental debts. Unlike the earlier cordial interregnum between Coolidge and Hoover, this one between Hoover and FDR was most unpleasant for both men. Hostile and suspicious of one another after the hard-fought campaign, they disagreed over everything from the gold standard and the origins of the depression to the banking and farm problems and the role of congressional initiative. Hoover wanted nothing less from Roosevelt than "the abandonment of 90 percent of the so-called new deal." Naturally such capitulation was not forthcoming from the president-elect.

More convinced than ever of the foreign origins of the worldwide crisis, Hoover began insisting that the roots of postwar economic problems extended back to World War I and the inadequate settlement negotiated at Versailles in 1919. Conveniently forgetting that he had once seen defects in the American economy and the depression as American in origin, he now went to the opposite extreme, blaming the country's continued ills first on foreigners, then on Republicans who opposed him in Congress and during the campaign, and finally more and more on the Democrats and FDR's monetary views. He also exaggerated the importance of the economic advance recorded in the late summer of 1932, never admitting even in later years the judgment of most economic historians that the temporary upswing "came too late to prevent the disaster and was on an entirely inadequate scale to produce real economic revival." All in all Hoover's capacity for self-delusion reached new heights when he wrote to a friend shortly after leaving office: "This country started out of the Depression in August 1932 . . . all the rest of the principal commercial countries started out at the same time . . . all of them have gone along smoothly making steady progress; [only] the United States slipped backwards and came into a banking panic because the New Deal began on November 9, 1932."

All such private tirades during and immediately following his last months in office reflected what Hoover dared not admit publicly or to himself. His dream for a new America had failed. Socially responsible corporatism based on voluntarism and associationalism among countervailing business, labor and farm groups had collapsed. There had been no value change based on less materialism and the practice of cooperative individualism among average citizens. The closest Hoover probably ever came to admitting the truth was when he bitterly confided to Mark Sullivan: "You know, the only trouble with capitalism is capitalists; they're too damn greedy."

The great engineer and humanitarian still lived beneath the new mantle of the Great Depression president, but few Americans realized this or cared. Some were openly vindictive — personally blaming Hoover for the national economic collapse. Such vengefulness had been amply demonstrated when a Republican congressman introduced a resolution of impeachment *after Hoover had already been defeated for reelection.* The resolution, charging that he had mishandled economic foreign policy, was defeated in the House on November 13, 1931, by a vote of 361 to 8. A few days earlier ill will had even been more evident when Hoover returned to California to vote in the presidential election. The crowd that gathered to greet him in San Francisco spitefully released stink bombs as his entourage made its way slowly up Market Street.

VI

The Progressive
as Diplomatist

*". . . however internationalist in experience, [he] is in
conduct nationalistic almost to a fault."*

THE DIPLOMATIC COUNTERPART to Hoover's domestic concept of
cooperative individualism was "independent internationalism." They were similar in a number of ways. Both were considered progressive by contemporary standards because they
tried to synthesize some of the existing paradoxes of American
society; both required the expert services of professionals; both
demonstrated the Chief's commitment to find apolitical, economic solutions to complex foreign and domestic problems;
both reflected a noncoercive brand of corporatism based on
voluntary associationalism between nations and individuals;
both reflected his use of conferences, fact-finding commissions,
and public relations as administrative techniques; and finally,
both were key factors in his attempt to devise new institutional
means upon which to build a new socioeconomic order for the
United States and the world in the postwar era.

In the formulation of foreign, as opposed to domestic,
policy, however, Hoover initially found his task more complicated as secretary of commerce because of jurisdictional disputes with the State Department, especially while Charles

Evans Hughes was secretary of state from 1921 through 1925. His work as a diplomatist was further complicated in a much more subtle manner by the uncontrolled bureaucratic growth within government circles that was accompanying the search for greater rationalization of the political economies of all postwar industrialized nations. Thus, it became evident during the 1920s that diplomacy often resulted not from the accountable, personal decisions of individual specialists, but from institutionalized, anonymous attitudes within the labyrinth of governmental bureaucracies. This has become a much more common and disturbing feature of the formulation of foreign policy in the United States and other highly developed countries since that time, but it was present in a nascent form even when men like Hoover were trying to control bureaucratic growth and warn against its dangers.

Interdepartmental rivalry, rigid bureaucratic procedures (often based on obsolete information or inefficient operational methods), and the usually haphazard and semiconscious search for world peace and order after 1920 by various elements of society — all affected Hoover's foreign policy views as secretary of commerce and later as president. In addition, of course, he had come to certain conclusions about world affairs because of his childhood, educational, professional, and wartime experiences. As with his domestic views, consistency was his hallmark in diplomatic matters. While a few of his ideas did evolve slowly over the years, particularly those concerning the Soviet Union, most of his basic diplomatic attitudes were formed by the time he entered Harding's cabinet and tried to obtain control over all aspects of economic foreign policy.

In fact, his career as a diplomatist had begun during the war with his famine relief work. The Hoover food distribution organization abroad amounted to a skeleton government that negotiated directly with hostile military and civilian leaders on both sides, using what Hoover called the "club of public opinion." His extensive international activities as chairman of the Commission for the Relief of Belgium finally led Senator

Henry Cabot Lodge in 1915 to consider charging Hoover with violating the Logan Act for conducting American foreign policy as a private citizen.

But it was not until the Paris Peace Conference of 1919 that Hoover formally emerged as a major force in the formulation of United States diplomacy. During that conference he personally advised President Wilson as Director-General of Relief for Europe and as a member of the President's Committee of Economic Advisers. It was, for example, at Hoover's suggestion that the Supreme Economic Council was established for the coordination of all former interallied economic activity. He also drafted the constitution for it, and as secretary became its most powerful member because of the vast economic information and control over scarce resources and transportation-communication systems that his relief organization gave him.

Like all of Wilson's economic advisers, Hoover wanted an American-led world economic community following World War I. Only the Open Door policy, they believed, could achieve this, because it represented unrestricted equal economic opportunity. Such a policy automatically favored the strongest postwar competitor, the United States. Wilson was advised by Hoover and others to liquidate all interallied economic controls after the armistice. So it was no surprise when the president rejected John Maynard Keynes' plan for cooperative reconstruction financing of Europe based on multigovernment guaranteed bonds.

Hoover was even more personally opposed than his colleagues to permanent postwar association with the former allied powers, because of his desire to see America become as economically self-sufficient as possible. So he urged Wilson on April 11, 1919, to announce that the United States would not participate in the various economic and military commissions to be established under the Treaty of Versailles after ratification. At best, Hoover favored economic coordination between major nations under strong American leadership, rather than an obligatory commission system which would have subordinated the immediate self-interest and the future self-sufficiency of the United States to the cause of European recovery.

Thus, his economic and political advice to President Wilson about foreign affairs during and immediately following World War I generally followed the lines of loose associationalism he so strongly endorsed at home and committed him to the private financing of European reconstruction. Such financing was to be based, as were his domestic economic policies, on the principles of voluntary cooperation and self-regulation among individual, multinational American corporations with a minimum of federal intervention. This type of associationalism at home and abroad would not only lessen the chance of future wars based on state-directed economic competition, according to Hoover, but it would also allow the United States to take the lead in organizing the world's economy, preserve its own future economic self-sufficiency, and still provide the means for harmonious global trade.

While he contributed to the work of the American delegation as chairman of six committees and a member of twenty others, Hoover did not formally participate in drafting the exact terms of peace. As usual he preferred the low-profile role of a behind-the-scenes adviser. But in the process he inadvertently alienated Wilson before the conference ended, by criticizing "anti–Open Door" provisions of the treaty concerning the economic treatment of Germany. Hoover and most members of the President's Committee of Economic Advisers doubted the wisdom of the sections on reparations (no reasonable sum had been set for Germany to pay), on mandates (especially in oil-rich areas), and on restricting German economic development. Serious doubt was also expressed about the ability of Article Ten of the League of Nations' charter, which provided for collective security, to preserve an Open Door for American economic expansion. Because Hoover privately made his views known to the president at Paris and later publicly criticized these portions of the treaty during the

campaign for ratification in the United States, Wilson personally singled him out for condemnation. Writing to
Norman H. Davis in December 1920, the President described
Hoover as a Republican defector who "is no friend of mind
[*sic*] and I do not care to do anything to assist him in any way
in any undertaking whatever."

Wilson's condemnation was unwarranted. As a member of
the League to Enforce Peace, Hoover initially took a stand
against amending the peace settlement, saying on October 28,
1919, that if "we attempt now to revise the Treaty we shall
tread a road through European chaos." By the end of the debate over ratification, however, he asked Wilson to accept all
of the Republican reservations, since even the "undesirable"
ones "do not seem to me to imperil the great principle of the
League of Nations to prevent war." Moreover, after Hoover
returned to the United States in September 1919 he pointed
out the dangers and the advantages of the peace settlement by
concentrating not on the "moral idealism of the League" but
on the "issues of self-interest" which he thought could best be
used to appeal to the American people. This was in keeping
with his own ideological conviction that altruism alone was
not usually sufficient to motivate support for an abstract
cause — a concept the Wilsonians in general and Wilson in
particular found irritating.

One of the major potential dangers he reiterated in numerous private communications was the possibility that even with
American participation the League could turn into a "super-
government" or an "armed alliance" that would ultimately
threaten "the very essential principle of nationalism upon
which our patriotism and progress is founded." Specifically he
urged some reservation on Article Ten because he thought
collective security might be used to preserve the rigid territorial boundaries established by the treaty. On the other hand
he was equally fearful that if the United States *did not* join
the League it might develop "into an organization for the
advancement of certain national interests, and we may find it

an economic, if not a political, league against us." In one 1920 telegram he even stressed that certain domestic problems — military expenditures, taxation, unemployment in agriculture and industry — all were dependent upon "stability abroad and upon our access to the world's markets which today are endangered by discrimination against us through our inability to exercise our veto under the Treaty."

Despite these private reservations about the League and all the imperfections of the treaty, Hoover always insisted in his public statements that approval was in the self-interest of the United States, because Americans no longer enjoyed the "pretense of an insularity that we do not possess." He believed that such a peace-keeping agency, with its World Council, could "minimize war" by marshalling public opinion and moral and economic sanctions against aggressive nations and by providing a new institutionalized means for airing international differences. Finally, he justified League membership as a means for "joining the moral forces of the world to reduce the dangers of growing armies, navies, national antagonism, . . . the spread of Bolshevism," and the necessity of sending American soldiers outside the United States. When Warren G. Harding, the GOP presidential candidate in 1920, seemed to be wavering on the subject of ratification Hoover emphatically told him: "No one except the former enemy and the Bolsheviki and their sympathizers advocate abandonment of the Treaty."

Hoover remained so suspicious of Harding's commitment to the League that he joined thirty other prominent Republicans in signing the October 1920 Declaration. This document attempted to assure the American people that a vote for the Republican party in November would be a vote for entrance into the League. Hoover was personally convinced that the "sincerity, integrity and statesmanship of the Republican party" was at stake on the League issue. After Harding won the election and denounced the League, Hoover continued to insist that the 1920 election was "distinctly in favor of the participation of the country in some form of international agreement for the maintenance of peace." Even after all hope for American entrance faded in the course of the decade, as secretary of commerce he unsuccessfully continued to press for close cooperation with the new international body. Later, in his *Memoirs,* he noted that as president he finally succeeded in establishing "systematic cooperation with the League in all of its nonpolitical functions . . . [and] its non-force activities . . . , conferences." In 1933 Hoover permitted the first on-site League investigation of a controversy between two Latin American nations. Until then the United States had prevented the League from investigating any diplomatic disputes in the western hemisphere.

As a diplomatist Hoover was characteristically seeking a middle or buffer course between extremes — in this case between the "ideal of isolationism" and "moral domination" of the world through internationalism. "Many of us want neither extreme," he said at Johns Hopkins University on February 23, 1920. This middle position rested on a foreign policy principle to which Hoover remained true the rest of his life: the idea that limited moral and political involvement with the world, accompanied by controlled economic expansion, was valid and could be distinguished from the less desirable extremes of overly righteous internationalism (associated with the Wilsonian position) or the extreme nationalism of irreconcilables like Hiram Johnson and William E. Borah. During the fight over ratification before 1920, however, he had not developed or articulated this particular brand of independent internationalism clearly enough to appreciably influence foreign policy by uniting the country's business interests — the one segment of American society with which he was most identified.

In retrospect it is clear that if Hoover, at the height of his wartime popularity, could not unite the American business community behind his League stand (with all of its economic implications), the odds were against his later achieving such backing for his plans to reconstruct Europe and to solve the world's economic problems through a system of loose associationalism under American leadership. Nonetheless, from two very important Washington positions he made a valiant effort to do just this between 1921 and 1933.

Hoover knew that the economic foreign policy of the United States following World War I was complicated because the country had become a creditor nation for the first time in its history. This situation, along with certain prewar problems, worsened from 1914 to 1918, and ultimately altered the entire equilibrium of international payments. These economic maladjustments between nations were largely the result of overproduction in agriculture, increased competition for dwindling foreign markets, and the failure of the United States to adapt its commercial policies to its new creditor status. World War I, then, accelerated an existing international balance-of-payments problem with Allied war debts and German reparations, and created the opportunity for the United States to replace British domination in world trade and finance. Many American business and government leaders agreed with Hoover that the United States had both the moral and economic right to seize such an opportunity, because of its unique world mission. But unlike most, Hoover had a comprehensive plan for dealing with the postwar balance-of-payment problems. Its major feature was coordination of the tariff, foreign loans and Allied debt, and international currency stabilization with the domestic commercial policies of the United States.

Hoover's tariff views were significant at the time not only because of the influential national offices he occupied between 1921 and 1933. He was also one of the internationally prominent business spokesmen of the period who simultaneously supported what appeared to be contradictory positions of tariff policy. Hoover took a nationalist position by favoring high protective duties, especially on farm products; and at the same time he supported the internationalist principle of scientifically determined flexibility, an increase in the investigatory powers of the Federal Tariff Commission, and the expansion of American trade through the negotiation of commercial treaties with unconditional most-favored-nation clauses.

Because the tariff was only one part of his comprehensive plan for the reconstruction of the war-torn world, Hoover maintained that there was no contradiction in his tariff views. Tariff policy never became an end in itself for Hoover, as it did with certain protectionist groups like the Boston Home Market Club and some agricultural interests. He always realized that by itself tariff policy could accomplish little in the way of transforming "the whole superorganization of our economic life" at home and abroad. Its effectiveness depended upon how well it was integrated into a general plan for world-wide economic reconstruction and reform, based on equality of opportunity under American leadership.

So Hoover and most of the officials in the Commerce Department under his influence believed that the volume of imports to the United States depended more upon the internal prosperity of this country than on high or low customs duties. But they did not opt for low duties; they were convinced by their own statistical data that the protective system was one of the major ways of maintaining a high standard of living, domestic prosperity, and some semblance of economic autonomy. High tariff duties would help to control imports and to expand the domestic market for greater consumption of American agricultural and manufactured goods. They were also convinced that an indiscriminate lowering of the tariff would not increase American imports enough to help European nations pay their debts to this country or to help sick industries like agriculture and textiles export their surpluses.

It is worth noting that at least on one occasion in 1927 as secretary of commerce Hoover privately confessed to a group of businessmen that only time and experience would prove whether his theories about the value of a high tariff were right or wrong. Publicly, however, he insisted in the 1928 presidential campaign that "there is no practical force in the contention that we cannot have a protective tariff and a growing foreign trade. We have both today." What Hoover and his economic advisers ignored in the course of the 1920s was the broader question of whether the United States was importing enough to offset profits from past foreign investments, or to equalize the large surplus of payments on current account that had built up since the war, and the degree to which increased American exports, especially those to South America, were responsible for the overall decline in the postwar exports of western European nations and the disruption of the triangular nature of international commerce. (Triangular trade referred to American exports to Europe; European exports to the tropics; and tropical exports to the United States.)

Also, Hoover personally overestimated what were called "invisible exports" in his defense of high import duties. These included the money newly arrived immigrants sent back to their native lands, the dollars American tourists spent abroad, the freight and insurance charges paid to European companies, and interest payments of foreign investments in the United States. With the exception of the money spent by tourists each year, the monetary value of these "invisible" expenditures constituted a more significant portion of the American trade balance *before* World War I than afterward. Although committed to bringing about a closer balance between American exports and imports, he refused to admit that the disparity between the two had significantly increased in the last half of the 1920s.

As secretary of commerce and as a depression president, Hoover defended the high tariff policy of the Republican party for reasons that were not completely justified by available economic statistics. But he did not do so out of blind faith in protectionism, even after the depression began. Commerce Department reports, and no little amount of chauvinism, for example, had convinced him by 1930 that high American rates would not harm world trade even in time of depression. What Hoover did not see was that once the United States ceased to export capital as a result of the Great Depression, the high American tariff would become a major obstacle to the adjustment of payments between nations — not simply a symptom of the international balance-of-payment problems that he had correctly perceived it to be up to 1929. Hoover's nationalist nature also did not allow him to see between 1921 and 1933 that high American duties were in fact "artificial restraints" of trade and often "deprived foreign producers of a 'fair price' for their goods," as did the international cartels and Soviet-controlled marketing agencies which he so vehemently attacked.

He never appreciated, therefore, the logical insistence by countries like England and France that their preferential tariff systems and national commodity monopolies were no more discriminatory than the protective American tariff. In part this was because he regarded dependence on foreign sources of raw materials as more critical to American internal prosperity than dependence on overseas markets. The former was threatened by international cartels and commodity monopolies more than the latter was affected by retaliation against high American tariff duties. Accordingly, Hoover unequivocally proclaimed in 1926 that the United States could more easily survive a loss of agricultural and manufactured exports than the loss of strategic raw material imports.

Finally, he did not consider the Hawley-Smoot tariff a depression issue. When he originally called for tariff revision in the spring of 1930, it was to obtain higher rates exclusively for agricultural products — as a complement to his Farm Board legislation — not to ameliorate depressed conditions generally. Political expediency demanded that he revise the tariff as early as possible in his first year in office. So Hoover ended up supporting high rates and flexible provisions because he wanted party unity and aid for farmers, and because of his long-standing nationalist concern for preserving the American standard of living. He did so over the opposition of business internationalists of both parties, of over a thousand economists, of almost 40 percent of the Republican newspapers across the country, and of twenty-four foreign nations — all of whom formally complained about Hawley-Smoot legislation.

At no point did Hoover think the Hawley-Smoot bill was perfect. Yet he signed it on June 17, 1930, much to the joy of the protectionists in the country, though his reasons for supporting the tariff were not the same as theirs. In fact, where other presidents had failed, he thought he could make both the Federal Tariff Commission and the flexible provisions work scientifically in the interest of internationalism by increasing imports. During the 1928 campaign the tariff had been regarded by many as "the touchstone for the foreign policy of the Hoover administration," and Hoover said on October 15, 1928, that it was "one of the most important economic issues of this campaign." His stand on tariff policy in 1930 was indeed indicative of how he would try as president to combine nationalism with internationalism in his foreign policy. It also reflected how, according to William Hard's biographical account, his nationalist sentiments sometimes interfered with his internationalist experiences and his objective interpretation of economic data.

There were two other economic foreign policy issues that played important roles in Hoover's postwar reconstruction plans. They were the related issues of foreign loans and Allied debts. Washington officials had to determine whether the former should be controlled by the federal government, and whether the latter should be cancelled as the financial contribution of the United States to the Allied cause during World War I.

There had been no systematic attempt to supervise private foreign loans until Hoover became secretary of commerce in 1921. Before that he had urged American bankers to begin voluntarily to set up their own standards for foreign loans. But when the financial community did not take the initiative to prevent "fraud, waste, and loss" in providing private financing for postwar reconstruction, he sought effective government supervision over such transactions as a member of Harding's cabinet. His failure to obtain this federal control should not diminish the significance of his attempt and the understanding of economic foreign policy upon which it was based.

Aside from bankers themselves, the greatest opposition to Hoover's attempt to establish government controls over foreign financing came from the Department of State under Charles Evans Hughes. Immediately following Harding's inauguration the two departments began to clash over control of commercial personnel abroad; Hoover insisted that those diplomatic matters which were largely economic (e.g., foreign loans) fall exclusively under the purview of the Commerce Department. By the end of 1921 an uneasy truce had been reached between the two rival departments for exchanging information on loans, but Hughes retained final jurisdiction over all proposed loans. But no such truce was ever reached over loan standards. When Hughes said the State Department should respond to the "imperative demands of American business," he did not think this entitled the government to channel private investment abroad through direct economic control. Neither did his successors, Frank B. Kellogg and Henry L. Stimson. All three secretaries of state between 1920 and 1933 preferred not to comment on the "economic feasibility" or "validity" of private loans. They were primarily concerned with establishing only very vague political controls over economic relations between the United States and other nations.

In contrast, not only did Hoover want stronger political controls, but he also thought that loans should be restricted both at home and abroad according to "their security, their reproductive character, and their methods of promotion." By "reproductive" he meant that loans should be earmarked for projects which would improve living standards, increase consumer consumption, and contribute to social stability. Loans used for military expenditures, for balancing spendthrift budgets, or for bolstering inflated currencies represented a waste of American surplus capital, he thought, and "generally would be disastrous" — such loans would not increase productivity or contribute to the economic rehabilitation of the world, and might involve the United States in the domestic affairs of unstable foreign nations. To avoid unnecessary foreign entanglement, such as American military intervention to protect unsound loans, and to insure that American bankers did not succumb to the temptation of high foreign interest rates and neglect needed capital investment at home, Hoover fought in vain for foreign loan supervision as secretary of commerce.

Although the State Department proved the major stumbling block to Hoover's loan control program, members of the Senate can be added to the list of government officials who indirectly helped to undermine his plans for supervision. In 1925 and again in 1927 a subcommittee of the Senate Foreign Relations Committee conducted hearings on the role the government was playing in guaranteeing foreign economic investments. These hearings stimulated public criticism of using the military power of the United States in foreign economic transactions, and of the practice of assuming internal financial functions in parts of Central America and the Caribbean. To the degree that such interference in the economic affairs of foreign countries was misconstrued to be part of Hoover's desire to obtain government approval of foreign loans, the hearings increased the pressure upon Washington officials outside of the Commerce Department to soft-pedal loan control.

This was ironic; Hoover had warned more strongly against loans to Latin America than to any other part of the world, and was on record in opposition to the use of armed intervention against foreign governments over economic matters. He also did not believe that American financial resources were unlimited. Indeed, these had been fundamental points of disagreement from the beginning of the decade between Hoover on the one hand and Hughes and the international bankers on the other. The latter thought it the duty of government to protect all American loans and investments abroad, while Hoover wanted to insure the soundness of such transactions to avoid the United States' being called upon to intervene. His failure meant, in essence, that America's private economic empire expanded in an open-ended, unsupervised fashion after 1920, with increasingly less concern for the productivity of foreign investments and with little political foresight or coordination between the country's economic and political foreign policies. It also meant that American bankers had successfully defied all of Hoover's suggestions for systematizing the country's foreign loan policy, first through voluntary and then through federal means.

Therefore, unlimited American loans abroad following World War I obscured the prevailing international economic instability, temporarily allowing foreign nations to meet their postwar debt payments and to purchase unprecedented amounts of goods from the United States. Only strong loan control in conjunction with lower tariffs increased imports on the part of the United States, and cancellation of the outstanding intergovernmental debts would have improved the world's economic health before 1929. Hoover's views on these intergovernmental debts were not as internationalist in the early 1920s as were his views on the other aspects of economic foreign policy, but he was ultimately more successful in moderating the institutionalized nationalist tendencies within government and business circles on the debt question than he was on the tariff and loan supervision issues.

Ignoring for the moment the contemporary moral arguments for and against payment, it is now clear that all war-related debts, whatever their exact origins, could be satisfactorily settled only if they were considered a common problem to be worked out at international conferences. Unfortunately for the international balance-of-payments problem, the United States insisted on handling these debts strictly on a commercial basis, and never officially recognized the connection between any of them. Operating on the assumption that international obligations had to be honored, the government chose to deal with each as a separate economic issue.

The attempts by the Harding, Coolidge, and Hoover administrations to collect the war debts, however, were less greedy than is usually contended. Much of the "Shylock" interpretation of the American position comes from the less than forthright way in which the issue was presented to the American people by leading government and business spokesmen. Subsequently this misrepresentation was perpetuated among the public by less knowledgeable bureaucrats and politicians. For example, in 1922 during the height of the cancellation controversy, as a member of the World War Foreign Debt Commission, Hoover initially supported writing off the prearmistice debts in order to strengthen "our moral position" and enhance the probabilities of payment. Told by his colleagues on the commission that Congress would never accept such a proposal, he then recommended that the United States forgo collecting interest payments and spread the repayment of the principal over an undetermined number of years based on each debtor's capacity to pay. Again the plan was considered unacceptable by other members of the commission, who insisted that Congress would never approve a debt-funding agreement which did not at least "preserve the appearance of repayment of both principal and interest."

Beginning in 1923, debt-funding agreements were negotiated by the commission which did indeed give the appearance of repayment, while in fact they reduced the combined outstanding indebtedness of the Allied nations by approximately 43 percent. This was a form of partial cancellation which was accepted in practice, but not in name, by Congress and other government officials who were convinced that popular opinion would not tolerate open cancellation.

For the same reason Hoover always referred to these reductions as "concessions," never as cancellations, because there had been no cancellation of the capital sum of any debt. Throughout the decade he privately remained willing to sacrifice interest payments for short periods of time, as long as the funding agreements were based on a scientifically determined capacity-to-pay formula that only temporarily deferred payment of the principal. Publicly, however, he encouraged the anticancellation forces in the country, and refused to admit there was any legal or economic connection between German reparations and American war debts. His irritation over the reluctance of the debtor nations to comply with what he considered very generous debt-funding agreements made him a leading critic, while secretary of commerce, of those "Americans who loved Europe more and America less . . . [and like] our international bankers agitated for cancellation night and day."

As a result in the course of the 1920s he also increasingly violated his commitment to the scientific capacity formula by using debt payments in attempts to obtain agreements from foreign governments over arms limitation and currency stabilization, or other political and economic concessions. For example, in 1929 he verbally offered to exchange most of the remaining English war debt for Bermuda, British Honduras, and the island of Trinidad, but Prime Minister Ramsay MacDonald refused to consider his proposal. After the depression began, Hoover's principled opposition to cancellation became more rigid in the face of French and British propaganda calling for repudiation of all intergovernmental debts, but his international responsibilities as president finally forced him to modify his earlier, more nationalist position.

By the spring of 1931 the financial situation in Germany was deteriorating at an alarming rate. Hoover's personal record of the events leading to the proclamation of his moratorium on all intergovernmental debts clearly indicates that he conferred almost daily during May and June with the

United States ambassador to Germany, Frederic M. Sackett, with Secretary of State Henry L. Stimson, Secretary of the Treasury Andrew Mellon, Undersecretary of the Treasury Ogden L. Mills, Senator and House of Morgan partner Dwight Morrow, and Chairman of the Federal Reserve Board Eugene Meyer about this impending economic crisis in Germany. Beginning on May 11 Hoover suggested to Secretaries Stimson and Mellon that since both the funding agreements with the United States and German reparation payments were "predicated upon capacity to pay in normal times," possibly the depression had now made such payment impossible. He still insisted, however, that "there was no relationship between reparations and the debts due the American government," although within weeks his actions were to belie these words. The two secretaries apparently made no concrete replies to this suggestion, but Hoover was aware that they differed with each other on the war debt question. Mellon was as firm an anticancellationist as Stimson was a cancellationist, and Hoover was caught in the middle of this interdepartmental dispute. The upshot of subsequent conferences was Hoover's proposal on June 20 of a one-year moratorium on the war debts in return for reciprocal action by the Allies with respect to reparation payments.

This June 1931 moratorium fell far short of solving Europe's financial difficulties. It came too late to prevent a general banking panic in Germany, and soon enormous sums of short-term credits were frozen — the very thing that Hoover had hoped his moratorium would prevent. He immediately arranged a "stabilization" or "standstill" conference in London to prevent further withdrawal of short-term credit from Germany. After considerable haggling with the French and the House of Morgan, a standstill agreement went into effect in September, 1931.

Both actions are significant; they represent Hoover's belated recognition in practice, if not in theory, of the relationship between the war debts and reparations. He continued, nevertheless, to deny this relationship in public, apparently never realizing that this position on the part of the United States had retarded the development of international monetary equilibrium for over a decade. Unfortunately for his oversold reputation as a businessman with an impeccable understanding of the world's political economy, Hoover's moratorium program did not restore international confidence in the face of the deepening depression. At best the moratorium and the standstill agreement stabilizing short-term credit to Germany only temporarily delayed the inevitable — the repudiation of both the interallied debt and the reparation payments that took place at Lausanne in the summer of 1932. Reparations, therefore, represented the last problem of economic foreign policy facing Hoover in his remaining months as president.

Having been one of the most vocal critics of the reparations section of the Versailles Peace Treaty, Hoover thought throughout the 1920s that the reparations arrangement was "entirely unworkable." He even acknowledged privately at the beginning of 1923 that European "continental stability cannot be secured unless there is a settlement of interlocked debts, reparations and disarmament." But it was not until 1931 that he was forced by the worldwide depression to formulate and try to implement such a coordinated settlement.

Until that time his actions with respect to reparations had been restricted, as were those of other major Washington officials, to supporting the Dawes and Young plans of 1924 and 1929. Under both plans American money was loaned to Germany to prevent default on reparation payments. In actuality, the loans represented the inescapable fact that the success of the funding agreements signed with Washington depended upon the Germans paying reparations to the Allies with United States money. But this unsound circular financial relationship was never admitted or explained to the public, and the Dawes and Young plans generated much false hope among Americans.

After issuing his moratorium Hoover worked frantically to

prevent permanent cancellation of German reparation payments as well as interallied debts. Privately financiers and politicians in the United States no longer made any attempt to insist that debts and reparations were not linked. These same business and government leaders also privately acknowledged that drastic reductions in both types of payments were inevitable. But the decade-long refusal of leading American officials to take a candid position on the debts resulting from the war and to mold intelligent congressional and public opinion on the subject placed Hoover in a difficult position, further complicated by the impending presidential elections. As with the Allied debt problem, Hoover seems to have had no hope that the public could be reeducated to accept a reversal in a policy that had become so entrenched both in the popular folklore and within the bureaucratic structure of the federal government.

The president and his advisers employed two standard tactics in the face of the growing threat of debt cancellation. They first unsuccessfully attempted to have European nations concentrate on the relationship between reparations and land armaments at international conferences. This tactic failed at the Geneva and Lausanne Conferences in the early 1930s. The other course, simultaneously pursued by the Hoover administration, had been initiated earlier by Secretary Hughes — the use of private financial experts to supplement normal diplomatic communication about economic problems. In this case Thomas W. Lamont was the unofficial liaison, who tried before the opening of the Lausanne Conference in June 1932 to present an economic alternative to total cancellation, and at the same time to impress foreign leaders with the delicate position of the Republicans in an election year. Hoover and other party leaders were convinced that if the United States negotiated new debt settlements with the Allies or extended the moratorium before the nation went to the polls in November, the Democrats would hang a "cancellation tag" on the Republican party. But despite Lamont's efforts, the Allies repudiated all intergovernmental debts arising from World War I.

Hoover's last and most original attempt to salvage the debt and reparations debacle came after his defeat for reelection. During the winter depression months of 1932–1933 he tried to obtain the cooperation of President-elect Roosevelt in reviving the Debt Funding Commission. A year earlier the Democratic Congress had refused to approve such action, and so Hoover thought Roosevelt's endorsement was necessary if the commission was to be recreated. More significantly, Hoover also wanted Roosevelt to help him appoint a nonpartisan delegation to the forthcoming London Economic Conference, and to agree to coordinate all future discussions with European nations about disarmament, debts, and other economic and monetary problems, including a commitment to an international gold standard. To achieve coordination, the president proposed the creation of an "interlocking directorate" selected by himself and Roosevelt from the delegates to the Geneva Disarmament and London Economic Conferences. With these suggestions, Hoover implicitly acknowledged the reciprocal relationship between the major economic problems confronting the world. A comprehensive settlement was now the only solution.

Obviously Hoover's emphasis on the importance of the London Conference and on the coordinated economic discussions underscored his belief by 1932 that the causes of the depression were foreign, not domestic, and therefore that international financial measures were necessary for recovery in the United States. In vain he sought Roosevelt's concurrence on these theoretical points that would have drastically limited FDR's options for dealing with the depression. At the same time Hoover tried to obtain Roosevelt's consent to diplomatic methods that would insure a continuation of the broadly internationalist position on debts and reparations that had evolved in the last years of his administration. Since the summer of 1932 this plan had included lowering the war debt payments of England in return for British trade concessions and restoration of the gold standard. Labeled "Hoover's harebrained scheme" by the Foreign Office, this effort to exchange debt concessions for a trade agreement had no chance of succeeding.

Nonetheless, Hoover remained rightly convinced that no kind of comprehensive agreement could be reached before March 4, 1933, unless the president-elect made it abundantly clear to Congress and Europe that there be no basic change in economic foreign policy after his inauguration. By this time Hoover was all the more convinced that the American gold standard could only be maintained through international cooperation, but Europe and, as it turned out, Roosevelt did not share his stubborn commitment to gold. This was particularly true of the British — who had no intention of either paying anymore on their war debt or bargaining away the advantage that devaluation of the pound had given them over the United States in the depressed markets of the world. So Hoover's belated attempt to forge a comprehensive international economic agreement at the end of his term in office failed, and along with it, his efforts to bring Roosevelt over to his point of view on domestic and foreign matters.

While it has taken Americans several decades to begin to appreciate the scope of some of Hoover's views about economic foreign policy, revisionist historians have long held that his political foreign policies were progressively modern for the period. This is true not simply because of his relief work during and after World War I, or even because of his pro-League stand during the battle over ratification. It is true also because of the positions he took in favor of such issues as disarmament, the Kellogg-Briand Pact, and the World Court, and generally against the use of force in world affairs, especially in Latin America and the Far East.

The United States participated in four major disarmament conferences between 1921 and 1933, so Hoover was in an excellent position to express his views on this question both as

secretary of commerce and as president. At the first one — the
Washington Conference on the Limitation of Armament,
1921–1922 — the Department of Commerce provided the
American delegation with economic data; Hoover viewed it
much in the same way he viewed the conferences he called on
domestic problems, as essentially ritualistic and educational in
nature. On the eve of what was to become the most successful
of all the disarmament conferences between the two world
wars, he advised Secretary Hughes to work out all the details
in advance. When Hughes jokingly accused Hoover of want-
ing to "have the Conference before the Conference," the secretary of commerce quickly confirmed that this, indeed, was
exactly what he had in mind. And to a large degree the success
of the conference rested upon the surprisingly detailed naval
limitations proposals Hughes made at the first plenary session.

In keeping with his preference to serve behind the scenes,
Hoover's only official role at the Washington Disarmament
conference was as a member of the highly publicized Advisory
Board to the American Delegation. Hughes said at that time
that he advised President Harding to appoint this committee
so that the American delegation "might have the support of
sound and well-informed opinion." Hoover, however, recalled
later in his *Memoirs* that the board was simply a "political
repository for some twenty persons who thought they ought to
be on the main delegation." Hughes, he said, urged him to be
on it "in order to keep peace within that Committee," which
he did even after a few of the other members began to rebel at
their "window-dressing" roles.

Hoover's interpretation is probably closer to the truth.
Documentary evidence shows that Hughes decided to appoint
the Advisory Board only after the National Council on the
Limitation of Armament threatened to sponsor sessions which
would run concurrently with the official disarmament meetings in order "to stimulate intelligent interest in the stated
objects of the Conference. . . ." Hoover and Hughes both
opposed any outside public pressure of this nature being

brought to bear on the conference, and both later denied that public opinion had played any significant role in originating the conference. The Advisory Board under their influence functioned exclusively as a public relations buffer between the American public and the American delegation, a function with which Hoover was both familiar and comfortable.

Hoover generally approved of the results of the Washington Conference because he believed that arms limitation was essential to European financial stability and because all of the treaties and agreements were based on voluntary international cooperation, not coercion. However, he did not think that by itself the conference was enough to remedy the diplomatic and military problems arising among competing nations in the Far East. In particular, he quickly recognized that the major disarmament reductions of the Five Power Treaty applied to only 30 percent of the naval tonnage of the nations who signed it, leaving competitive building in auxiliary naval categories below the capital ship level untouched. At the end of the decade this discrepancy had resulted in naval "disparity not parity," even between friendly nations like England and the United States. By this time Hoover also had been influenced by the postwar disarmament and peace movement; he personally believed that excessive military expenditures were an economic drain, and that moral sanctions based on public opinion constituted the best way to preserve peace and bolster the Kellogg-Briand Pact of 1928.

Although he thought this pact, which supposedly outlawed war among nations, represented the beginning of a new peaceful order in international relations, he emphatically opposed using military or economic sanctions to enforce it. It would be, he said, "contrary to the policy and best judgment of the United States to build peace on military sanctions." He also deplored the hatred, demoralization, and starvation which had resulted from the use of economic sanctions during World War I, even though he had expressed approval of economic sanctions in his defense of the League in 1920. As president, however, his opposition to economic sanctions to implement the pact was so firm that it survived contrary advice not only from Secretary Stimson, but also from the International and United States Chambers of Commerce and from individual businessmen.

The 1930 London Disarmament Conference provided Hoover with his best opportunity to implement his views. Closely cooperating with British Prime Minister Ramsay MacDonald, he not only handpicked the naval officers who attended, but also made them subordinate to the civilian delegates, in order to avoid a deadlock between the two groups like the one that had occurred at the 1927 Geneva Disarmament Conference. He also capitalized on the exposure in 1927 of the antidisarmament lobbying activities of William B. Shearer, an employee of Bethlehem Steel, to silence the Navy League and other interest groups opposed to naval cutbacks. "It seems to me," Hoover confidently told Stimson in the midst of these meticulous preconference preparations, "that there is the most profound outlook for peace today that we have had in any time in the last half century."

Anticipating criticism of the London Naval Treaty, Hoover called a special session of the Senate on July 7, 1930, to obtain ratification as quickly as possible. Criticism developed nonetheless along the lines that he had predicted. Much of it came from the Naval Board and focused on the rather minor point of whether the United States should have been granted twenty-one instead of eighteen 10,000-ton cruisers with eight-inch guns in order to reach parity with England. Hoover pointed out that this involved less than 3 percent of the entire fleet, and that even the naval experts could not agree on the relative merits of the 30,000 tons of ships armed with eight-inch guns that the treaty did not accord the United States, and the 38,000 tons of ships with six-inch guns that it did.

The most difficult feature of the treaty to explain to the Senate and the public, however, was why the agreed ratios required the United States to increase rather than decrease its

overall cruiser tonnage. To many in the antiwar movement
this disarmament agreement encouraged preparedness, not
peace. The reason was obvious, according to Hoover. The
United States had "lagged behind" England and Japan in
building cruisers since 1922, and must now catch up in the
interests of parity and national defense. At the same time he
emphasized that the London Treaty would ultimately reduce
total naval building programs throughout the world by 12
percent and like Secretary Stimson, insisted that the "doctrine
of parity . . . was not a military doctrine but a doctrine of
statesmanship." When he finally pushed the treaty through a
procrastinating Senate on July 21, 1930, it represented not only
the end of the Anglo-American naval race and another temporary slowing of the worldwide naval race, but also a personal
triumph for Hoover — his greatest in the field of arms limitation.

Hoover's other activities in the area of arms limitation were
not so successful. He left office without significantly reducing
the American contribution to the international arms traffic —
even though he refused to endorse federally financed muni-
tions plants, limited the War and Navy Departments to the
sale of defensive weapons, and tried in vain to obtain discre-
tionary presidential authority over arms exports through congressional legislation. By permitting exceptions to the general
ban on government arms sales established under Harding in
1923, Hoover actually extended rather than limited government intervention in certain revolutionary situations, particularly in Latin America, although his original intent was to
change what he thought was an obsolete antirebel arms policy.
His approval of the War Policies Commission (WPC) in 1930
had a similarly reverse effect. Established by Congress to
investigate and reduce the possibility of war and unnecessary
arms production by reducing profits through taxation, the
WPC ended up furthering military preparation for mobilizing
the economy for war.

Finally, Hoover was committed to "economical preparedness," meaning a low-cost American military establishment. When he became president he introduced a new simplified budget to convey his alarm about rising military expenditures. This so-called "functional or pocket budget" lumped together current army and navy spending with veterans' benefits and the principal and interest on the national debt coming out of World War I. This, Hoover said, was the true cost of war: it came to some 72 percent of the projected fiscal budget for 1931. To say the least, the pocket budget was not appreciated by military spokesmen, who called it "misleading, overpublicized, and ill-motivated." Although this new cost accounting system did not lead to any major cuts in army and navy appropriations until the depression, it is a significant indication of Hoover's concept of the impact of the military on the entire American economy. Even before the depression, it is clear, he tried to keep military costs to the bare minimum consistent with national defense. He had originally intended to use any savings from defense appropriations to improve diplomatic services and domestic social conditions, saying that "nothing could be a finer or more vivid conversion of swords to plowshares."

By the time of the 1932 Disarmament Conference at Geneva, Hoover had finally come to endorse the limitation of land as well as naval forces in the interest of economic and political stability. Even in the midst of the depression, however, he perceived that disarmament was not the whole answer to world peace — only, as he said in a memorandum to Stimson on May 24, 1932, "one of the contributions to the dissolution of fear which haunts the world as a result of its massed armaments." Ultimately, economic and political fears caused the 1932 Geneva Disarmament Conference to falter and finally collapse, even though Hoover proposed in June a drastic one-third reduction of all "armies in excess of the level required to preserve internal order . . . and abolition of certain 'aggressive' arms." While Germany, Italy, and Russia accepted the idea, England and France procrastinated.

Since this disarmament conference, unlike the 1930 London meeting, was held under the auspices of the League of Nations, Hoover was unable to exert the effective personal leadership he had in planning the earlier one. In desperation as the Democratic convention approached, Hoover asked the Democratic members of the delegation, Norman H. Davis and Senator Claude Swanson, to use their influence to get a plank into the party platform favoring his one-third plan. But neither the Democrats nor the Geneva conference delegates accepted this suggestion. Hoover pursued disarmament, like his other goals, with consistency and as much advance planning and educational publicity as possible. The loss of a Republican-dominated Congress in 1930, however, and his defeat for the presidency in 1932 prevented him from realizing long-term, comprehensive results.

Hoover's stand on the World Court in the course of his careers as secretary of commerce and president is perhaps the least overtly progressive of all his political foreign policy positions. Ironically, nationalists in Congress most feared his leadership role on this question. Hoover did not oppose the concept of such an international judicial body, nor did he oppose American participation. But from the beginning of the 1920s his advocacy of the World Court lacked originality, spirit, and commitment. Telling the National League of Women Voters in 1923 that the court was not a "back door" to League of Nations membership, he undercut the overall significance of American entrance when he added that the World Court was only a "minimum possible step in eliminating the causes of war" and not the "total solution of international cooperation for peace." His one original contribution to the debate over the World Court was to say that American membership would be one way of strengthening the Kellogg-Briand Pact.

Much of this can be explained by Hoover's foreign policy priorities, especially during his first months in the White House. The World Court issue was low on such a list; he placed both the tariff and the London Treaty ahead of it. By the time he had tangled with Congress on these two issues, Hoover was not eager to take on a difficult question that a strong bipartisan minority in the Senate had opposed for an entire decade. Most important, the depression intervened, followed by the Manchurian crisis and numerous complications in Latin America. Even Secretary Stimson lost his eagerness for World Court membership with the onset of all these other issues, and Hoover became all the more certain that there was no time to prepare a convincing defense to present to the Senate. The depression made him particularly pessimistic about such an encounter, and even less tactful than usual in dealing with both proponents and opponents of the court.

So Hoover pursued a "strategy of delay"; the more he procrastinated in presenting the Court Protocol to the Senate the less chance there was of passage. The procourt publicists found themselves victims of the lack of funds and heightened nationalism that accompanied the Great Depression. Although he formally submitted the new Court Protocol negotiated by Elihu Root to the Senate on December 10, 1930, Hoover was really making a perfunctory gesture. By that time it was evident, even to the strongest Senate proponents of the court, that it would be defeated. Thus, Hoover came close to deserting the court issue, in practice if not in theory, in the last years of his ill-fated presidency. His *Memoirs* are less than accurate when he takes credit for the Root Protocol and places full blame for the lack of positive Senate action on the bipartisan group of court opponents in the upper house. Action from the White House had also left much to be desired, as Hoover concentrated on the other demands of his depression presidency.

The remaining important aspects of Hoover's foreign policy between 1921 and 1933 represent a combination of economic and political decisions; they pertain to specific geographical locations — Russia, Latin America, and the Far East. Hoover's attitude toward communism and the Soviet Union was a complex one, taking various forms between the Bolshevik Revolution of 1917 and recognition of the USSR in 1933. It continued to evolve, albeit more gradually, for the rest of his life. Although he started out taking a strong public stand against bolshevism as a private citizen during World War I, there were frequent discrepancies between his excessive anti-Communist rhetoric and his official diplomatic actions as secretary of commerce and as president.

For one thing, Hoover was unable to resolve his ideological opposition to communism with the unqualified promotion by his Department of Commerce of American trade all over the world. In addition to his reluctance to trade with the Soviet Union — which appeared to contradict Hoover's general goal of controlled economic expansion for the United States — interdepartmental rivalry with Secretary Hughes over who should direct American political and economic relations with the USSR also accounted for the lack of a coordinated foreign policy in this area. Finally, between 1917 and 1933 key career personnel within the bureaucratic structure of both the State and Commerce Departments contributed to the institutionalization of a strong anti-Soviet diplomacy — one that prevailed regardless of the individual predilections of the secretaries of state or commerce or the presidents who held office during those years.

The original nonrecognition policy of the United States toward the Soviet Union was passed on to Hoover and Hughes from the administration of Woodrow Wilson. The Chief initially dominated the implementation of policy toward Russia because, as secretary of commerce, he directed the activities of the American Relief Administration (ARA) there. Hoover saw no contradiction between his ideological denunciation of bolshevism and his support for Russian relief programs. In fact, he hoped that such programs would contribute to the downfall of the young Communist regime, either by directly forcing a modification of its economic and military policies, or at least by leaving a lasting impression of good will and efficiency that would lay the groundwork for future American leadership in the reconstruction of the postwar Russian economy. Hoover also hoped that his relief efforts would effect the release of American political prisoners held by the Bolsheviks, and help alleviate the postwar agricultural depression in the United States by reducing supplies of American surplus wheat.

Amazingly enough, he was able to convince the other members of Harding's cabinet and Congress that these goals could be accomplished *without* formal recognition of the Soviet Union — a nation that refused to adopt acceptable western socioeconomic views, namely, Hoover's own version of corporate liberalism based on associational activity. In the long run, except for the return of American citizens held by the Bolsheviks, the ARA operation accomplished none of these objectives. If anything, American relief served instead to bolster the Soviet economy and so indirectly helped to stabilize Bolshevik rule during the crucial civil war years of the early 1920s. Hoover himself later admitted to reporter Henry C. Wolfe that through his Russian relief activities "we may have helped to set the Soviet Government up in business," but that saving lives was worth such a political risk. So he remained convinced of the basic soundness of his action on humanitarian and ideological grounds.

The true significance of the ARA was that it revealed Hoover's ability to temper his ideological opposition to communism in order to carry on humanitarian work inside Russia, even though it meant daily contact and sometimes compromise with Soviet leaders. He did this despite strong opposition from many liberals and radicals in the United States who correctly suspected that he had, on occasion, used food relief to aid foreign counterrevolutionary groups in Eastern Europe during the armistice period. He had, for example, recommended that Allied food supplies be withheld from the proletarian dictatorship established in Hungary by Bela Kun until the Hungarians could be convinced to "throw off the Communist regime." Recent Soviet sources document that he did arrange at least one food agreement with a White Guard army fighting the Bolsheviks. Nonetheless, ARA food distribution was not entirely onesided and ultimately did benefit the Communists, despite Hoover's original intentions.

However, he steadfastly opposed military intervention into the Russian civil war, always maintaining that the best way to counter one ideology was with a better one, namely the American system. Never fearing the spread of postwar communism to the United States, Hoover spoke out in favor of protecting the civil liberties of Bolshevik sympathizers in this country during the Red Scare. Also, as secretary of commerce he retreated from his initial opposition to trading with the Soviets. Later as president he refused to engage in "Red hunting" or to arrest peaceful Communist picketers, and reportedly told a group of businessmen en route to the USSR in July 1929 that he was reconsidering the question of recognition because he did not want Americans to lose potential Soviet trade to foreign competitors. Finally, he tacitly supported indirect government financing of exports to the Soviet Union in 1932 and 1933 through short-term credit advances from the Reconstruction Finance Corporation to certain ailing financial institutions.

Despite these modifications in his attitude and actions toward the Soviet Union, Hoover never altered his views enough during the 1920s to take definite steps toward recognition. With the onset of the Great Depression, furthermore, he became rigidly defensive about any action that might seem to repudiate his earlier ideological or economic positions. Instead, he retreated to the bureaucratized anticommunism that he had initially helped to create in both the Commerce and State Departments. Consequently he imposed his depression-bred defensiveness about maintaining the nonrecognition policy on Secretary of State Stimson, who appeared inclined toward reconciliation with the Soviets.

Hoover's Latin American policy was less ideological, and

more economically based than his Russian policy. As secretary of commerce he obtained control in December 1921 of the Inter-American High Commission from Treasury Secretary Andrew Mellon, largely because of Mellon's lack of interest in it and Hughes' refusal to fight for it. The purpose of this commission was "to act in common as an advisory body to various [Latin American] countries in perfecting [their] commercial and financial practices. . . ." As a result of this transfer Hoover steadily established his hegemony over Latin American economic affairs, except in the areas of oil and cable development and bank loans, where the State Department retained basic control.

Gradually in the course of the 1920s Hoover began to sense the growing resentment in Latin America against what were deemed to be spurious legalistic arguments, political inter- ference, financial imperialism, and unwarranted unilateral use of force on the part of the United States. There was also growing dissatisfaction within the United States about the government's Latin American policies, as evidenced by the Senate hearings of 1925 and 1927. Realizing by the end of the decade that such resentment at home and abroad might harm future economic relations between the United States and Latin America, government officials such as Hoover, Kellogg, and Stimson, and to an even greater degree, business inter- nationalists Thomas W. Lamont and Dwight Morrow, began to register dissatisfaction with the policy of dollar diplomacy based on arbitrary military and political intervention.

In particular, Hoover's practical, businesslike nature prompted him to become publicly more critical of twentieth- century policies of military intervention. He had expressed serious reservations about such police action in 1922, and later came to view the American experience in Haiti and Nicaragua as too expensive, ineffective, and a negative means of protect- ing lives and property and advancing the cause of democracy and capitalism. The Kellogg-Briand Pact further compromised the presence of American marines in Haiti and Nicaragua.

Beginning with his tour of Latin America as president-elect in 1928–1929, therefore, Hoover began to refer to the United States as a "good neighbor" of the southern republics, while emphasizing more and more the reciprocal cultural and economic interests of the two regions.

After assuming the presidency he found support for his good neighbor philosophy within the State Department, from Secretary of State Stimson and Undersecretary William R. Castle, Jr. But his good intentions in the area of political foreign policy were hampered by his economic policy; he was never able to overcome his reputation for supporting high tariffs and loan standards, which appeared contrary to the economic interests of certain Latin American countries.

Although the Hoover administration did not change its high tariff policy or make any significant attempts to collaborate economically on an equal basis with individual Latin American nations, the president and his secretary of state did begin to act like better, if not good, neighbors in political affairs. They directed the marines, for example, to protect only those Americans in coastal areas after new violence broke out in Nicaragua in the spring of 1931. This refusal to deploy troops into the interior for the protection of lives and property represented a departure from previous policy. Military action was also not taken against the growing tyranny of the Machado regime in Cuba in the early 1930s, despite the existence of the Platt Amendment and despite strong recommendations from the United States ambassador to Cuba. It was also during the Hoover administration that arrangements were made for the removal of the marines from Haiti and Nicaragua, although this was not done with any great haste.

Yet despite his refusal to intervene militarily in revolutionary situations or to use nonrecognition as a means of undermining revolutionary governments (except in Central America where the United States continued to honor a 1923 nonrecognition treaty), it was only upon Stimson's insistence that Hoover hesitantly accepted the J. Reuben Clark memorandum, which separated the Roosevelt Corollary from the Monroe Doctrine. This separation denied the United States the right to intervene in Latin America under the Monroe Doctrine, and returned to the original anti-European interpretation of that doctrine. Apparently in the summer of 1930 Hoover feared the effect the Clark memorandum would have on England and the Senate which was then considering the London Naval Treaty. But at no time before leaving office did he approve of the distribution of this memorandum, and he continued to insist that American arms would be used to defend the entire western hemisphere if necessary.

While the good neighbor mutuality that Hoover wanted to forge between the United States and Latin America was far from perfect when he left office, together with Stimson he had achieved a relatively successful Latin American political foreign policy. They significantly improved the quality of diplomatic appointments, placed the recognition policy of the United States toward South America on a *de facto* rather than *de jure* basis, withdrew the marines from Nicaragua, and tried to revise the policy governing arms sales by refusing to apply it indiscriminately against all rebel groups. To their credit, they also did not permit the principle of American supervision of free elections in Latin America, which like military occupation proved more expensive and time-consuming than it was worth, to become an institutionalized end in itself — as American government since 1933 has tended to do.

Their economic foreign policy was more inflexible and less successful in Latin America, because the depression defied the traditional economic principles entrenched in the bureaucratic structures of both private business and government. Hoover and Stimson, for example, continued to insist that nations of the southern hemisphere honor their contractual obligations — at the very time when default had become the rule rather than the exception in this part of the world.

Hoover's economic and political foreign policies for the Far East epitomize all of the ideological and methodological principles he tried to employ as a diplomatist from World War I to the end of his life. Because of his engineering experience in China around the turn of the century, he was considered an expert on that country and the Far East in general, as well as Russia.

China, with all of its internal disorder, was by Hoover's standards a very inefficient, nonproductive nation in the first quarter of the twentieth century. Although he supported the efforts of Charles Evans Hughes at the Washington Conference of 1921–1922, he warned that codification of the Open Door policy, which essentially meant a "negative hands-off policy" while China set her house in order, would not be enough. What was needed in addition, he told the secretary of state, was something "to strengthen the Kuomintang government of Sun Yat-sen against internal as well as foreign pressures . . . conditional upon the elimination of the communists and the creation of much stiffer internal administration."

So Hoover recommended a $250 million bankers' loan to China. When this recommendation failed to obtain the approval of the State Department and the Second China Consortium did not provide enough money to finance American enterprises in China, the Commerce Department tentatively proposed that an industrial consortium be set up to help create order in China through private trade and investment. But there was so much conflict within the Commerce Department over how to structure such an independent consortium and so much opposition from the American Group of the Second China Consortium, that the project did not develop beyond the planning stages.

At this point Hoover turned to what he considered only a secondary way to help China get back on her feet — the promotion of various China Trade Acts between 1921 and 1933. This legislation was intended to encourage trade and investment by providing federal incorporation for companies operating in China, and to exempt such firms from most

federal taxation. The secretary of commerce was determined
to overcome the absence of financial support from the American banking community for such trade. In contrast to his
usual insistence that European nations improve internally
before receiving American aid and trade, Hoover attempted to
stimulate economic development artificially in a politically
unstable part of the world – although he was never wholly
taken in by the institutionalized myth of the China market.
But despite these China Trade Acts, by the time Hoover
became president he had tacitly assented to the anti-Chinese
loan policy of both the State Department bureaucracy and the
American Group of the Second China Consortium. With the
exception of his agreement to Japanese exclusion by the 1924
Immigration Act, his actions in the Far East were implicitly
pro-Japanese, because that country exhibited so much more
economic and political stability after World War I than
China. His favoritism became explicit during the Manchurian
crisis of 1931–1932.

The crisis began with the Japanese invasion of Manchuria
in September 1931, ended with the creation of the puppet
state of Manchukuo in Southern Manchuria a year later, and
finally led to Japan's withdrawal from the League of Nations
in March 1933. At its beginning the president, his cabinet, the
Department of Commerce, and most senators, including the
influential Senator William E. Borah, opposed collective or
unilateral economic sanctions. Early in December 1931 there
was some vacillation within the State Department on the part
of Stimson and a few of his State Department advisers, but the
firm opposition of Hoover and Castle prevailed.

In the first few weeks of the Japanese invasion of Manchuria, neither Hoover nor Stimson publicly appeared to favor
either side; the secretary of state had previously made it clear
in the Sino-Soviet dispute of 1929 that the United States did
not intend to intervene militarily in such crises. Given the pro-
Japanese sentiments of Hoover's closest personal adviser on
the Far East, Undersecretary of State William Castle, and

Hoover's own admiration for the economic achievements of Japan, it is not surprising to find the president cautiously defending Japan's action at a cabinet meeting in the middle of October 1931. He viewed the increasing lack of order in China and Bolshevik infiltration as reasonable Japanese justifications for violating the Nine Power Treaty.

As Japanese aggression intensified in 1932, a tactical dispute revived between Hoover and Stimson that had been temporarily settled in the last months of 1931. The two men found themselves at odds not over the principles contained in the January 7 proclamation of nonrecognition (the Stimson Doctrine), nor over Hoover's informal offer to Prime Minister MacDonald on January 30 that the United States and Britain appeal directly to Japan and China for a cessation of hostilities and an arbitrated settlement of their outstanding differences. It was not even a question of Stimson's letter of February 23 to Senator Borah, stressing the applicability of the Nine Power Treaty as well as that of the Kellogg-Briand Pact to the Manchurian situation. Their misunderstanding, rather, was rooted in their personal estimations of one another and their temperamental differences. Generally speaking, Hoover thought Stimson was acting more like a "warrior than a diplomat" when he tried to put teeth into nonrecognition and the Nine Power Treaty through the use of veiled threats about military and economic sanctions. Stimson, for his part, thought Hoover lacked combativeness because of his Quaker background, and was not firmly enough committed to the Open Door to try to bluff Japan into compliance with it.

In other words, neither man was prepared to stand alone against Japan in view of the reluctance of England and France to take decisive action in the League of Nations, and both agreed that moral sanctions were all the United States could bring to bear in the Far East. Nonetheless, Stimson was definitely more disposed than Hoover toward a bellicose public posture. According to Stimson's published account of the incident, the only difference between his views and the president's "was the reliance which I felt we could put upon America's strength both economically and militarily. . . . I thought we had a right to rely upon the unconscious elements of our great size and military strength; that I knew Japan was afraid of that, and I was willing to let her be afraid of that without telling her that we were not going to use it against her."

Consequently, the secretary of state was angered in May 1932 to find that Hoover and Castle had taken advantage of his absence from Washington at the Geneva Disarmament Conference, to announce that the United States had no intention of supporting an independent boycott movement on the part of private citizens against Japan, or of pursuing by other than peaceful means a settlement of the Sino-Japanese conflict. Stimson resented this public rejection of all sanctions; it undermined the implicit threat he had made in his letter to Borah about fortifying Guam and the Philippines if Japan continued to violate the Nine Power Treaty. Hoover's and Castle's collusion, however, did not prevent Stimson from privately telling Walter Lippmann he was in "full agreement with the essentials of the president's position," for whatever second thoughts Stimson may have had about appeasement as a result of World War II, in 1931–1932 he was as convinced as Hoover of the foolishness of pushing ahead with unilateral economic sanctions in time of depression. Both men also realized there was no chance of collective action by the League or unilateral action by England or France. Their individual estimations of the situation were, therefore, neither unrealistic nor naive. Compounded by the worldwide depression, the situation simply defied either an independent or an international solution.

Stimson was, however, willing to endorse the use of sanctions as a diplomatic ploy, while Hoover was not. In this sense their misunderstanding, although of relatively minor significance during the Manchurian crisis, became enormously important in terms of subsequent application of the Stimson Doctrine and the Open Door it was intended to protect. The policy of nonrecognition of the fruits of aggression was significant to Hoover as an end in itself (so much so that he tried to insist upon calling it the Hoover Doctrine); to Stimson it was simply a means to an end that required concrete implementation. Thus, Hoover continued to praise the doctrine because it "avoids precipitant action and allows time to work out proper solutions," while Stimson thought of it as not yet an "effective living reality" and ultimately as an ideological justification for war.

By August 1932 it was evident that the Stimson Doctrine and an unofficial loan ban against Japan recommended by the State Department were not preventing Japan from taking over Manchuria. At this point the secretary of state made his last major bid to "implement the Kellogg Pact" with a declaration of cooperation with the League against aggressor nations. He did so in a far-reaching public pronouncement on the meaning of the Paris Pact before the Council on Foreign Relations in New York on August 8. For political as well as philosophical reasons Hoover censored the last three pages of the speech, in which Stimson had said the United States was willing to join in League sanctions.

No sooner had the secretary of state delivered this address than the president further weakened its impact by accepting his party's renomination for the presidency on August 11. Hoover took the occasion to agree with Stimson that the United States was obliged by the terms of the Kellogg-Briand Pact to consult with other nations, but he reiterated that the United States would not use force to preserve peace. He also narrowed the scope of the Stimson Doctrine by limiting nonrecognition to the "title to possession of territory," whereas the original January 7 proclamation had encompassed "any situation, treaty or agreement" in violation of the pact. Thus, the Manchurian crisis brought out Hoover's basically pro-Japanese attitudes, which stemmed from his engineering days and were reinforced by the ideas of his friend and adviser Undersecretary Castle.

The major reason behind Hoover's refusal to sanction the use of force in revolutionary situations in Latin America or to uphold the Open Door during the Manchurian crisis was his belief that no world economic community under American leadership could be permanently established by such means. He was no less a nationalist in 1932 than he had been in 1919 or 1900, but as an internationalist as well, he was also no less committed to the *peaceful* promotion of American capitalism and democracy abroad. He had never pursued an openended, devil-take-the-hindmost course in foreign or domestic affairs. Consequently, even though he considered the Stimson doctrine of nonrecognition to be one of the most important developments of American policy, Hoover privately informed his secretary of state in January 1933 that he would not back it with force: to build peace on military sanctions was "contrary to the policy and best judgment of the United States." Today this position symbolizes what many consider the most progressive and modern feature of Hoover's diplomacy — its noncoerciveness.

VII

The Republican
as Forgotten Progressive

*"Out of the debacle arises the shining thought that
you will reorganize the Republican party and lead it
again to victory. . . ."*

HERBERT HOOVER'S CONVERSION to strong party loyalty was the
single new ingredient in his domestic views after 1933; he did
not really become a regular party man until after he was no
longer president. Until then his political affiliation had always
been secondary, first to his private career and later to his
duties as a public servant. As an "independent" in the best
prewar progressive tradition, he had earned the animosity of
many old guard regulars in 1918. Their hostility combined
with that of some Republican Progressives in the course of the
1920s and finally broke out into open attacks on the president
during the first years of the Great Depression. Opposition to
Hoover within GOP leadership remained so strong throughout
the 1930s that he did not enjoy the usual influence and respect
as titular head of the party out of power.

During the thirty-one years Hoover lived after leaving the
White House he resumed the activities for which he was best
suited by training and temperament: mining, and educating
the American people through public relations techniques that

did not draw attention to him personally. In neither field did he keep to the pace he had set immediately before and after World War I. In fact, his mining endeavors between 1933 and 1937 amounted to little more than an avocation, and were carried out in partnership with two old friends, Mark Requa and Jeremiah Milbank. He invested primarily in gold, lead, zinc, and mercury mines in Idaho, Nevada, Utah, and Guatemala. Hoover told Requa's son Lawrence that he went into mining again as an investment to leave to his boys, but Lawrence thought he really wanted "something to take his mind off politics."

As educator and ideologue, he now suffered from a tremendous handicap he had not had in the 1920s: a reputation as a heartless reactionary who would not aid his own people in time of duress. Gone were the memories of the Great Humanitarian and Super Businessman. Hoover contributed to this unprogressive image in his private and public statements by talking more about moving the country to the "right" — away from the "left" represented by the New Deal. Small wonder that people forgot he ever had been considered progressive as an engineer or a public figure. Although his views remained what they had been at the height of his progressive reputation, his rhetoric changed in a desperate attempt to ward off what Hoover considered the first indigenous postwar threat to the American system — the New Deal of Franklin Delano Roosevelt.

Hoover also cultivated new friends within the newspaper world to replace those who had turned against him during the depression. These journalistic contacts not only provided him with a means for disseminating his ideas from behind the scenes, but also with much needed information about domestic and foreign affairs, and partisan politics. He privately corresponded with such editors and journalists as John Callan O'Laughlin, Ashmun Brown, and Theodore G. Joslin. Possibly because he had more time on his hands than before, Hoover revealed his opinions about domestic and foreign affairs with a new frequency and frankness. O'Laughlin, an adamant critic of the New Deal and FDR, edited the *Army-Navy Journal;* in 1933 he began to send out an exclusive, private newsletter of six to ten pages to a select group of Republicans, keeping them informed of inside developments in Washington politics. The mailing list included, in addition to Hoover, Generals Pershing and MacArthur, and a number of other anti–New Deal military and political leaders. Throughout the 1930s O'Laughlin also repeatedly predicted that Hoover would rise to party leadership once again. Ashmun Brown was the Washington correspondent for *The Providence Journal* and *The Evening Bulletin,* while Theodore Joslin wrote the weekly *Babson's Washington Reports* in the 1930s.

Most of Hoover's public and private statements throughout the 1930s were devoted to attacking the New Deal. He raised two crucial critical points about the New Deal. First, its policies did not bring the United States out of the depression; World War II did. Second, socialism and capitalism could not be mixed indiscriminately without destroying the traditional initiative, freedom, and independence of the average American and his uniquely productive economic system.

Hoover continually attacked the "totalitarian liberals" of the 1930s and 1940s, whose patchwork attempts to mix economic systems and excessive use of state power had only "succeeded in stabilizing the depression." The result, he finally argued in the 1950s, was a dependence on government expenditures that too easily led into justifications of massive federal purchases for hot or cold war purposes. Such expenditures were necessary, according to Hoover, to keep the bastardized New Deal economy going. On numerous occasions he equated New Deal liberalism with a "coercive economy."

During the first hundred days of Roosevelt's new administration Hoover kept quiet in public, but privately his language was shrill. On March 25, 1933, for example, he wrote to O'Laughlin: "February, March and April, 1933, will someday be known as the winter of the Roosevelt hysteria." He labeled as "white rabbits" such New Deal measures as the "unnecessary closing of the Banks for dramatic purposes" and fiscal measures which increased government expenditures. He condemned Congress as well, for abdicating its responsibilities to the White House. But until the hysteria passed, he thought, the Republican party could "do little else than show that it kept its head." Four days later he said: "Our fight is going to be to stop this move to gigantic Socialism of America. That is what is being done under the demagogic terms of 'planned industry,' etc. Correction of abuse has ever been a principle of Republicanism. But Socialism never has been. It has been a subsidiary in the evident intent to break down the currency. The whole gamut is Bryanism under new words and methods. It seems to take some time even for intelligent people to realize it."

In addition, Hoover privately castigated the economy-of-scarcity concept of the early New Deal, the devaluation of the dollar, reciprocal tariffs, deficit spending, and the general lack of any defined limits to the experimental programs Roosevelt undertook. But it was obvious that he was most concerned with the possible loss of individual rights. "To me the Bill of Rights is the heart of the Constitution," he wrote to his friend and diplomat William R. Castle, Jr. on November 15, 1933. "All the rest is a method and a framework for its guardianship and development." Hoover repeatedly referred to the Bill of Rights in his private letters, saying that it created "an ordered individual liberty," and expressing the fear that the "whole temper and attitude of the Democratic Party is to break down this system and to substitute a regimentation of men and collectivism instead of a nation of freemen." Writing to Brown in March 1934 he claimed that the New Deal was transforming the government — from one where the individual has certain rights which could not be transgressed even by the state, into one "where the individual is solely the pawn of the state. It is a lot worse than communism."

Later in 1934 as he continued to watch the New Deal take form, he was more explicit in *The Challenge to Liberty* about the effect of collectivism on American institutions. He noted that the "penetration of Socialist methods even to a partial degree will demoralize the economic system, the legislative bodies, and in fact the whole system of ordered Liberty." He went on to predict that the reaction to such demoralization "will not be more Socialism but will be toward Fascism because it has been the invariable turn in foreign countries where there is a considerable economic middle class. And this group is proportionately larger in the United States than in any other country in the world."

Hoover sometimes simplistically equated loss of freedom with any federal intervention into the economy; to him freedom was synonymous with decentralization. Nevertheless, he also expressed fears about the subtle expropriation of private rights and property, which has indeed taken place in almost all twentieth-century industrialized nations, through the pacification or elimination of all the diverse, cooperative groupings which formerly provided the individual with protection and security. He talked about the loss of freedom, for this reason, in conjunction with the rise of elitist socialist or capitalist bureaucracies, and stressed the importance of the decline of associationalism and participatory democracy. Unless this is understood, his view of the New Deal as a threat to the Bill of Rights and his comparisons of the political economy of the New Deal with that of Fascist, Communist, or Socialist regimes do indeed seem hyperbolic. Today, however, comparisons between monopoly capitalism and state socialism are becoming commonplace — and this, after all, is what Hoover was talking about in the early 1930s. The Watergate scandal in particular has given rise to statements by Democrats and Republicans alike about the dangers of an "imperial presidency" or of a "Gestapo frame of mind" in government — a tendency that has been building up since the New Deal and World War II.

But most liberal intellectuals in the 1930s did not foresee, as did Hoover, that subtle expropriation, and did not fear as he did the consequences for American democracy and values. Nor did they believe that a "gimme" attitude would become prevalent among increasingly atomized, alienated citizens, or that presidential power could reach dictatorial proportions. Yet Hoover wrote about these things in his private correspondence, immediately after leaving office. His friends as well as his enemies, therefore, portrayed him as an archconservative or even a reactionary after 1933, because he was so out of tune with the urban brand of liberalism arising out of the depression. Not only does this indicate how forgotten Hoover's progressivism was, but also how far New Deal liberals strayed from some of the basic prewar tenets of progressive neoguildist corporatism: Jeffersonian agrarian values; faith in direct, decentralized government, in the possibility of cooperation between labor and management in the name of economy and efficiency, and in the significance and dignity of each individual.

Hoover's ideas appeared perhaps more outmoded than forgotten after he left office. To his way of thinking, the American people were selling their traditional freedoms for government subsidies, while to the New Dealers this was not a relevant consideration. Few would argue that what took place in the 1930s plunged the United States into a Fascist or Communist dictatorship, but more are now questioning how truly progressive the period was in its promotion of increased dependence on the state (Hoover was calling it "State-ism" by 1940, "with its political bureaucracy, directing, dictating and competing with farmers, labor and business"). People are also questioning today, as Hoover did then, how progressive it was to extol materialistic values almost exclusively, and to condone the use of centralized, public power based on impersonal expertise without regard for some sense of the concept of community that had been so important to one segment of the progressive movement. Such questions, now common, were behind all Hoover's hyperbole in the 1930s, 1940s, and 1950s.

The ex-president broke his self-imposed public silence just before the congressional elections of 1934, with the publication of his most comprehensive philosophical treatise, *The Challenge to Liberty*. He said privately at the time that it was intended for "the thinking people" who "need to have their thought realigned," because "through their influence and transmittal of ideas, the country could be put right." Hoover's attitude toward public opinion, always reserved, became most negative in the years when the New Deal was most popular. He harbored great disappointment at how gullible Americans had proven when offered material salvation and depersonalized security at the price of their supposedly unique, independent, and innovative characters, and at how easily they had allowed another world war to take their minds off domestic problems. He felt that he had failed as a propagandist in the 1920s. So he tried once more.

The Challenge to Liberty contained an elaboration of Hoover's standard ideological views; it is basic to an understanding of his fears about "national regimentation" versus "liberty" and collectivism versus individualism. Hoover defined national regimentation as the "old, very, very old, idea that the good of men arises from the direction of centralized executive power, whether it be exercised through bureaucracies, mild dictatorship or despotism, monarchies or autocracies." Liberty was the "emancipation of men from power and servitude and the substitution of freedom for force of government"; it guaranteed "that men possessed fundamental liberties apart from the state, that they were not the pawns but the masters of the state." Hoover insisted in *The Challenge to Liberty* that it was true human liberty he was talking about — not some partisan ploy to win votes. In a series of anti–New Deal addresses beginning in Sacramento on March 22, 1935, he warned his audience against becoming "pawns or dependents of a centralized self-perpetuating government," the primary danger of the New Deal. But he could not even get members of his own party to listen to him in the 1930s. About the only influence Hoover claimed for his book was that it had provided the basis for the work of the Republican Resolutions Committee meeting in Springfield that year. Once again he had failed to convince Americans to accept his personal philosophy.

Although *The Challenge to Liberty* was circulated by the Book-of-the-Month Club just before the 1934 midterm elections, it had no positive political effect. In fact, the Democrats gained seats in Congress, unusual for the party in power during the off-term year. Nonetheless, right after this election Hoover was surprisingly optimistic, writing privately to both Brown and O'Laughlin: "The 45.6 percent in the last election that voted *against* the New Deal absolutely and from conviction so deep they could not be bought, were obviously to the 'right' of the New Deal in the social spectrum; and that group (which is within 5 percent of commanding the nation) would never accept any leadership which squints or trifles with that stuff. My belief is that it likewise will not for many years accept leadership from New York either. Its center point of emotional stability lies in the midwest."

This optimism and this analysis reflect his political isolation: neither was generally shared by his fellow Republicans. As a politician, Hoover had in 1920 and 1928 faced serious opposition from Republican leaders on both the right and the left. Beginning in 1933 a number of them once again openly dissociated themselves from his name and leadership. Hoover was incensed throughout the 1930s to find his Republican colleagues trying to win back majority status for their party, in face of the growing popularity of the Democrats, by "some partial adherence to the planned economy and other features of the New Deal." Although his reporter friends assured him that he was "the controlling factor in the Republican Party," clearly he was not.

He did try to be. For example, Hoover expressed continued dissatisfaction with the Republican National Chairman Everett Sanders, the 1932 campaign manager, and wanted him replaced with a "new face . . . from the Middle West." Hope for the party, he told O'Laughlin in March 1934, lay in a grass-roots "younger Republican movement." He noted, however, that this idea was too radical for the present National Committee. Yet later that spring Hoover prevailed when Henry P. Fletcher was selected as the new party chairman.

This temporary control of the National Committee by anti–New Deal Hoover forces proved futile. It came at the very time that the Democratic party was becoming the nation's majority party as a result of the demographic shift to the cities that had taken place in the 1920s and the recent triumph under FDR of the New Deal coalition among urban groups. This major political realignment in favor of the Democrats could not have been countered by any reorganization of Republican party structure. Consequently, Hoover's initial success in controlling the National Committee meant little, especially as more and more GOP senators and congressmen refused to acknowledge its jurisdiction over them.

As the 1936 presidential election approached, Hoover received conflicting advice from his friends inside and outside of the journalism profession. Some, like Theodore Joslin, thought Hoover's stock was rising and urged him in 1935 to disclose his political intentions; but Hoover refused, saying that to do so would only please the Democratic administration and his Republican enemies. He was no more receptive to others, like Eugene Meyer and Ogden Mills, who said as early as 1934 that Hoover should make it clear he would not run in 1936 on the outside chance that his prestige would be reestablished by 1940. Both were "excommunicated" for this suggestion, according to Meyer, by "small" men like Henry M. Robinson and Mark Requa — who apparently advised Hoover to keep his counsel before the nominating convention and above all not to issue a statement of unavailability. Hoover had already fallen out with Meyer over whether or not to proclaim a bank holiday in March 1933 and over Meyer's initial accommodation of the New Deal, so there was little likelihood he would follow his advice. As usual, the Chief preferred to remain silent and to influence developments indirectly, if possible.

His enemies in Congress, however, were not content; they let it be known that if Hoover were nominated again he could not possibly win. Nonetheless, the former president stubbornly toured the country in 1935, ostensibly defining party policy. In 1936 and again in 1940, Hoover seemed to be hoping for a deadlocked nominating convention that would enhance his own candidacy. In each case, backers of Alfred M. Landon thwarted his attempts to line up unpledged delegates.

His speech to the nominating convention on June 10, 1936, was well received, but there was little chance that party leaders would nominate him. So he resigned himself to insisting on the defeat of the New Deal at the polls and acceptance of his philosophy of cooperative individualism by the Republican standard-bearer. Landon was not his favorite. Hoover would have preferred Frank Knox, Frank O. Lowden, or Arthur Vandenberg. Also, Landon's campaign staff later angered him by first accepting and later refusing his offer to help with the campaign.

To O'Laughlin and others after the election Hoover privately explained Roosevelt's landslide victory by the political advantage the Democrats enjoyed because of slightly improved economic conditions; by the enormous expansion of government employees under the New Deal; by the usual solid South vote; by the vague popular feeling that FDR opposed big business; and by the movement in America and other parts of the world "toward personal economic security against the competitive system — the promise of personal government." In addition FDR had been aided by misguided Republican strategy. Landon was an honest man but with no public career and little knowledge of the important forces in government, unknown views, and poor ability to express himself. Hoover believed that "Alf" had been nominated at the behest of large

eastern banking and business groups and that he had subsequently made the grave error of accepting the support of the
American Liberty League, "the very emblem of big business."

Hoover's contempt for the Liberty League knew no bounds.
Among the men who founded it in 1934 were the DuPonts,
John J. Raskob, Democratic National Committee chairman in
1928, Jouett Shouse, executive director of the 1928 committee,
and Al Smith himself. All had opposed Hoover in 1928 and
1932 by marshalling money and propaganda against him. So
he refused to join this ultra-conservative "smear brigade" of
disaffected Democrats even though it claimed to oppose the
New Deal for one of the same reasons that Hoover did: individual liberty.

In Hoover's mind, however, his position and that of the
members of the Liberty League were worlds apart. For one
thing they emphasized property rights to the exclusion of the
other provisions protecting personal liberty. Hoover saw himself occupying a middle position between this Wall Street view
of the Liberty League and the New Deal view emanating from
Washington. His administration he once told O'Laughlin was
a "centrist" one between the "reactionary and moneyed ring,"
and the "radical elements," with the result that it had preserved the "great middle class of the United States right
through the depression." Thus he had no sympathy what-
soever for leaders of the Liberty League in their belated
opposition to FDR for they were partially to blame for his rise
to power. By accepting their support Landon had lost the
"moderate progressives of the country" who were more afraid
of big business than Roosevelt.

Another strategic error Landon made, according to Hoover,
was one GOP candidates had been making since 1932 when, he
told Castle, they had begun to run as "50% Republicans . . .
against 100% Democrats." Landon ignored or apologized for
the Republican party in many of his campaign speeches. Some
of them even implied support for New Deal measures like
relief, contrary to the Republican platform. Others were poorly

prepared and delivered without conviction and in some instances they contradicted one another especially on such complicated topics as tariff reciprocity, foreign affairs, labor and farm legislation, and social security. The ex-president also thought it was a mistake to compare the 1936 GOP candidate with Theodore Roosevelt in order to "make Landon look Progressive." By clinging to the spirit of TR, Hoover said, Landon opened himself to the charge that he was for defying judicial decisions and so he lost the force of the constitutional issue in the campaign arising from Supreme Court decisions against New Deal legislation in 1935.

Finally Hoover believed that there had been no real defense of his own administration so that misrepresentations mounted during the campaign, making all Republicans "look black . . . including Landon himself." An aggressive campaign, he said to O'Laughlin, should have been waged defending his administration on the basis of "its economy, its statesmanship, its constitutional practices, its real courage and genuine liberalism . . . [and] the fact that of the practical depression measures the only effective things left of the New Deal by the Supreme Court were Hoover's measures." Instead Landon lost the constitutional issue, lacked party courage and party conscience, did an injustice to former leaders (namely Hoover), and alienated Republican voters in general by making "the Liberty League and Big Business the mainstay of the Party instead of its own accomplishments and traditions." Had Lowden, Knox, or Vandenberg been the GOP standard-bearer the party would have obtained three million more votes because they were the real intellectual leadership of the party. Seeing that the real principles of the party were not contained in the Republican platform any of these three men would have realized that the true philosophical base of the party was contained in his own 1936 addresses and would have endorsed them during the campaign.

Thus his analysis of the 1936 election convinced Hoover more than ever that only his philosophy offered the country a reasonable alternative to "New Deal radicalism." Like most of his Republican contemporaries he did not admit the "revolt of the cities," which had been working against GOP candidates since at least the election of 1924, and so with minor variations this was the position he took in all of the presidential elections up through Eisenhower's victory in 1952. The results of his efforts during this period were always the same. Audiences at the various Republican National conventions roundly applauded his addresses and then nominated men who were not principled enough to gain Hoover's wholehearted approval. Moreover, Republican presidential aspirants in the 1930s and 1940s often indicated implicit approval first of New Deal domestic measures and later of New Deal foreign policy.

Therefore as a rabid anti–New Dealer, a loyal Republican, and titular head of the party, Hoover found himself consistently uninfluential between 1933 and 1952. He had consummated his partisan loyalties late in life, at the very moment when his party began to move away from him, and a majority of the country's voters was moving away from the GOP.

This swing away from the Chief in particular and from Republicans in general deepened an old split present within the party since the prewar Progressive Era. It reflected both the differences between Republican ideologues and Republican pragmatists and the emergence of what is known as the Republican Old Right by the late 1930s. The original division had been obscured by the prosperity of the 1920s, but it returned in full force with the Great Depression. Hoover did not simply imagine, therefore, that eastern moneyed interests within the party had turned against him in 1928 and in 1932. This trend had begun much earlier, as big businessmen increasingly joined the ranks of the Republican pragmatists opposing the ideologues headed by Hoover. Their financial support insured that this wing of the GOP would dominate in the early 1930s. Hoover was fighting not only the taint that the depression had left upon him, but a historical trend involving long-term realignment — within the power structure of the Republican party and between the two major parties.

The struggle he understood best was the one which finally produced the Republican Old Right at the end of the decade. By that time the Old Right was composed largely of the least conservative Republicans who were drawn together by their common opposition to the New Deal. Although they were labeled conservatives by their Democratic opponents, this term is misleading; by the late 1930s the ultraconservatives in the party — the leaders of big business and banking interests, who were also members of the Liberty League — had retired from the battle against the New Deal, discovering they had little to fear from its moderate reforms. Thus, moderate Republicans and leftover Republican Progressives like Hoover composed the bulk of the Old Right by 1940, with a sprinkling of former members of the Farmer-Labor party, Non-Partisan League, and even a few midwestern prairie Socialists. It was this middle or left-of-center group of Old Right Republicans that New Dealers, in conjunction with the eastern advertising and media establishment, first characterized as conservatives (because of their opposition to FDR's domestic policies) and later renamed isolationists (because of their opposition to FDR's foreign policies before and after World War II). Led by men like Hoover and Senator Robert A. Taft, the Old Right did indeed constitute the ideological wing of the Republican party after 1940 — as opposed to the opportunistic, pragmatic branch of the GOP — but they were not necessarily the most conservative or the least progressive of the two groups.

Naturally, throughout the 1930s, 1940s, and 1950s Hoover never ceased to support Republican ideologues for presidential candidates. As he told the 1936 convention: "There are some principles that cannot be compromised. Either we shall have a society based on ordered liberty and the initiative of the individual, or we shall have a planned society that means dictation [sic] no matter what you call it or who does it. There is no halfway ground." With the nomination of

Landon Hoover faced the pragmatists' first national victory within the party. In 1936, only Lowden, Knox, and preferably Vandenberg were ideologically acceptable to him. After Landon's humiliating defeat by FDR, the Republican faction that he symbolized remained in control of the party and this prompted Hoover to privately castigate the "dozen pinheads" in charge of the GOP for their lack of leadership.

But the pattern of 1936 was repeated in every Republican nominating convention until Hoover's death in 1964, when Senator Barry Goldwater became the first Republican ideologue to be nominated since Hoover in 1928. Throughout these years Hoover complained to friends about the lack of qualified candidates for upcoming elections. His choice in 1940 was not Wilkie or Dewey. Privately, he pushed Vandenberg's candidacy, although he would have approved had Taft become the standard bearer. By that time Taft had become an Old Right leader on both domestic and foreign policy. In 1944 the ex-president supported Taft, as he did again in 1948 and 1952. But only in this last year did he quietly inform party leaders of his choice before the nominating convention met.

During these years Hoover always addressed the national conventions and made some campaign speeches, whether or not the chosen pragmatist wanted him to. Publicly he always supported the ticket no matter what his personal misgivings were. He was, of course, pleased with the Republican victory in 1952, even though Eisenhower, whose party loyalty and foreign policy he questioned among other things, was not his first choice. This election represented "a turning in American life away from bad taste, corruption, communism and to some extent from socialism," he told his friend Joseph N. Pew, Jr. But he worried over the fact that the general had run so far ahead of other Republican candidates, and privately he warned Pew: "What I get of this is that the left wing opposition in the country will be stronger in the future than might appear now."

The most interesting proposal Hoover made during these

years was that the Republicans begin holding a national midterm convention to strengthen unity and principles. But like his advocacy of Old Rightist ideologues as candidates, nothing came of this call for an ideological refresher course at the national level between presidential elections. Similar calls for "biennial national conventions to provide a forum in nonpresidential election years," by Democrats and Republicans alike, failed to gain acceptance among professional politicians until March 1974, when the Democratic Charter Commission voted to hold midterm party conferences between national conventions.

In the realm of bipartisan activity, Hoover's outstanding contribution in the 1940s and 1950s was the direction he gave to two commissions on the Organization of the Executive Branch of Government. In each case, the changes along functionally efficient lines that he recommended were very similar to the ones he had been advocating since the early 1920s. Needless to say, they were not designed to enhance the independent power of the president. Instead, they were aimed at increasing the responsibility and accountability of the executive branch to the people and Congress by instituting "adequate staff aids . . . to assemble facts and records . . . and report upon the execution of decisions." There had to be a clear line of command because the president needed structural authority to direct his office efficiently, but not capricious personal power. Big government was bad enough, according to Hoover; unrestrained presidential prerogative, even worse.

The need for reorganization of the executive branch had arisen in both instances out of wartime expansion, first during World War II and later in the Korean War. The first commission Hoover headed, from 1947 to 1949, confined its recommendations "to the organization and structure of the various agencies under inquiry in an effort to promote greater efficiency and to effect economies." Because it did not deal with policy matters, the 1949 report created less controversy than the 1955 one, which openly investigated and criticized governmental policies and functions as well as practices. Also, Hoover's private correspondence about reorganization with President Truman indicates a cordial meeting of the minds that did not exist in his correspondence with President Eisenhower on the same subject. "I feel," Hoover wrote to Truman on February 14, 1949, "there are fields here where direct cooperation between you and me might contribute to successful reorganization . . . [and] that such personal understanding from time to time would forward our common purpose."

Hoover and Truman were in complete agreement on the following recommendations: legislation allowing the president to effect executive changes; removal of the quasi-judicial and quasi-legislative functions from the executive branch; unification of public works projects under one agency; consolidation of all medical services and medical research programs; grouping of all transportation agencies under the commerce department, and "of certain lending agencies under the Secretary of the Treasury;" and opposition to exempting the defense services from reorganization. While Truman did not act on all of the suggestions in the first report on executive reorganization, Hoover and his friends privately estimated that over 72 percent of the 273 recommendations for vertical reorganization had been instituted by Truman, while at best only 64 percent of the 314 recommendations of the second report had been instituted by Eisenhower as of October 1958.

A number of things account for Eisenhower's poorer record, including both less personal communication between the Chief and the General and recommendations for horizontal as well as vertical reorganization that were more difficult to implement. The determining factor, however, was Hoover's deliberate attempt to take advantage of the broader policy-making powers of the second commission in order to set specific goals or tests for the proper functioning of executive agencies — based on views he had first expounded in 1921 before the House and Senate Joint-Sponsored Committee on Reorganization of Government Departments. Had he suc-

ceeded, there would have been significant reduction of governmental functions and expenditures in the 1950s — all designed to purge the federal government of its New Deal
machinery and restore the informal corporatism of the New
Era.

That such an attempt should have failed is not surprising,
nor is it surprising that the tenacious Hoover should have tried
it between 1953 and 1955, when he was over 80 years old.
All of his standard progressive views about government and
American life can be found in the work of the second commission and its task forces, which although ostensibly bipartisan
were dominated by anti–New Deal representatives. Moreover,
unlike the first commission, no liberal Democratic vice-chairman was appointed to give greater political balance to its final
decisions. In fact, there was no vice-chairman. This placed
Hoover in greater control than had been the case previously,
under the Truman administration.

The standards by which these task forces judged various
agencies of the executive branch were intended to maintain
separation of powers, rule of law, congressional control over
the powers of the purse, civilian control of the armed services,
minimum government competition with private enterprise,
and finally to restore efficiency and economy. Some of the most
controversial of all the recommendations were those affecting
the Department of Defense — especially those where the main
concern was economy rather than combat effectiveness, and
those placing discipline matters under civilian rather than
military jurisdiction. Others involved limiting federal lending
to those areas where private agencies would not act, and then
proceeding only when there was some clear federal purpose for
doing so.

Probably the most controversial of all the recommendations
never went beyond the original task force which suggested it:
that federal power projects such as the Tennessee Valley
Authority be sold, leased, or dissolved. Ultimately the commission simply suggested that the government sponsor no more

power-generating projects unless state, municipal, or private funds were absolutely not available. The commission also noted that it had found approximately 3,000 examples of governmental competition with private enterprise, and recommended that 1,000 of them be summarily terminated. Personally Hoover remained adamant on the subject. "I would sell the TVA if I could only get a dollar for it," he reportedly told Senator Barry Goldwater. Federally sponsored projects such as transportation systems like the St. Lawrence Seaway he had long approved; but never those that produced a salable commodity.

While the commission's criticism of foreign aid was less severe than expected, its position on domestic federal lending was extreme, calling for the liquidation of the twelve Production Credit Corporations, the Agricultural Marketing Act Revolving Fund, the Federal Farm Mortgage Corporation, and college housing loans. Mutualization was recommended for those lending agencies that had "demonstrated merit and financial success" following the example of Federal Reserve Banks, the home-loan banks, and the Federal Deposit Insurance Corporation. Agencies which were not self-supporting, e.g., the Rural Electrification Administration, were "required to stand on their own feet" or be converted into private enterprise operations.

Clearly most of Hoover's lifelong progressive views on economics and politics were in this 1955 report on reorganization — from the attack on big government in the name of economy, efficiency, and cooperative individualism, to the demand for more intelligence information about Communist countries. Insisting on the educational value of the commission's investigations and the need for informed discussion of its findings, Hoover repeatedly tried to persuade Eisenhower to lend his personal support and prestige to its most controversial recommendations. He even drafted a special message for Eisenhower to deliver to Congress on the need to reduce expenditures through the commission's recommendations; the president ignored it. His failure represented the last major attempt of Old Rightist anti–New Dealers to repudiate FDR's domestic policies and to insure responsible executive authority. From then on most Republicans, including the president, tacitly accepted the permanence of a huge federal bureaucracy and the variety of centralized economic and social welfare functions that had arisen from the Great Depression.

Hoover recognized both his failure to rally public or political opinion to his cause and Eisenhower's obvious dominance as a national father figure within the Republican party in a decade of complacency. Combined with his own advanced age, this finally induced him to retire from active partisan politics in the last half of the 1950s. Nonetheless, he remained cognizant of political trends and major events, as his correspondence with Richard M. Nixon, General Wedmeyer and others indicates. The last detailed advice he offered the GOP during a campaign came in 1952, when he outlined seven points of attack against the Democrats and sent them to Nixon and other prominent Republicans.

These were the "centralization of arbitrary power over free men," as reflected by the increase in the bureaucracy during the previous twenty years; the fact that there was no peace even though the war was technically over; the existence of high debts, taxation and inflation; the creeping socialism of the New Deal; the implications of the charges of communism and conspiracies among government officials (here Hoover went back to the recognition of the USSR as the basic cause for the increased influence of the Communist party on government officials, labor leaders, and intellectuals) ; the rumors of corruption within the Democratic party; and finally, the intellectual dishonesty that had prevailed under the Democrats. He noted that liberalism was now a term that only "applied to those who would deny the same freedom to others which they demand for themselves — a good word turned pink inside." He concluded this detailed plan of attack with a statement repeated in a variety of forms since 1952 by disgruntled members of both parties: "To demand secret documents is helping Russia; to disclose waste in military spending is to hamper defense; to question price supports is to hate farmers; to worry about Communists in Government is a red-herring; to worry about the national debt is reactionary; to think that the President of the United States should obey both the letter and spirit of the Constitution is rank heresy." Portions of this summary of his dissatisfaction with the liberalism of the New Deal in 1952 have now been taken up by leftist and rightist critics of the respective Republican and Democratic administrations since World War II. But there was no such bipolar or even bipartisan acceptance to console Hoover prior to his death in 1964.

"You will discover," he told Nixon cynically in 1961, "that elder statesmen are little regarded . . . until they are over 80 years of age — and thus harmless." Perhaps the best advice he could have given Nixon he had already stated in 1923 when President Harding had asked him what he would do if he "knew of a great scandal in our administration." Hoover's abrupt reply was: "Blow it out at once! The blowing will prove the integrity of the administration."

Hoover's comments on the 1960 Kennedy-Nixon debates were reminiscent of his analytical post-mortem of the 1936 election, but with inevitable signs of age and increased ideological rigidity. In particular he noted not only Nixon's poor physical appearance but also the fatal mistake he made, as a Republican pragmatist, in repeatedly saying that he agreed with Kennedy on major domestic issues. Hoover was convinced that "Kennedy's goals were evil" because the "stupendous spending" he proposed amounted to "socialism disguised as a welfare state," and therefore simply a "new, New Deal."

The ex-president's contact with Nixon was enduring, if not particularly close, during the 1950s and early 1960s. Periodically as senator and vice-president, Nixon wrote "dear Chief" letters thanking Hoover for his advice and support, but both seem to have been nominal from the existing records. Specif-

ically, Hoover had sent Nixon letters of support or congratu-
lations at three crucial times in his career: after his successful
1950 anti-Communist campaign in California against Helen
Gahagan Douglas; during the 1952 GOP slush fund incident;
and during the Harold Stassen attack on Joseph McCarthy,
which Nixon opposed, in 1953. In return Nixon supplied
Hoover upon request with private lists of suspected Communists in government during the early 1950s. At the very most
their common bond was anti-Communism and not much else;
Nixon was clearly not a member of the Old Right.

Significantly, Hoover did not tender Nixon advance support
for the Republican nomination in 1964. Instead, he privately
encouraged Senator Goldwater to try to become the party's
standard-bearer. Telling Nixon that he was too old and sick
and "under instruction not to get into any more controversies," he nonetheless offered Goldwater all the support he
could muster. "There is not much that I can do in this campaign," he telegrammed the Senator on July 22 after he had
received the nomination. Then he offered him the services of
his son Herbert, Jr., "for your success . . . means the success
of our country." In truth, however, not even Goldwater was
all that Hoover wanted in a GOP presidential candidate,
especially in the area of foreign policy where he was much
more inclined to use force than the former president. Nonetheless, Goldwater the ideologue was preferable to Nixon the
pragmatist.

In general, Hoover's relationship with Nixon reflects his
typical behind-the-scenes type of anti-Communist activity in
the post–World War II period, rather than any endorsement
of Nixon's other political or economic views. A misleading
attempt has been made in the 1970s to confound Nixonomics
with Hoover's New Era economics because of the difficulties
inherent in understanding either. Hoover's was in fact a
comprehensive voluntary approach to national planning;
Nixon's was a piecemeal, vacillating approach without any
discernible philosophical or moral commitment. The same is

true of their views on foreign policy, although many have also mistakenly assumed that Hoover was as rabid an anti-Communist and vociferous Cold Warrior after World War II as Nixon. The following chapter clearly indicates that this was not so.

Although his political star had risen slightly after Roosevelt's death when presidents and leaders of both parties appeared more willing to consult with him about national policy, even this recognition came too late in Hoover's life to make him a truly influential political figure once again. Realizing this, he told Joseph P. Kennedy on September 19, 1956: "I don't see how we can do anything about things. At least we can take satisfaction in two sons in public life who are carrying on the battle." A forgotten Progressive in the last years of his political career as a loyal Republican, Hoover symbolized conservative reaction to New Deal liberalism until his death on October 20, 1964.

VIII

The Quaker Out of Tune
with the World

*"There is no doubt in my mind that you will prove to
be a wise [foreign-policy] prophet."*

BOTH FOREIGN AND DOMESTIC affairs after 1933, in Herbert
Hoover's view, were mishandled by the New Dealers. Charging
FDR with intellectual dishonesty in the conduct of American
diplomacy, he predicted that the new president's bellicose attitude toward Japan, should it lead to war, would hasten the
appearance of socialism in the United States. As in domestic
affairs, Hoover urged his fellow Republicans to launch national propaganda campaigns against the foreign policy of the
Roosevelt administrations, but increasingly in the late 1930s
he expressed fear about the decline of free speech and the
growth of news management under the Democrats.

Hoover was probably better informed about events affecting
American policy abroad after he left the White House than he
was about the details of domestic issues; his contacts in
Washington often were more knowledgeable on diplomatic
than on domestic matters. John Callan O'Laughlin, editor of
the *Army-Navy Journal,* provided him with invaluable inside
information, as did the career diplomats William R. Castle,
Jr. and Hugh Gibson, Walter Trohan, chief of the Washing-

ton bureau of the *Chicago Tribune* from 1935 to 1967, and Generals Albert C. Wedemeyer and Patrick J. Hurley. Castle provided the ex-president with access not only to his own diaries, but those of another career diplomat, Joseph C. Grew, with whom Castle regularly exchanged diaries until 1937. Hoover also had limited access to the diaries of diplomats Sumner Welles and Chauncey McCormack, and later in the 1950s his son Herbert, Jr., became Undersecretary of State to John Foster Dulles.

Hoover's interest in foreign policy after 1933 focused on *relief* for the small western democracies victimized by totalitarian aggression; *resistance* to American entrance into World War II; *reconstruction* of Europe after 1945 in light of the Cold War; and *revisionist interpretations* of the foreign policy of the United States for the 1930s and 1940s. But his ideas and actions in these four areas of diplomacy seldom found acceptance in official circles between 1933 and 1964, because as a consistent pre–World War I Progressive he was a noninterventionist, an Old Right Republican, and an anti–New Dealer. He was completely out of step with the bipartisan foreign policy devised by post–World War II liberal Democrats, and was conveniently written off by them as a conservative isolationist.

While secretary of commerce and president Hoover had always placed domestic affairs above foreign ones as a matter of course; he continued to do so after 1933 until war threatened in Europe at the end of the decade. From time to time after leaving the White House, however, he commented on isolated foreign policy issues. For example, he opposed Roosevelt's vague proposal of May 16, 1933, urging the "nations of the world . . . [to] enter into a solemn and definite pact of non-aggression." This "consultative pact would lead to trouble," he said, because "it has been given one interpretation in Europe and another in the United States." To Europe it meant joining the League in determining an "aggressor," in embargoes and boycotts, and ultimately in military action. To the American people it meant "pious advice with no liabilities." Hoover wanted Congress, therefore, to demand a clarification of Roosevelt's May 16 communique.

Hoover reserved his strongest criticism of New Deal foreign policy in the early 1930s for the decision to recognize the Soviet Union. His initial opposition to recognition during World War I had been tempered slightly in the 1920s — because of increased American-Soviet trade after 1923 and because of the reliable credit records the USSR established in Europe. Nonetheless, during the 1932 presidential campaign Hoover had tried for partisan reasons to discredit any move on FDR's part in the direction of recognition, even though he himself had toyed with the idea in the summer of 1929 for economic reasons. Under the influence of his friend and Undersecretary of State Castle, Hoover prepared a press release on the attitude of his administration toward Russian trade and recognition, to use in the event the Democrats raised the issue. This proved an unnecessary precaution, but the unreleased press statement is significant; it underplayed the issues of Soviet propaganda and the unpaid Russian debt from World War I as reasons for continued nonrecognition. Instead, it stated that "trade with Russia is not a matter of recognition, but of credit" and denied that the United States government opposed economic relations with the Soviets. It noted, however, that organized labor in America opposed recognition "because they clearly understand that communism means class warfare, the degradation of the standards of living of the working class, [and] the loss of independence, individuality and opportunity for self-betterment;" and it pointed out that only a few manufacturers urged recognition for purely selfish reasons.

A press release of November 16, 1933, the day that the Roosevelt administration accorded the Soviets recognition, again denied that Hoover's opposition to recognition had ever been primarily economic, but rather had always been "moral" (meaning ideological). This statement, also written with

Castle's advice, denied that there was any contradiction between the Hoover policy of recognizing Latin American dictatorships while not recognizing the Soviet Union, because all despots in the southern hemisphere "acknowledged the normal and established obligations . . . which the whole thesis of the Russian government defied." It also deplored the "moral acceptance of the respectability of Communism with all of its destruction of Christianity, of human liberty, and other fundamental moral foundations upon which our nation rests." Furthermore, it asserted that recognition had obvious anti-Japanese overtones and that the stability of the Far East certainly did not gain from encouraging communism there with such a diplomatic act.

Hoover's books, his campaign statements in 1928 and 1932, his press releases and speeches immediately following recognition in 1933 and still later after World War II — if taken at their face value — seem to indicate no change in his original ideological opposition to communism. In fact, however, if they are analyzed closely in terms of both language and action recommended or taken, it becomes evident that they exhibit an excessive rhetorical commitment to anticommunism, rather than practical or effective guides to action. Increasingly over the years, this became Hoover's typical position against the USSR; it occupied a good deal of his private time, but not his public actions.

Once recognition was an accomplished fact, for example, Hoover began a lifelong personal project of compiling public documents and confidential evidence on Communists and the USSR from diaries and other private sources. From these he composed over the years a mammoth work tentatively entitled "Freedom Betrayed," about how the world position of the United States had suffered "because of our attitude on the Communist world conspiracy." (In time his personal staff came to call this compilation the Chief's "Magnum Opus" — it approached almost three volumes before his death in 1964 and Hoover had intended it to be four.) According to Neil Mac-

Neil, a former *New York Times* editor and editorial director of the second Hoover Commission on the Organization of the Executive Branch of Government, the work was so filled with potentially libelous statements that it could not be published in its original form. "It was not written for popular consumption," MacNeil said in an interview in 1967. "It was written for the record and should be of great interest to historians, because there are documents . . . and . . . information there that I don't think [are] available anywhere else. . . ." Even after MacNeil helped Hoover edit out the worst charges, he still recommended against publication. Now the property of the Hoover Foundation, this controversial manuscript remains unpublished.

While "Freedom Betrayed" expressed the theoretical and often excessive ideological hatred that Hoover harbored toward communism, he did not, contrary to standard interpretations and popular impressions, become a rampant Cold Warrior after World War II. In fact, despite his periodic verbal attacks on communism he did not affiliate with any anti-Communist groups like the American Liberty League or the China Lobby — any more than he did with isolationist groups like the America First Committee. Hoover always recognized such organizations for what they were: irrationally extreme and often composed of opportunists who had not been members of the Old Right within the Republican party of the late 1930s.

He refused to join the America First movement, therefore, or to speak under its auspices to prevent the United States from entering World War II — despite his friendship with one of its leaders, Charles A. Lindbergh. When Gerard P. Nye asked Hoover to participate in a Lindbergh–America First rally in May 1941, Hoover declined, saying: "[I] can be of more service by taking my own independent line than being associated with any particular committee on such issues as these." During World War II as well he turned down offers to speak for various single-minded isolationist and pacifist groups, even when they were also promoting a project such as relief for war-stricken peoples.

Likewise, he turned down Congressman Parnell Thomas, chairman of the House Un-American Activities Committee (HUAC), in March 1947 when he was asked to appear before the initial session of these hearings in order to start them off "with a bang." Hoover excused himself by claiming that he had no special knowledge on the subject of legislation to curb or outlaw communism. Three years later, during the McCarthy anticommunism hysteria, Hoover refused to become chairman of President Truman's bipartisan commission "to report on the question of infiltration of Communists in the Government." (Nonetheless his association with strong anti-Communists such as Richard M. Nixon and Generals Patrick Hurley, Arthur Douglas MacArthur, and Robert E. Wood, as well as others of similar persuasion, increased after his wife's death in 1944. This alone did indirectly lend his name and reputation to that infamous postwar phenomenon.)

This was truly a case of guilt by association; Hoover's anticommunism was so nonmilitaristic that he was later called "a tool of the Kremlin" by Cold Warriors during the Truman and Eisenhower administrations of the early 1950s. His anticommunism, like his other theories and ideas, was tempered by statistical analysis and precise ideological definitions. He was no public witch hunter after either World War; he did not fear any Communist takeover of the State Department, other branches of government, or the country. What concerned him, and other Old Right so-called isolationists of the late 1940s and early 1950s, was the permissive attitude toward communism that he was convinced had come into government with the New Dealers. As a result, Hoover was not so obsessed with rooting out individuals as he was with rooting out a misguided value judgment that was perverting American diplomacy. While "I doubt," he told Truman on November 26, 1950, "if there are any consequential card-carrying Communists in the Government . . . there are men in Government (not Communists) whose attitudes are such that they have disastrously advised on policies in relation to Communist Russia." Here was Hoover, an anti-Communist, opposing what he considered to be the excessive anti-Communist domestic (and foreign) policies of the Truman administration. This attitude was to make him a leading critic of the Cold War.

Characteristically, Hoover insisted that punitive measures were not the answer. The only way "to restore . . . confidence in the Administration's Foreign Policy makers" was with moral suasion, education, and domestic value change through national, educational propaganda. He did not, therefore, advocate the use of coercion against communism at home or abroad. As he said in a radio broadcast on June 29, 1941, World War I had taught him that "we cannot slay an idea or an ideology with machine guns. Ideas live in men's minds in spite of military defeat. They live until they have proved themselves right or wrong." Rarely, therefore, did Hoover suggest taking overtly hostile diplomatic actions against countries with unacceptable foreign ideologies like the USSR. Usually he preferred indirect, propagandistic actions, arguing in speeches and articles in the late 1930s that the United States had to "keep peace with dictatorships as well as with popular governments," and denouncing those who wanted to go to war to save democracy from communism *or* fascism.

The major deviation from this personal foreign-policy guideline came in December 1939 after the Russian invasion of Finland, when he urged that the United States withdraw its ambassador from the Soviet Union. He suggested this privately to O'Laughlin and Castle, noting that Roosevelt had taken that action against Germany when Hitler invaded Poland and should now act similarly despite "his friendly leanings toward the Communists." Castle ultimately convinced him that this would be as much a step in the direction of war as an economic embargo.

A "sentimental journey" in February and March 1938 to the European countries he had aided with food supplies during World War I expanded Hoover's interest in foreign affairs beyond relations with the USSR. This trip included an unplanned, hour-long meeting with Hitler during which Hoover silently acceded to the Führer's anti-Communist remarks, but vigorously protested when democracy was also attacked. Returning to the United States, he wrote a series of private letters, foreign addresses, and articles, in which he asserted that there was no immediate prospect of general war because European war preparations were not complete. In any case he was convinced that Britain would keep the United States "out of war whether we want to get into it or not." Approving of the Munich Agreement of September 29, 1939, he praised the English for having the "only outstanding skillful group of world diplomats," and lauded the moderating influence of their Prime Minister Neville Chamberlain.

In contrast, Hoover viewed Roosevelt's statements on foreign policy as intemperate, especially his October 5, 1937 "Quarantine" speech from Chicago. Even though he thought that the League of Nations was "in a coma," Hoover contended that FDR should not have by-passed the League as he did in this speech with the suggestion that the United States join France and England in an ideological war against Germany and Italy. As late as July 18, 1939, he did not think either France or England in danger of direct German attack. Instead he charged that FDR's annual message to Congress earlier in January promising to use all "methods short of war" to aid these two nations would tend to make their citizens "precipitate a world war instead of some sort of accommodation." (By October 1940 he wanted to "furnish all support to England that we can within the law," but it was not until September 1941 that he was willing to send England all aid short of American soldiers.)

While Hoover had little faith in Roosevelt's ability to keep the nation out of war, he had even less in the various neutrality bills Congress had passed since 1935. Believing that neutrality differed with each time and circumstance and that Congress

should not legislate tactics and strategy in advance, he perspi-
caciously predicted the 1937 neutrality legislation would
"sometime place us in practical economic alliance with the
aggressor. If we wanted to be neutral in other people's wars,"
he stated on January 15, 1938, "we should not tie our hands so
that we are forced to favor one side or the other." In addition,
Hoover remained as opposed to forcing peace on other nations
by the use of economic sanctions, embargoes, or boycotts as he
had during the Manchurian crisis of 1931–1932.

Although he never had opposed adequate national defense,
Hoover insisted in January 1938 in an address to Republican
Women's Clubs that the United States should limit its arms
"solely to repel aggression against the Western Hemisphere"
(after World War II, this was to become known as his "Gibraltar" concept of defense). The first mission of America, he
declared, was "to maintain its own independence"; the second, "to maintain a society of free men and women"; and only
last should it "cooperate with the rest of the world to lift the
burdens of war." Nonetheless, in a July 1939 article in *American Magazine* he was recommending cooperation "with other
nations to relieve the economic pressures which are driving the
world constantly to instability. . . . The greatest healing
force that could come to the world is prosperity." Specifically,
he wanted the United States to organize international economic conferences similar to the ones he had promoted in
1932; such action was "free from political entanglements."

But as his personal letters to O'Laughlin indicated, Hoover
always thought the most effective way the United States could
preserve peace was by establishing a nonpolitical organization
that would function as a "neutral propaganda machine," to
counter statements by any nation or combination of nations
that tried to convince people to go to war, including the
United States and the western democracies. Despite his disappointment over the American people's acceptance of New
Deal domestic programs, he still believed they could be convinced that war would lead to a disastrous Fascist-like mobili-

zation that would be next to impossible to abandon in peacetime.

Hoover's commitment to educational propaganda was all the more evident after war broke out in Europe in September 1939, beginning with his refusal to accept either of the "present alternatives of embargo or no embargo for arms shipments abroad." His position in the debate over whether to repeal neutrality legislation depended on the acceptance of the dubious distinction between aggressive and defensive weapons, just as he had outlined it to the 1932 Geneva Disarmament Conference. To Hoover, aggressive weapons meant those used against civilian populations — such as "bombing planes, large mobile cannon, submarines, tanks, and poison gas" — while defensive weapons were "airplanes for observation and pursuit purposes, anti-aircraft guns . . . [for] defensive action against bombing planes, fixed cannon for fortifications, cannon of small caliber, small arms and ammunition." So he privately suggested to Castle on September 14, 1939, that the Neutrality Act of 1937 be amended to prevent the sale of aggressive weapons "to all nations at all times and irrespective of whether a state of war exists or not."

By allowing the purchase only of defensive weapons, Hoover later noted in a radio address in October, the United States could not be charged in the propaganda statements of foreign nations with "favoritism or unneutrality or intervention in this war," nor the American people with "killing women and children of any race. . . ." Furthermore, he suggested amending the Neutrality Act far beyond insistence on "cash and carry." For example, he wanted provisions made whereby "some part of the sale price of all manufactured commodities shipped to belligerents is placed in a fund to support unemployment insurance after the war." Finally, because he believed that war could not be prevented by regulations and that a "democratic nation gets into a war because of popular demand," he called for strict controls on domestic propaganda, prohibiting "any public criticism of foreign nations and . . . any public discussion of the purposes and plans of the belligerents by appointed officials of the American Government."

Congress gave little consideration to this public advice. Instead, on November 4 it repealed the embargo on all arms, stipulating that sales had to be strictly on a "cash and carry" basis. By that time Hoover was already convinced that if Roosevelt was "not bent on getting us into this war [he] is bent on getting us as close into it as he can." Upon learning of the repeal of the arms embargo and the passage of the "cash and carry" provision, he confided to O'Laughlin in an October 2, 1939, letter: "We must now await the next step toward taking us into war. I imagine it will revolve around either extending government credit to the Allies or presenting them with ammunitions."

Several months earlier he had told this same friend that in the summer of 1939 the abrogation of the commercial treaty with Japan had aroused his foreboding: "We have taken on a situation from which sooner or later we will see outrages upon American citizens and other incidents which will inflame the country and draw us into war in the east. It may be that the Japanese are surrounded by circumstances that will make them grin and bear it, but having regard for the war groups [in Japan], things are likely to get out of hand. Unless it is our desire to go to war with Japan, it is one step on the road."

With the signing of the Soviet-German Pact on August 23, 1939, and the subsequent invasions of Poland by the Germans and of Finland by the Russians, Hoover futilely advised that American ambassadors should be withdrawn from both countries, not just Germany. Initially he seemed more concerned with the plight of the Finns than with that of the Poles, probably because he was more ideologically anti-Soviet than anti-German, and also because Finland was the only European nation to have continued to make payments on its World War I debt. In neither instance, however, did he indicate privately or publicly that the United States should militarily defend these two countries; neither invasion posed a threat to the western hemisphere, as far as Hoover was concerned. In fact, in the April 27, 1940, issue of *Colliers* Hoover explicitly opposed any consideration of war with Russia, and denied that there was any threat of a Communist revolution in the United States. But he feared that redbaiters would try to convince the American people that there was such a danger, and that "in a rage" they would "go Fascist . . . or in a milder form . . . go vigilante." To Hoover, either reaction would mean the "defeat of liberty."

His immediate personal reaction to these two unprovoked invasions was to take up relief work again, quickly raising some $6 million to aid Poland and Finland. Then, as war spread, the small western democracies of Belgium, Luxembourg, Greece, central Poland, Finland, Holland, and Norway officially called upon Hoover in August 1940 to help them transport necessary supplies. This was not charity. They had money outside their borders and ships for carrying the needed materiel. The major obstacle to such relief operations remained what it had been during World War I: opposition from Germany and Britain and their respective allies. Another serious problem, according to Hoover, was the Roosevelt administration. In *An American Epic* he speaks of "four years of frustration" beginning in 1940, for he found that he did not have the opportunity to operate as an unofficial diplomatist under FDR that he had had under Wilson over a quarter of a century earlier.

In particular, trouble developed between Hoover's National Committee on Food for the Small Democracies and the President's Committee on War Relief Agencies headed by Joseph E. Davies. Hoover told Lewis L. Strauss in August 1941 that Davies and others working for the administration such as Secretary of State Cordell Hull were "under instructions not to do anything." He also faced serious opposition across the Atlantic from Winston Churchill. Hoover had referred to

Churchill back in 1919 as a "hardened militarist," and he did not change his opinion of the English prime minister during World War II. Once the United States entered the war in December 1941, Hoover's national committee had to suspend operations; it could not act without cooperation from top Washington and London officials — none of whom was willing to accept the responsibility of trying to feed peoples in German-occupied areas as Hoover advocated.

Although his own relief activities had to wait until the war ended, Hoover continued to be vocal on this and other aspects of American diplomacy. One theme in particular became increasingly prominent in his thought: economic self-sufficiency or self-containment for the United States. As secretary of commerce he had sporadically talked about the country's potential for economic independence. But it was his conclusion as president about the foreign origins of the Great Depression that finally led him to announce proudly to Congress in his annual message on December 8, 1931: "The redeeming strength of the United States is that we are economically more self-contained than any other great nation." In other public statements in 1930 and 1931, Hoover argued that because "we consume an average of about 90 percent of our own production of commodities," the country could boost domestic consumption to include 97 percent of all domestic agricultural and manufactured products, regardless of the economic or diplomatic climate in the rest of the world. His increasing fears about "totalitarian economic hegemony" in the late 1930s made Hoover even more determined to see the United States achieve a greater amount of self-sufficiency. To him, it was a question of self-defense against the "totalitarian economics" threatening the normal flow of world trade.

Hoover took up this theme with renewed vigor in 1940 and 1941. He began insisting that even if Hitler and his allies (including Japan and Russia) ended up in control of all of Europe, East Asia and Africa — that is, if they dominated 60 percent of the world's population and 40 percent of the world's trade — the United States could still maintain a "greater period of prosperity than ever before in its history" and preserve its basic freedoms. Moreover, he asserted, if more countries became "self-contained in raw materials and their production of goods," a basic cause of war would be eliminated. Applied technology, according to Hoover, had already made America 93 percent self-contained and could make it 97 percent, at less cost than it would take to fight one year of war.

Whereas in the 1920s he had usually subordinated his nationalistic dream of economic self-containment for the United States to his internationalistic dream of world economic interdependency and cooperation, now he did not. "We could produce about three-fourths of our present imports if we had to," Hoover asserted in a September 18, 1940, address. "Certainly it is time we exhaustively examined our own possibilities in this direction." He also recommended the use of import quotas (a tactic he had opposed as secretary of commerce and president) because he believed they would be more effective than reciprocal tariffs — in protecting domestic industry from cheap goods produced under totalitarian conditions, and in obtaining secure foreign markets for American exports. Although Hoover admitted that none of these negative, artificial ways to build up home production and stabilize foreign markets were ideal, he considered them a necessary, if temporary, economic form of self-defense. Given the outbreak of war in Europe, he believed, this type of immediate defense was as important as military preparedness.

Far Eastern affairs also occupied much of Hoover's attention after World War II began; it became evident to him by the summer of 1940 that the Roosevelt administration had embarked on a "get tough" policy toward Japan far exceeding the abrogation of the commercial treaty between the two nations a year earlier. When he told O'Laughlin in July that he was "a good deal disturbed by the change in attitude toward Japan as it may make a serious situation," he apparently had inside information about an impending embargo on petroleum products, scrap iron, and steel to Japan. The White House announced such an embargo on July 25, but after more debate within the executive branch failed to implement it that year, except for aviation gasoline and the highest grades of scrap iron and steel.

Hoover reacted to this modified embargo rather mildly. He compared it to "sticking a pin in a rattlesnake," because Japan could obtain the restricted commodities elsewhere. He added, however: "Either we should leave this thing alone, or we will be drawn into real trouble." It was clear to Hoover and his correspondent-informants that the United States was rapidly becoming the guardian of French and British interests in the Far East, applying the "same old principle of denial of trade that we are enforcing with respect to the Old World." Hoover at least was convinced that Japan would make no move until after the Battle of Britain (which took place beginning in August through September). Some of his friends were not so sanguine. A year later in August 1941 Hoover's interpretation of New Deal Far Eastern policy was considerably more negative.

In the intervening months the Tripartite Pact had been signed between Germany, Japan, and Italy on September 27, 1940; Roosevelt had been reelected; and Hoover had opposed both Roosevelt's destroyer-base deal with England of September 3, 1940, and the open-endedness of the Lend-Lease Act of March 1, 1941. He suggested to Castle that the best thing the United States could do for the English would be "to give them all of our accumulated defense material which we could spare; to give them an appropriation of anywhere from two to three billions with which to buy other things; to allow them to spend the money directly themselves and to conduct their own war in the way that seems to them to be the wisest. The whole of these sums should be secured upon such collateral or such properties as they possess irrespective of whether it is enough to cover these sums." Above all, however, Hoover expressed the fear in March and April 1941 letters to both Castle and O'Laughlin that the president would take advantage of lend-lease to "project the American people further out into the emotional rapids which lead to the cataract of war;" to employ the American navy for convoy duty in the Atlantic, thus starting an undeclared naval war; and ultimately to make "the world safe for Stalin."

By August 1941 he was openly denouncing Roosevelt's "diplomacy of the deed," because it also increased the power of the president at the expense of Congress. By this diplomatic method, FDR waited until an American ship had been sunk or an Allied setback had occurred to announce some previously negotiated executive agreement binding the interests of the United States more closely than ever with the war in Europe. Hoover had also begun to refer privately to the president's "fireside chats" as "fire-provoking chats." However his spirits temporarily rose after Germany turned on its ally Russia in June 1941; he took great pleasure in believing that the Nazis would win and that Hitler would then come to terms with Britain. Hope for the United States to escape war under Roosevelt rested upon a quick German victory over the Russians, according to Hoover. He told Castle that if the United States could keep from entering a "shooting stage" until the end of the year, "we may keep safely out of this mess."

This brief ray of hope quickly faded in August, however, when his attention was once again diverted to the deteriorating Far Eastern scene. In the fall of 1941 Hoover made the following confidential comments to various friends about American relations with Japan: "The handling of the Jap situation is appalling to me. It is based upon bluffing. In the meantime, the Japs occupy Indo-China and stay there. . . . The Japs will hold their takings, we will threaten and fulminate. When Hitler wins in Russia — and he will eventually — and when the British make their peace with him, or when we go to war and in the end make peace with him, the Japs will still be there. We will then probably go to war with them and when we will have made peace with them, they will still be in China and way stations. As a matter of fact, if we had kept still these last years they would have gone to pieces internally. There is nothing so good for the dictators of Japan as outside pressure. . . . If we go to war with Japan it would be God's gift to Hitler. . . . There is no sense in having a war with Japan. But I am afraid that our people are so anxious to get into the war somewhere that they will project it. They know there will be less public resistance to this than to expeditionary forces to Europe." Hoover summed up these gloomy predictions on September 4, 1941, when he asserted in a letter to Castle that the president and his advisers were "doing everything they can to get us into war through the Japanese back door."

Given his premonitions about Far Eastern policy, Hoover privately reacted to Pearl Harbor almost as though it were anticlimactic. He said approximately the same thing in several different letters on the day after it took place: "You and I know that this continuous putting pins in rattlesnakes finally got this country bitten. We also know that if Japan had been allowed to go on without these trade restrictions and provocations, she would have collapsed from internal economic reasons alone within a couple of years." Publicly, however, on December 8, 1941, he denounced the attack, saying war had been forced on the United States. But at the same time he told his correspondents to begin to collect every record they could about the event because he was sure there would be an investigation of it.

When Congress finally did investigate the Pearl Harbor attack after the war, Hoover played an important role behind the scenes, suggesting witnesses and helping to provide documents (such as a portion of Sumner Welles' diary) to prove civilian mismanagement of the affair. As early as December 31, 1941, he had anticipated the later revisionist claim that Secretary of State Hull's November 26, 1941, answer to the latest offer of the Japanese to negotiate a settlement constituted an ultimatum. "I assume he knew that it would mean war," Hoover said at the time.

After the United States officially entered the war, Hoover largely confined his actions to planning for postwar food relief abroad and to attacking New Deal economic policies at home. Among other things, he opposed any obligatory price and wage freeze, even as a war measure. Instead he unsuccessfully recommended to a Senate committee in December 1941 that an administrative agency under a single head with an independent review board be established to obtain acceptable wartime prices voluntarily. All of his suggestions and criticisms were made on the basis of his experiences as Food Administrator during World War I. This had convinced him that wage and price restraints had to be flexible, not rigid (as implied by a "freeze"), in order to be maintained without bureaucratic coerciveness, injustices, and inadequacies.

While the domestic impact of the war remained his major concern, Hoover did find time to collaborate with Hugh Gibson from 1942 to 1945 on several articles and books — all suggesting ways to bring about a peace which would avoid the mistakes made after World War I. Two works in particular, *The Problems of Lasting Peace* (1942) and *The Basis of Lasting Peace* (1945), represent the ex-president's most publicly ambitious wartime attempts to influence conditions of peace following World War II. The first, an approximately 300-page study, is the more significant of the two; the latter was simply a brief 44-page essay analyzing and criticizing the 1944 Dumbarton Oaks Plan for organizing the United Nations.

Unlike *America's First Crusade,* a short polemic he also published in 1942 that criticized the Versailles peace settlement, Hoover's collaboration with the retired diplomat Hugh Gibson on *The Problems of Lasting Peace* was a reasoned appeal to the American people and government officials to remember that "military victory alone will not give us peace." Urging the government to make specific postwar plans while waging war, Hoover and Gibson made over fifty suggestions for preserving peace and personal liberty in the aftermath of World War II. They called for the acceptance by the defeated powers of representative government, as the best but by no means perfect guarantee of lasting peace. This suggestion was not in contradiction of Hoover's long-held conviction that "ideologies of personal liberty and freedom cannot be imposed by machine guns." Hoover and Gibson hoped simply that a decent peace, which was not vengeful and which did not impose economic hardships on the vanquished, would provide the proper soil for the growth of democracy abroad.

The two also wanted preliminary or conditional terms of peace worked out in advance of any armistice, so that nations would have time to "cool off" before attempting any comprehensive peace settlement. Above all else they opposed an omnibus conference like the Versailles Peace Conference, recommending instead that the details of a general peace be worked out by separate, specialized commissions of experts. In addition they called for drastic disarmament by both sides, a general ban on military alliances in the future, protection of oppressed minorities (even if it meant the transference of entire populations to different locations) and of small states in general, and the prosecution and punishment of national leaders who had wilfully provoked war or committed wholesale murder.

Finally, Hoover and Gibson favored subsequent, but not immediate, creation of a cooperative international peacekeeping body based on a charter which eliminated all of the coercive clauses of the original Covenant of the League of Nations. They did not want to see the new world organization, like the League, overwhelmed with immediate postwar problems. To avoid this, the new body should be established only after these emergency crises had been solved by commissions of experts, and it should then stress "regional policies of peace" rather than global ones. They viewed this proposed world body as a "clearinghouse and roundtable" for the discussion of all international questions with enforcement of its recommendations ultimately relying on friendly persuasion and the pressure of public opinion. Since the use of force could not be entirely eliminated in international affairs, Hoover and Gibson recommended the creation of separate military organizations in the three major continental areas of the world — the western hemisphere, Europe, and Asia — for the independent preservation of order, but without the right to enter into military cooperation or alliances with each other.

Both men also agreed that satisfactory postwar economic arrangements were essential. Consequently, a good portion of *The Problems of Lasting Peace* was devoted to suggestions for eliminating the barriers to trade after World War II — governmental buying and selling, unstable currencies, special agreements like reciprocal or preferential treaties, tariff quotas, monopolies or cartels which prevented equal access to raw materials, and high tariff rates which hindered the "reasonable competition between imports with domestic production." With the exception of the tariff question, all of these suggestions exactly corresponded to Hoover's ideas in the 1920s. Even here it was a difference of degree, not kind, when he insisted that tariff rates were now not such an important factor in world trade. He never completely abandoned his nationalist commitment to the "protective principle" as necessary for the preservation of high American standards of living, however, and he ultimately returned to his traditional position against import quotas as a protective device (presumably on the assumption that they would be unnecessary after the defeat of the enemy and their totalitarian economic policies) .

Likewise, Hoover and Gibson thought that the relation of raw materials to lasting peace had been "entirely overestimated from an international point of view" by the New Dealers, especially before the outbreak of World War II. In part this was because they believed that the United States could achieve a substantial degree of economic self-sufficiency, even though it was not possible for Americans to produce or control all of the raw materials they consumed. The problem was not one of scarcity, but of access. So *The Problems of Lasting Peace* reiterated the stand Hoover had taken as secretary of commerce against international cartels: "The whole experience of the past hundred years shows that the assurance of supplies of raw material requires only a dissolution of monopoly controls, an assurance of equal prices, open markets — and peace." Here was the ideal of the cooperative Open Door policy of the 1920s all over again.

At the heart of all these economic proposals lay concern for what Hoover had referred to in earlier prewar statements as the "Fifth Freedom." This meant the economic freedom "for men to choose their own calling, to accumulate property in protection of their children and old age, [and] freedom of enterprise that does not injure others." In direct reference to Roosevelt's Four Freedoms pronouncement of January 6, 1941, Hoover said in September of that year that the "other four freedoms will not survive without this [fifth] one." He had repeated this claim several times in articles. Now in *The Problems of Lasting Peace* he and Gibson further clarified the terms economic freedom, free enterprise, and the "Fifth Freedom" by saying that none of them meant *"laissez faire* or capitalistic exploitation . . . [or] going back to [old] abuses." The importance to Hoover of this concept of the "Fifth Freedom" should not be overlooked; as he repeatedly told General Albert C. Wedemeyer and others, unless the postwar peace continued to guarantee this to Americans any military victory would prove a Pyrrhic one.

Most of the specific suggestions made by Hoover and Gibson for preserving the "Fifth Freedom" through a noninterventionist diplomacy fell upon deaf ears among policy makers in both parties. This same fate greeted their general exhortations about learning to live with dictatorships, conserving American domestic resources instead of promising to save the rest of the world with them, and preserving economic and political freedom in the United States. In the case of the latter, admittedly, their rhetoric was so excessive and so paranoid about the internal political impact of the New Deal and the war that it was difficult to take seriously. Hoover privately insisted to O'Laughlin in November 1943 that his proposals for making peace in transitional stages — with "no general peace conference, no long armistice, no long-term military alliances" — were being followed by Secretary of State Cordell Hull. But less than a year later at the Republican National Convention he complained, in what amounted to a public display of petulance if not actual anger, that both parties were ignoring his advice on domestic and foreign policy. Nonetheless, in May 1945 he conferred with top government officials about food relief operations and other diplomatic problems. The result of these meetings was a series of confidential memoranda designed as Hoover's last efforts to influence the peace settlement.

The first was a position paper on world affairs sent to Secretary of War Henry L. Stimson on May 15, 1945. A handwritten postscript said that Hoover "did not agree with Baruch's idea of destroying either Japanese or German nonmilitary industry." More specifically, he turned his attention immediately after V-E Day to "Stalin's sphere of political domination" in Eastern Europe with its estimated 200 million people. He predicted that "economic life of those countries under Russian sphere [sic] will be socialized, and there will no longer be an opportunity for American or British private enterprise therein." This would leave "only three great areas in the world where the Americans and British might have freedom and opportunity in economic life" — the British, French, Belgian, and Dutch "empires;" the western hemisphere; and Asia outside of Russia. In this memorandum Hoover also predicted the defeat of Japan, expressed the fear that Russia could take what she wanted after such a defeat, and gloomily concluded that in both the European and Far Eastern military theaters the Allies were winning the "war for Russia's benefit."

In view of these dismal conclusions, Hoover argued on May 15 that America and Britain needed a "revolution in policies." He suggested to Stimson that the United States, England, and China make a separate and lenient peace in the Far East without consulting the Soviet Union and before Stalin committed troops to that war zone. Later in a 55-minute meeting with Truman on May 28, 1945, ostensibly to discuss the world food situation, Hoover repeated his ideas about a separate peace in the Far East and his fears about Soviet ideological aggression, stressing above all that the United States should not go to war with the USSR, but that "our position should be to persuade . . . [to] hold up the banner of free peoples and let it go at that for the present." Criticizing those who had "formulated policies in respect to other nations 'short of war' because they always lead to war," Hoover clearly indicated to Truman that his objections to ideological war as having "no ending and no victory" had not diminished since the 1920s — nor had his belief in America's unique world role.

His urgent desire to convince Truman of a separate peace with Japan made him oblivious to the dubious diplomatic propriety of ditching an unwanted ally on the eve of victory. But it did not blind him to the slim chances of persuading the president. For even after Truman asked him to submit his foreign policy proposals in writing, Hoover ended the private memorandum on his May 28 conversation with the president thus: "My conclusions were that he was simply endeavoring to establish a feeling of good will in the country, that nothing more would come of it so far as I or my views were concerned." Despite this pessimism, on May 30, 1945, Hoover submitted the confidential memorandum on foreign policy requested by the president.

This one emphasized the undesirability of further depleting American manpower and natural resources by fighting to the finish in the Far East. In addition to the lenient territorial terms suggested in the first memorandum, Hoover now stressed the fact that the Japanese should be assured that the settlement would not deprive them of their emperor, "who is the spiritual head of the nation." Later former Secretary of War Stimson publicly acknowledged that if such an assurance about the emperor had been made to the Japanese, the war in the Far East could have ended six months to a year earlier *without* the use of either massive American ground forces or the atomic bomb. At the time, however, civilian leaders in the government, including Stimson, found themselves trapped in the illogical syndrome of unconditional surrender that technically denied the Japanese their emperor. They subsequently justified using the atomic bomb against the Japanese as a way to end the war as quickly as possible, to prevent the Soviet Union from entering the Far Eastern theater, and to impress Stalin with America's postwar nuclear power. Like later revisionist historians, Hoover deplored the excesses fostered by the open-ended concepts of unconditional surrender and ideological warfare. "The use of the Atomic bomb, with its indiscriminate killing of women and children, revolts me," he confided to O'Laughlin on August 8, 1945. "The only difference between this and the use of poison gas is the fear of retaliation. We alone have the bomb . . . [it] is no doubt being exploited beyond its real [military] possibilities."

Hoover was convinced that these position papers to both Stimson and Truman in May 1945 were of great historical value. On November 15, 1945, he sent them to historian Charles A. Beard, indicating that he did not think either the Potsdam Declaration (calling for Japan's unconditional surrender) or the use of the atomic bomb against the Japanese had been necessary. Both, he thought, could have been obviated by the offer of a separate peace by Britain, America, and China. "For obvious reasons," he told Beard, "I ask you to keep my memoranda confidential until I am dead or until I sooner release them. They may serve someday as reminders of the blundering in our foreign roles." Hoover died without releasing these documents, and while Beard's family have faithfully honored this confidence since his death in 1948, there is little doubt that knowledge of these memoranda and Hoover's cogent evaluation of international affairs at the end of World War II reinforced the historian's revisionist ideas about the diplomatic conduct of the United States in the 1930s and 1940s.

In three other confidential memoranda to Truman on May 30, 1945, Hoover called for the United States Army, instead of the United Nations Relief and Rehabilitation Administration (UNRRA), to administer foreign relief and organize the economic rehabilitation of postwar Europe. He also suggested changes in wartime food-rationing agencies and the creation of a European Economic Council. While the army did assume emergency control of relief operations in Western Europe, which had the effect of terminating UNRRA operations, none of Hoover's other suggestions were implemented. At the beginning of 1946, however, the president asked him to draft a comprehensive program to alleviate world famine. By this time, Hoover and Truman agreed on one basic point: no relief attempt would be made in the part of Eastern Europe occupied by the Russians, but immediate remedial action should be taken elsewhere in Europe.

Traveling 50,000 miles from March through June 1946, Hoover and his voluntary staff visited thirty-eight surplus and nonsurplus producing countries, trying to relieve discrepancies between supply and demand — through better internal distribution in some countries, reduced consumption in producing countries, substitution of other cereal products for rice and wheat, and loans of other cereal products. As a result, the gap between supply and demand was reduced from 11 million tons to 3.6 million. Hoover's original optimism after returning from this trip was not warranted; there was a limit to what could be accomplished by rationalizing administrative procedures. In the next few years, bad harvests continued to plague the world's food supplies. Conditions were so bad in Central Europe alone that Truman sent Hoover on another economic mission to Austria and Germany in 1947.

Hoover had never advocated a harsh settlement for either Germany or Japan after World War II, but at the end of 1946 he told Truman that American charity and government credits to foreign countries had to cease "except to prevent starvation — and even here we should require some percentage of their exports at some future date to be set aside to repay us." Both Germany and Japan therefore would have to become more self-sufficient; the United States was overexporting and placing a strain on its natural resources. Hoover even suggested after visiting Germany that Americans might have to be convinced to voluntarily reduce their own food consumption and change manufacturing patterns in order to aid the economy of the world. Foreign nations continuing to receive American credit would have to do likewise, of course. But nothing ever came of this modified version of cooperative individualism on a worldwide scale.

Rather than support an attempt by the United States to revive the wartorn, famine-stricken world through massive foreign aid programs, Hoover appealed for private funds to send food to needy countries. Once again people at home and abroad failed to see the wisdom of self-sacrifice and cooperation. Once again nations transgressed the limits of economic behavior Hoover thought appropriate. At the end of this last food relief phase of his life, he opposed international control of the distribution of American food and relief abroad, except for the rehabilitation of children, because he feared it would end "in foreign control of American farmers' prices and production." As after World War I, Hoover recommended coordinating relief actions by the United States with those of other nations, but he continued as before to oppose "any joint control" which might threaten his dream of American economic independence. By 1947, he thought American domestic resources so diminished that no more outright charity should be granted Europeans. While Truman was willing to listen to Hoover as Roosevelt had not been, the ex-president's influence still remained minimal.

Hoover's ideas on economic foreign policy fared better during the drafting of the Marshall Plan in 1947 and 1948 than they had during his earlier attempts to influence the peace settlement, relief operations, and the general direction of American diplomacy following World War II. He expressed relief that he was not a member of the factfinding committee headed by General George C. Marshall to determine how much economic aid the United States could provide for Europe; he felt it lacked the breadth and authority to deal with greedy European politicians. According to Hoover, Marshall originally intended for him and Bernard Baruch to act as co-chairmen of this study group; after consulting they decided not to accept the joint responsibility because of the committee's limited power. He did nonetheless exert indirect influence over the final form of the Marshall Plan through private correspondence with Baruch, Representatives Christian Herter and John Taber, Speaker of the House Joseph W. Martin, and Senators Arthur H. Vandenberg, Robert Taft, and Styles Bridges.

Hoover criticized the original plan on two basic premises: the United States was already overexporting as a result of the war, and "the need for rapid rehabilitation and food of [sic] the war-torn areas are much greater than the United States can carry." In the interest of conserving American resources and fostering economic self-sufficiency, Hoover wanted to control future exports "to protect our own stability;" he refused to endorse any proposals for unilateral or "blank check" relief for Europe. Even if such open-ended actions saved Europe from communism, reasoned Hoover, it would not be worth the domestic economic drain on the United States.

In June 1947 Hoover confided to Baruch that he preferred to make further postwar European reconstruction a cooperative venture on the part of the United States and other nations, with favorable trade balances through the World Bank. Almost all of his very technical and complicated criticisms of the original Marshall Plan, consequently, were aimed at reducing its unilateral economic features and minimizing the proportion of food contributed by the United States. He insisted to Vandenberg, Taber, Bridges, and Martin that while he approved of aiding Europe, if the relief plan finally approved by Congress actually weakened the American economy, it would "defeat all world recovery."

This argument about keeping the United States as economically stable and independent as possible was certainly not new to Hoover's thinking. But he did place greater emphasis on it in the post–World War II period than he had after World War I. As in the 1920s, however, he realized that such a condition could only come about through government regulation of loans and exports, and through coordination of economic and political foreign policies. His relief missions to Europe from 1946 to 1948 had convinced him of the need for extending aid to Europe, but they also heightened his concern about increasing the tax burden of American citizens, and about making areas of Europe unnecessarily dependent upon the United States.

Hoover therefore recommended limiting Marshall Plan aid to fifteen months subject to review and extension, instead of guaranteeing it for four years from the very beginning. He also wanted it stipulated that American gifts or grants of consumption (as opposed to loans) would be strictly limited to this country's surpluses in any given year. Even so, he still thought that to prevent overstraining the American economy the government would have to encourage federal programs for promoting voluntary conservation of national resources, voluntary price and wage controls, and greater individual productivity. With such restrictions and cooperation, he thought that Marshall Plan aid could safely include China, Germany, Japan, Korea, Greece, and Turkey, as well as the sixteen European countries originally singled out by the president's factfinding commitee. Germany in particular, he thought, should begin to pay in part for American relief by increasing its exports and having a tax in dollars placed upon them as of

July 1, 1949. Generally speaking, he wanted a disarmed Germany integrated as quickly as possible into the European economy (even if this meant trading with the satellite countries of Eastern Europe) so that the entire continent could assume some sense of economic self-sufficiency.

Congress followed a good number of Hoover's suggestions, especially those technical ones concerning the administration of funds and goods. It rejected, however, his proposal for an "offshore guarantee." This idea was so important to Hoover he personally recommended it to General Marshall through Christian Herter. It called upon the "offshore" western hemisphere nations of Argentina, Canada, and Brazil, that had favorable postwar balances of trade like the United States, to guarantee credit to the Marshall Plan states. This would allow Europeans to buy agricultural products from these surplus producing countries, and would relieve the United States of the entire burden for rehabilitating Europe and Japan.

Above all else Hoover viewed the vanquished powers of Germany and Japan as "major fronts of Western Civilization" in the ideological Cold War that began in the later 1940s. But instead of concentrating exclusively on relief in these two key countries with only scattered efforts throughout the rest of the world, he wanted the United States to systematically build up its independent domestic productivity. He neither wanted the country to fall victim to "unlimited demands and subsequent disappointments and recriminations," nor to become a "competitive Santa Claus" in a gift-giving contest with the USSR.

Outside of Germany and Japan and the Communist countries, Hoover wanted to see most other nations of the world undertake their own defense. Typically, he did not want American or international loans used for unnecessarily large military expenditures; he remained convinced that "military strength is no substitute for sound policy." But on the other hand he did not want the United States to provide a military shield against communism for all of Europe and Asia. So he opposed sending large numbers of American troops abroad after the war, fearing it would slow down the return to self-defense of the recipient nations. While he continued to believe as in the 1920s that "disarmament flows only from peace, not peace from disarmament," he became increasingly discouraged after 1945 about the prospects of world disarmament, as the Cold War prevented peace from returning. He placed his hopes instead in quick European rearmament, only to be disappointed on that score as well.

By the end of 1950 Hoover was convinced that America's military aid program had to be reevaluated. Europe's military contributions both to the North Atlantic Treaty Organization (NATO) and to the United Nations endorsed war in Korea had been inadequate. While the productivity of European nations was rapidly returning to prewar levels, Hoover noted with irritation that, with the exception of England, their capacity or willingness for self-defense was not. "The North Atlantic Pact was ratified on the promise of no American ground armies in Europe" and on the assumption that "Western Continental Nations were going to arm," he declared, but in twenty-one months "they have done nothing consequential." All of this, of course, only confirmed Hoover's long-held suspicions about the unreliability of European nations. Thus, beginning with an address on December 20, 1950, entitled "Our National Policies in this Crisis," the ex-president threw himself into the "Great Debate" of the decade over American foreign policy.

America had been progressing toward this confrontation since World War I. Most broadly stated from Hoover's point of view,* the Great Debate concerned whether or not

---

* More specifically, the Great Debate revolved in the early 1950s around the question of whether Asia should rank with Europe in terms of American diplomatic priorities. This aspect of the debate was greatly intensified by the Communist victory in China, the Korean War, and the resulting dispute between Truman and General MacArthur. In general Republicans favored an "Asia First" policy, while Democrats looked to Europe more as a prime area of expansion and defense. Hoover opposed unlimited extension of American military and economic power in either area of the world.

the United States should continue to base its economic foreign policy on the principle of open-ended expansion abroad, and its political foreign policy on increasing military and political intervention in world affairs. The alternative was to moderate and control American economic expansion in the interests of domestic development and reform, thereby abandoning the role of self-appointed policeman for the world, and establishing instead a defensive perimeter for the western hemisphere — a region Hoover called "this final Gibraltar of freedom." Both approaches recognized a relationship between foreign affairs and internal conditions. The Hooverian one did not want external, international problems to determine the quality and character of American life and realized that domestic reforms would have to be undertaken to insure the continued semi-independent and self-contained existence of the United States. The opposite point of view was that traditional American institutions could not change or survive unless the United States adopted an expansionist foreign policy after World War II. Dean Acheson probably best summarized the latter approach when he said in 1944: "If you wish to control the entire trade and income of the United States, which means the life of the people, you could probably fix it so that everything produced here would be consumed here, but that would completely change our Constitution, our relations to property, human liberty, our very conception of law . . . you find [instead] you must look to other markets and those markets are abroad." Later in 1969 Acheson reflected in his memoirs that for the United States to try to confine itself to the western hemisphere would change "the spacious freedom of American life" and in doing so would "undermine its cultural, moral, political, and constitutional bases."

In contrast to what was to become the prevailing postwar foreign policy of the United States, Hoover had increasingly stressed the desirability of national economic sufficiency and a hemispheric or "Gibraltar" concept of military defense based largely on air power. Since the late 1930s he believed that political and economic freedom at home would be destroyed by too much expansion and intervention abroad. He now insisted that the high American standard of living was basically the result of production efficiency through the elimination of waste, low prices for consumer goods, high wages, and cooperative individualism at all political and economic levels; not of uncontrolled exports and military establishments abroad. Continuing to hold out the ideal of an America that was not dependent on foreign markets and vulnerable boundaries, but that instead consumed most of what it produced and defended only its own hemisphere, Hoover found himself totally out of step with the bipartisan internationalist or globalist diplomacy that developed to combat the Cold War. In fact, he equated bipartisanship with one-party, Communist organization. "The whole history of bipartisanship in foreign affairs," he wrote in 1951, "is a record of failures for lack of proper ventilation and criticism. . . ."

In particular he found himself at odds with the man who became President Eisenhower's secretary of state — John Foster Dulles. During World War I Dulles had agreed with Hoover about protecting the economic independence of the United States, and as late as the fall of 1943 Dulles appeared to agree with Hoover's "Gibraltar" concept of economic and hemispheric self-containment; they both opposed Walter Lippmann's thesis about the danger to the United States if England were defeated. But in the early 1950s Dulles believed in massive military retaliation against ideological enemies, in the economic and political dependence of the United States upon the rest of the free world, and in the impossibility of simply a hemispheric or area air defense. Secretary Dulles no longer thought that the best test of American diplomacy was how it affected the domestic standard of living and individual liberties at home. No longer did he fear the domestic impact of "irresistible forces of inflation" caused by the deficit financing of defense expenditures which were "bleeding us economically to impotence" and encouraging the trend toward so-

cialism. Or so it appeared to Hoover and his friends such as
General Albert C. Wedemeyer, Patrick J. Hurley, Hugh
Gibson, and Robert Taft.

Hoover and his friends deplored most the lack of American
diplomatic initiative in the burgeoning Cold War. Hoover, for
example, urged Eisenhower to go before the people and say:
"This costly European experiment [meaning NATO] has
now demonstrated its failure to secure our objectives. We can
no longer leave 400,000 American boys and 50,000 women and
children in such jeopardy. We will withdraw at once and leave
them our arms. We will endeavor to erect air and naval deter-
rents. But we have been trifled with long enough." He also
wanted it made clear to the American people that the "United
States *can* survive in the Western Hemisphere." Hoover and
his friends were convinced that Nationalist China had been
sold out by Roosevelt at Yalta; they wanted stronger leadership from the United States in opposing the recognition of
Communist China. Hoover personally began collecting documents on the reasons for Chiang's fall from power; he looked
upon Mao's government as simply a satellite of Moscow and
upon recognition as "fatuous" and "unspeakable." Yet he also
expressed serious reservations about Chiang's leadership abil-
ities, never joined the China Lobby, and like Wedemeyer,
approved of very restricted trade with the Chinese Communists.

These attitudes combined with his earlier criticism of the
Marshall Plan and his advocacy of military withdrawal from
both Europe and Korea had caused the bipartisan Cold
Warriors of the late 1940s and early 1950s to doubt his
anticommunism. It was in fact moderate in comparison to
theirs, as was that of most of the Old Right critics of the Cold
War like Robert Taft and Charles A. Beard. Ironically,
Hoover and those who agreed with him are more often
charged with having encouraged McCarthyism and hence
having contributed to the Cold War syndrome than some of
the most vociferous Cold Warriors in both parties. Their

opponents also successfully labeled them conservative isolationists, and until recently historians have refused to consider
their most constructive foreign policy alternatives to the Cold
War — all because they thought that diplomatic reconciliation with the USSR was possible without sacrificing national
interest or their own ideological opposition to communism.

Hoover's criticism of the Korean war is a case in point. On
the one hand, despite his friendship with General MacArthur,
Hoover did not approve of his military conduct of the war. In
particular he had not wanted MacArthur to cross into North
Korea with his ground troops. Instead, he had wanted him to
"stop and dig in on the short line across Korea — and then use
his air force on any armies north of that area." In general,
however, he opposed the war for its ideological overtones, convinced that the "Reds just want to bleed us to death with
these small-scale wars." He also had little faith in South
Korean President Syngman Rhee, whom he once referred to as
a "menace," but he realized the United States was stuck with
him. While he had earlier approved of the Truman Doctrine
for aiding Turkey and Greece, the Korean war experience
convinced him that the open-ended declaration Truman had
made about opposing armed revolutionaries everywhere in the
world was totally impractical.

Given his dissatisfaction with the course and results of
American foreign policy by 1950, Hoover entered the Great
Debate with the following specific suggestions. The United
Nations should be reorganized, he proposed, without Communist participation, so as to "confine communism to the
people already enslaved." (Later in 1955 he abandoned this
idea, after concluding that the United Nations had at least
shown more strength than the League of Nations.) But in
1950 he had recommended arming the American air and naval
forces "to the teeth," to protect "sea lanes for our supplies"
and to protect a western hemisphere defense perimeter —
bordered by Japan, Formosa, and the Philippines in the east
and England (at the very most) in the west. Once such naval

and air supremacy was achieved, Hoover recommended that the foreign policy of the United States should be one of "watchful waiting before we take on any commitments." Subsequently he recommended to Dulles in 1954 that no more American foreign aid be granted outside of Korea except "upon request accompanied by detailed specifications and supporting data" in order to reduce and keep appropriations "within our available resources."

According to the ex-president, such suggestions as those listed above did not constitute isolationism or appeasement; he simply refused to accept the increasingly popular postwar premise that the collective security represented by internationalism had to be synonymous with endless foreign expansion and military intervention. "Indeed, they are the opposite," Hoover said of his ideas in a December 20, 1950 address. "They would avoid rash involvement of our military forces in hopeless campaigns. They do not relieve us of working to our utmost. They would preserve a stronghold of Christian civilization in the world against any peradventure. With the policies I have outlined, even without Europe, Americans have no reason for hysteria or loss of confidence in our security or our future. And in American security rests the future security of all mankind. . . . We shall not fail in this, even if we have to stand alone. . . . The Almighty is on our side." Admitting that it would be an "uneasy peace," Hoover insisted nonetheless that the United States could successfully pursue these policies indefinitely, "even if the Communists should attack our lines on the sea." As always he believed that the "evils of communism . . . will bring their own disintegration." As he said in a January 27, 1952 address, "It is contrary to the spiritual, moral, material aspirations of man. These very reasons give rise to my conviction that it will decay and die of its own poisons. But that may be many years away and, in the meantime, we must be prepared for a long journey."

Hoover's recommendations for disengaging the United

States from its overly committed position in the Cold War were based on an economic and ideological philosophy which had not basically changed since the 1920s. Largely because of this philosophic consistency, Hoover never succumbed to the Cold War paranoia about the military threat the United States faced from the proliferation of nuclear power, and especially from the development of intercontinental ballistic missile systems (ICBMs). While all his postwar disarmament proposals called for eliminating the production of both atomic bombs and nuclear warheads as "weapons of aggression," he continued to advocate the use of conventional weapons in a hemispheric defense system instead of a worldwide system of American military bases and personnel. To Hoover, for the United States to have permanent military forces abroad was equivalent to an internationalized dole for the rest of the world.

However, this same consistency did lead him to overestimate the monolithic features of communism in other parts of the world, and to exaggerate the economic disruption and political demoralization that were taking place in the United States because of its misguided foreign policy. Even so, he was not completely wrong in predicting such domestic problems, as the turbulent 1960s and 1970s would demonstrate. Above all else he had consistently maintained that the United States could not shoulder the responsibility for rehabilitating the world's economy after 1945. If it did, its democratic and corporatist institutions would become dependent on overseas expansion. And indeed they have. This is what his friend John Callan O'Laughlin meant when he predicted as early as 1941 that Hoover would "prove to be a wise prophet" in foreign affairs.

Thus, while Hoover's mind remained alert, his foreign and domestic views essentially unchanged, his body succumbed to age. After his wife died on January 7, 1944, there was no more talk of returning to California to live in the house that Lou Henry Hoover so loved, which today serves as the residence of the president of Stanford University. Instead, he set up permanent quarters in the Waldorf-Astoria Towers until his death (from ulceration of the lower esophagus near the entrance to the stomach) on October 20, 1964, at the age of ninety. One by one his old friends died, and his correspondence with those who remained increasingly concerned their illnesses or his. Although as late as June 1964 Hoover was still turning down speaking engagements, in his last months, according to Lewis L. Strauss, he "just went to sleep." He still enjoyed mystery stories, but now they had to be read to him while he lay in bed with one of his favorite cats sleeping beside him. The final book that Strauss read to him was *The Spy Who Came In From the Cold.*

Hoover continued to write letters and send telegrams until a few days before he died. Probably the most significant one in terms of summing up his own career went to the journalist Walter Trohan on April 13, 1962. "The world has gone bye [*sic*] you and me," Hoover wrote. "However it is some satisfaction that you and I have gone through the agonies of these years without 'deviations.' " No better epitaph for Herbert Clark Hoover has been written.

IX

The Old and New Hoover

"Even though the work fell at times to blind and incompetent successors, it must go on; for he has shown a new way."

THERE IS A GOOD DEAL OF TALK TODAY about a "new" Hoover. Disparate political groups ranging from the far right to the far left think they are rediscovering him, because his progressive philosophy contained ideas whose time has finally arrived. Americans had to experience the Great Depression, the New Deal, the Cold War, Vietnam, and Watergate before they could begin to contemplate a value change in domestic and foreign policies along the cooperative, decentralized, anti-interventionist lines Hoover suggested in the 1920s.

A large part of this "public amnesia" with respect to Herbert Hoover is due to the negative impression he created during the depression years, and to the ignominy Democrats continued to heap upon him after he left office in 1933. But the image of him as efficiently cold-blooded had been common in the public mind even before economic disaster struck the nation in 1929, and before Democratic hatchet men like Charley Michelson began to smear him with modern mass-media tactics. With time, even those who had suffered most during the Great Depression gradually began to suspect that Hoover's partisan enemies protested too vehemently and too long against an aging, but nonetheless devoted public servant.

Hoover's impersonal image cannot, however, be blamed exclusively on either the depression or his political enemies. His various publicity staffs had inadvertently oversold him between 1914 and 1928, while promoting the projects with which he was associated during those years. They had touted him first as an incomparable engineer, "human symbol of efficiency"; then as the unemotional savior of starving Europeans as well as the efficient Food Administrator during World War I; and still later as the super businessman and omniscient economist, who would be capable as president of solving any problems they might encounter. During the 1928 campaign his public-relations men realized the necessity of planting items in the press about his personableness ("charming to intimates and children, with a shyness appealing to women . . . ," proclaimed an article in the *North American Review* entitled, "Is Hoover Human?"). These attempts to reveal the "real" or human Hoover became all the more frantic and unconvincing after the depression began. What had not caught the public imagination during years of prosperity had little chance of succeeding in an anxious time of national economic crisis.

This ultimate failure in public relations was ironic; Hoover had been the first Washington official to systematically employ publicity techniques on a massive administrative scale. The problem was also compounded by the jealous way the Hoovers guarded their private lives from public view beginning with their marriage in 1899. Until the Lou Henry Hoover papers are opened no new light can be cast on the personal side of his life. But there is strong circumstantial evidence that, although he mellowed with age after 1933, at the height of Hoover's power and influence he was as cold and impersonal in his private life as he appeared in public. While his press agents tried to cover up or change this image in the mass media, Lou Henry Hoover tried to do the same by shielding both her husband and herself behind a wall of social decorum. The American people were provided only the barest glimpse of her natural warmth and gregariousness, which might have miti-

May 26, 1929 — *How Will Hoover Go Down in History?*

gated the impression of indifference and severity from their years in the White House.

Hoover's characteristic indifference to his physical surroundings, his years of travel and separation from family and friends, his asocial nature and inability to relate emotionally to the suffering of others, all confirm the suspicion that the mechanical quality of his professional and public work carried over into his personal life as well. He was not able to overcome this tendency even in his later years, although he did become more extroverted, and exhibited a gentle sense of humor to close friends and relatives. Even his generosity was usually disguised by a cloak of anonymity, as in the case of the private trust fund he set up to take care of any of his old friends from Food Administration and war relief days who fell upon hard times.

The available documents, however, create an almost too perfect picture of the ideal statesman, a figure of matchless integrity and boundless energy, devoted to the unselfish, apolitical service of his nation, but with little personal warmth. Hoover was indeed apolitical, in the sense that he had little faith in standard electoral politics or the congressional legislative process. Somehow he managed to succeed in American politics despite his refusal to backslap, fraternize with local supporters, kiss babies, or engage in any of the expected social and political amenities of the Roaring Twenties. While his proponents extolled his apolitical nature, his opponents condemned this characteristic as unnatural at worst and snobbish at best.

Between 1921 and 1928, however, he managed to make the Commerce Department more influential and powerful than at any time in its history. Moreover, during his first eight months as president, and even during the first year of the Great Depression, Hoover successfully dealt with Congress. If politics is in fact the "art of the possible," then he must be credited with considerable political success before 1933. Yet it was a particular and highly stylized type of nontraditional political success. It was largely administrative, economic, and public relations oriented, and it was unaccompanied by any personal or emotional mass commitment to him as an individual, for Hoover was in no way a charismatic figure. "He lacked a certain spark . . . the spark of leadership," Charles A. Lindbergh once said, "that intangible quality that makes men willing to follow a great leader even to death itself."

This lack of charisma and oversold public image, combined with his asocial personality and the secrecy surrounding his family life, have led most of his biographers to conclude that Hoover's career represented a paradox, an enigma, disturbingly enticing and undecipherable. New research, which began with the opening of the Herbert Hoover Presidential Library in 1966, is finally breaking down this myth about the mystifying Quaker. His public career is now being studied in depth as never before. While his private existence continues to elude historians because of research restrictions, Hoover's known personality traits can now be related to his public career, rather than made to appear in contradiction to it. Furthermore, his contributions to American domestic and foreign policies are undergoing a much needed reevaluation. That this reconsideration is largely positive without being eulogistic comes as a surprise, no doubt, both to his friends, relatives, and hagiologists who cherish the memory of a man who could do no wrong, and to those few unforgiving enemies who managed to outlive him.

Few enemies, or friends for that matter, did outlive the ninety-year-old Hoover. His reappraisal is now in the hands of a generation of historians who are too young to have personally experienced the height of his public career. Yet they are better able than his contemporaries were to see and appreciate the consistent patterns in his thought and actions. On the domestic scene it is now clear that Hoover avoided legislation whenever possible, and relied upon public and private cooperative forces outside normal political avenues — statistics, expert advice, and educational publicity — to accomplish his goals. The same was true in foreign affairs, where he avoided traditional international political agreements based on coercion, and sought instead to apply business principles by taking diplomacy out of the hands of politicians and putting it under the control of economic experts. He sought to institutionalize new administrative means at home and abroad for obtaining cooperation based on a scientific consensus and objective settlement of problems. As a transitional figure in a postwar decade of flux, Hoover tried to chart a new middle course — between obsolete laissez-faire economics and monopoly capitalism, between traditional American isolationism and future American global interventionism. Like most transitional public leaders, he failed.

As with everything Hoover did, however, even his failure was on a grand scale. No other twentieth-century American statesman has had his range of interests and breadth of understanding of domestic and foreign economic problems, or has developed such a consistent and comprehensive scientific, organizational approach for dealing with the political economy of the United States. For this reason, historians are reevaluating his ideas and his place in American economic and political thought.

Historians first began to reconsider Hoover's views on world affairs because so many of them (at least after World War II) were in keeping with the ideas of the original generation of revisionist historians who opposed FDR's diplomacy. His noncoercive approach to foreign policy, for example, not only prevented him from supporting the Red Scare hysteria after World War I and from becoming a redbaiter of the McCarthy ilk in the 1950s, but it also turned him into one of the most challenging critics of American foreign policy as it developed after 1890 along the lines of unlimited American intervention in world affairs. Without such limitations, he predicted, individual freedoms would be threatened at home by bureaucratic, corporate liberals who, in turn, would so overextend

America abroad that there would be no end to political and military intervention under their leadership.

According to William Appleman Williams, Hoover realized "the dangers of relying on the national government to solve every problem," and perceived that "military intervention . . . was a measure of last resort rather than a routine instrument of policy." Gradually Hoover is emerging as a major twentieth-century prophet to groups at opposite ends of the political spectrum. His assortment of socialistic and libertarian defenders cogently point out that it is no longer historically accurate to discredit Hoover's attempts "to evolve a more rational and moderate foreign policy" and to call attention to the dangers of New Deal corporate liberalism by simplistically condemning them as examples of "neoisolationism" or "laissez-faire individualism."

The talk in current political and historical circles about a "new" Hoover is largely because the "old" Hoover had been misunderstood or forgotten for so long by apologists and critics alike. In actuality, this rediscovery of Hoover is not as new or as incongruous as it first appears. Especially in the field of foreign affairs, revisionist historians have for some time respected his views. In some instances they were personally encouraged and aided by Hoover after he left office in 1933.

Exactly how much influence Hoover did exert over postwar revisionist scholarship is not yet fully known. There is evidence to show that several of his friends, such as John W. Blodgett, Jr. and members of the Pew family of Philadelphia, financed revisionist writing, but more research needs to be done to reconstruct the entire situation and Hoover's exact position and function within it. At present it appears as though he played his favorite role of "hidden catalyst," supplying some documents in his possession while withholding others for events in the Far East dating back to his own presidency and the Manchurian crisis. There was not complete agreement between Hoover and revisionist historians like

Charles A. Beard, Charles C. Tansill, or Henry Elmer Barnes, but they did concur that American foreign policy had been ill-conceived in the Far East during the late 1930s and early 1940s, and that a number of diplomatic errors had been committed during World War II and at the onset of the Cold War.

It is perhaps one of the ironies of history that Herbert Clark Hoover, forgotten Progressive and remembered reactionary, was once associated with the economic and ideological school of revisionist historical thought that has contributed to the rise today of the New Left criticism of American foreign policy. Although Hoover opposed Beard over domestic policy during the Great Depression, this did not prevent their agreeing on occasion when it came to foreign policy. "I was rather astonished to find an article by that left-winger, Professor Beard, in the 'American Mercury,'" he exclaimed to O'Laughlin in 1939. "It is worth reading. He is opposed to our going into war from a rather different point of view, but any anti-war point of view is good now." It is also conceivable that his private comment about Roosevelt getting the United States into war "through the Japanese back door," inspired the title to Charles Tansill's revisionist study, *Back Door to War: The Roosevelt Foreign Policy, 1933–1941.*

There is no doubt that Hoover sympathized with revisionist criticism of FDR's Far Eastern policy and later of what now appears to be a civilian, political decision to use two atomic bombs against the Japanese people. Like the early revisionist historians, he also insisted that Germany and Japan did not constitute a clear and present danger to the United States, and that in the long run the greatest ideological threat was posed by the Soviet Union, not by fascist countries. He was also convinced, like some of the more recent revisionist historians, that the United States had unnecessarily pressured Japan into striking out in the Far East and exaggerated the military aggressiveness of Russia after V-E Day.

Finally, Hoover's anxiety about the war's lingering effects

on domestic political and economic freedoms did not prove entirely unwarranted, however exaggerated they appeared at the time. He predicted, for example, that Americans would have to "adopt totalitarian methods to 'fight a war for freedom,'" that the standard of living would degenerate as a result of wartime inflation and postwar economic dislocation, and that restrictions would be placed on freedom of speech and economic opportunities as the economy became more subject to centralized control. Massive bombing of civilian populations was but one of the "totalitarian methods" emulated by the Allies that Hoover deplored. Indiscriminate firebombing of Japanese cities was another, and these violations of previous restraints on bombing civilians gradually inured the American people to the use of the atomic bomb. On the domestic scene it did prove impossible to dismantle the military-industrial complex that had arisen from wartime production, and to unravel the web of increased security surveillance and violation of civil liberties which finally reached a postwar climax in McCarthyism.

Hoover was not alone, of course, in anticipating the negative internal results of modern total warfare. These were commonly held fears among many old-time Progressives of both parties, the Republican Old Right, those concerned primarily with domestic reform, and knowledgeable isolationists and pacifists in the late 1930s. World War II did effectively put an end to New Deal reform — just as World War I had killed progressivism as a national movement and the Indochina war was to end Lyndon Johnson's attempt to create the Great Society. Most important, from Hoover's point of view, was the abandonment of noncoerciveness as a mainstay of American foreign policy in direct proportion to the acceptance of unlimited American intervention in world affairs. Stimsonianism rather than Hooverism became the most pervasive of all the diplomatic legacies of World War II, the defense of an American political, economic, and military empire abroad its major raison d'etre. Such an empire —

based on rigid ideological motivation and military tactics —
meant to Hoover the extinction of both international and
domestic cooperative communities. He had always defined
such communities as self-regulating entities. If self-serving
groups of political, business, and military bureaucrats were to
manage the governing process, then the people would no
longer be in control of the country or its foreign policy. The
Indochina war and the Watergate scandal have amply demonstrated his worst fears of a society and economy run from the
top down by a coercive system of expertise and by what has
recently been called an "arrogant elite guard of political
adolescents."

The real tragedy of World War II for Hoover lay ultimately, therefore, in its impact on his domestic dreams:
American self-sufficiency, cooperative individualism, associationalism, and a decentralized economy. Historians only recently have begun to reevaluate his comprehensive domestic
program in light of the unsatisfactory record of the New Deal
in solving the political and economic problems of the Cold
War era. This delay resulted in part from his own and his
family's reluctance to release his papers for research until
1966. Primarily, however, it was caused by the Great Depression, which retarded serious consideration of the merits of
public versus private power, of the importance of cooperative
versus elitist individual action in a modern, technological
nation, and of the impact on the democratic process of em-
ploying the immense power of a managerial, corporate state in
an unlimited fashion at home and abroad. Moreover, the
material benefits associated with the New Deal and World
War II further delayed consideration of these basic questions;
only most recently have domestic and foreign-policy problems
been increasingly attributed to a bureaucratic, elitist, com-
munity-destroying federal power that borders, some say, on
American fascism.

Like many Marxist and non-Marxist anti-establishment historians, Hoover had been asking these significant and endur-

ing questions about the domestic and foreign affairs of the United States since the 1920s. It is no wonder that he criticized the negative implications of such an arrogant, interventionist approach to reform and foreign policy before they were anything but the vaguest fears to most critics of the New Deal.

It is true that Hoover placed too much confidence in the ability of his own informal corporatism both to employ expertise in the public interest without succumbing to selfish elitism and to establish a proper balance between industry, agriculture, and labor. He also had too much faith in the willingness of capitalists to produce efficiently and maintain enough competition to insure that profits would pass on to the workers in the form of lower prices and higher wages. Hoover himself recognized that these ideals were unrealized, and that the problem of technological unemployment, for example, was very real. "We must work our machines heartlessly," he said in December 1937 to members of the Chicago Economic Club, "but not our men and women. . . . I have long believed that we cannot secure full economic security in the wage group until we face the question of assured annual income. . . . It would be a great demonstration of cooperation in industry to accomplish it," and one means of eliminating technological unemployment and "mistaken opposition to new improvements."

While his belief in a cooperative, humane, common-sense capitalism never materialized in the 1920s, it was rooted in the sound idea that only through scientifically controlled expansion could the best of individualism and neoguildist corporatism serve the people, the country, and the world. In other words, there were clearly defined limits to the American system that had to be honored if the United States was not to stumble onto the path of state socialism, fascism, or monopoly capitalism — all of which would destroy the material independence of people, their innovativeness, and their sense of significant political participation.

However correct his theories may appear in retrospect, there were serious defects in Hoover's methodology. Probably the most serious one was his failure to account for human irrationality and prejudices. Nations, no less than individuals, cannot function exclusively on the basis of economic principles — no matter how scientifically determined they may be. But Hoover was too much the capitalist and cold-blooded individual to recognize this fact of life and international affairs. He failed to understand why certain individuals and nations would not cooperate with his plans for providing them with economic security (as in the case of the farmers with respect to agricultural policy, and the French in their refusal to cooperate with the United States over war debts).

In addition, no single public figure could have mastered all the various foreign and domestic projects and problems that he attempted between 1921 and 1933. Inevitably he was swamped by the plethora of data gathered by the Department of Commerce and other agencies under his direction during those years and he resorted, on occasion, to the selective use of facts in violation of his own code of scientific objectivity. This was particularly evident in his defense of the high American protective tariff in 1930, on the question of Allied debts, and in his handling of the Bonus March. Finally, in the 1920s Hoover was not able to obtain the scientific consensus based on new institutional forms of organization at home or abroad that he so desired. Ultimately, therefore, he could not insure equality of opportunity or cooperation without resorting to traditional military or political power tactics — and this he refused to do. When his umpire concept of government, or neoguildist corporatism, or belief in the gold standard proved inadequate during the Great Depression, he stubbornly refused to consider other alternatives.

Nonetheless, there is much to be said for the best of the transitional ideas that Hoover came to embody. Despite the limitations of his personal philosophy and temperament, they did allow for an alternative foreign policy after *both* world

wars that was not based on unlimited interventionism or the
military suppression of revolutions based on communist ideology, but rather on disarmament and peaceful coexistence. His
views also recognized the relationship between domestic reform and international relations, and called for a coordination of national and international policies. They also
perceived the dangers of making individuals increasingly dependent upon government bureaucracies they no longer controlled, and the necessity of preserving a sense of community
participation. That such ideas were not endorsed by his
successors in the White House cannot be blamed on Hoover.
It simply has taken until the 1960s and 1970s for the most
constructive aspects of what Will Irwin in 1928 called
Hoover's "new way" to be appreciated. As a supporter predicted in 1944: "One hundred years from now the historians
will be quoting his words as final on the affairs and issues of
the past dozen years." And in 1971 Senator Barry Goldwater
commented that "had we followed his thinking we would not
be in the trouble we are today."

This does not mean that Hoover's enhanced reputation rests
on the successful promulgation of his own ideas about cooperative individualism, associationalism, tempered materialism,
or independent internationalism based on a modified application of the Open Door policy. It lies instead in his prophetic
and consistent criticism of the foreign and domestic policies of
the United States from 1933 through the mid-1950s. There is
no "new" Hoover, just an "old" one; he defies precise labeling
today just as his American system did fifty years ago. He is
coming into his own by default, long after he had stopped
trying to reshape traditional American values to guide the
organizational revolution started by modern technology, and
just as his apologists had despaired of rehabilitating his
reputation.

It is both sad and intriguing that this should be the fate of a
man who was both an inflexible and forgotten Progressive

during the course of his long life, and who began an autobiographical fragment sometime during World War I with the words:

There is little importance to men's lives except the accomplishments they leave to posterity. What a man accomplishes is of many categories and of many points of view; moral influence, example, leadership in thought and inspiration are difficult to measure, to prove or to treasure . . . and the proportion of success to be attributed to their effort is always indeterminate. *In the origination or administration of tangible institutions or constructive works men's parts can be more certainly defined. When all is said and done accomplishment is all that counts.* Record of failure may be warning, guiding information or vicarious sacrifice, but it [is] the progress marched that counts, not the description of the road or the conversation and gossip. [Emphasis added.]

Thus, by his own standards of success, Hoover failed. But the magnitude of his efforts and the significance of his best ideas have been revitalized with the passage of time. It is to be hoped that the serious attention they have not been given up to now will be justly accorded to them by history.

Acknowledgments and
Sources

DURING THE FIVE YEARS that I spent researching and writing this biography I received essential personal assistance from several sources. First, I want to thank Oscar Handlin and William Appleman Williams for reading the original manuscript in its entirety, and Ellis W. Hawley for reading extensive portions of it. The substantive criticisms and balanced, if differing, perspectives of Williams and Hawley helped me to clarify my own thinking and writing about Hoover. Their comments that I chose to incorporate into the text have strengthened and improved it more than I ever could recount or repay here. In particular, Oscar Handlin's detailed advice about style and organization proved invaluable during the first revision of the work.

Second, I am most indebted to various people who have worked with me at the Herbert Hoover Presidential Library in West Branch, Iowa, since I made my first trip there in 1967. They are Martha Smith, former Archivist; Dwight M. Miller, Senior Archivist; Ruth Dennis, former Librarian; Mildred Mather, Librarian and Archivist; Robert Wood, Assistant Director; and Thomas T. Thalken, Director. I was also aided in numerous ways at the Hoover Institution on War, Revolution and Peace in Stanford, California, by former Director of the Archives Dr. Franz G. Lassner and Archivist Crone C. Kernke. In addition, my thanks go to Judith A. Schiff, Chief Research Archivist at Yale University Library, for retrieving several obscure Hoover memoranda from the Henry L. Stimson

Papers; to Mrs. Alfred (Miriam) Vagts for corresponding with me about her father Charles A. Beard and his professional relationship with Hoover; and to Leah F. Freeman, Assistant Social Science Reference Librarian, California State University, Sacramento, for all her personal assistance in locating a wide variety of secondary source material.

Finally, there are those usually anonymous friends and relatives who have, at all the right times, encouraged, cajoled, and coerced me into finishing this book, despite numerous rewritings and production delays. They have, in some instances, served in various capacities as editors, typists, and proofreaders. Among them are Dave Wilson, who read and edited all of the different drafts; Mary Jean Brackmann, who helped me rewrite the final version of the first three chapters; Jean Roberts, a former graduate student who somehow has managed to be both a promising young historian and an excellent typist; Dee Scriven, a long-time friend and critic from Los Angeles; Kathy Barry, whose ever-present skepticism about Hoover was a welcome relief during the final stages of revision; the family of Irene and Tommy Jang of Vancouver, B.C., whose warmth and good meals I shall long remember; and Paula Eldot, whose work in progress on Al Smith has provided me with some interesting hypotheses about progressivism. Other scholars to whom I am indebted for allowing me to read their unpublished research on Hoover are credited in the following discussion of the major sources consulted for this biography of the thirty-first president of the United States.

The Herbert Hoover Presidential Library and Museum at West Branch, Iowa, constitutes the major primary-source collection for research into the life and activities of this much-misunderstood American figure. Although the museum was opened and personally dedicated by Hoover in 1962, the library was not ready for research purposes until 1966 — two years after his death. Processing and reclassification of the Hoover papers has continued since that time under several different directors and changes in administrative staff. For example, articles and books which first appeared based on research conducted in West Branch contain footnote references to box numbers which have since been discarded. Also, material in the "Official" and "Personal" files is now being combined, so that it is no longer necessary to make that distinction in requesting or citing documents. The current citation form suggested by the library staff is quite accurate, but somewhat cumbersome; so Hoover scholars have employed various abbreviations in footnote references for "folder title," file name, and major archival group (e.g., Pre-Commerce, Presidential, and Post-Presidential Papers) .

However, this continuing processing and reclassification has sometimes made it difficult to locate material cited in works resulting from early research at the library, especially in what originally was the 1-Q series containing personal data. Such is the case with the autobiographical fragment I refer to in several chapters of this biography. I learned of its existence from the works of other researchers, only to find that it still could not be located as of my last two trips to West Branch in 1974. I am indebted to Craig Lloyd for providing me with copies of a portion of his notes on this interesting document.

There is little available about Hoover's personal life in the entire West Branch collection, and almost nothing about his private career and business affairs up to 1914. All material about his finances is restricted, as are the 550 boxes constituting the papers of his wife, Lou Henry Hoover. The best source about his financial involvements remains an article in *Fortune* in August 1932. Minor additional information about financial matters can be found in the appendices of both Roy V. Peel and Thomas C. Connelly, *The 1932 Campaign: An Analysis* (New York: Farrar and Rinehart, Inc., 1935) and Walter W. Leggett, *The Rise of Herbert Hoover* (New York: H. K. Fly Company, 1932) . Historian David Burner arranged for the deposit in West Branch of microfilm copies of a letterpress copy book Hoover kept as manager of the Sons of Gwalia mine in Leonora, Western Australia from 1898 to 1899, and of other records about his business associations with Bewick, Moreing and Company from 1897 to 1926. These cast much needed light on Hoover's labor and business policies during his formative years as a young engineer.

Aside from these documentary deficiencies for his private affairs before 1914, the Hoover Library contains a wealth of material on Hoover's long public career beginning in 1914. Most of it is yet untapped, but it is already clear what the important areas of future research will be. Obviously, historians must still determine precisely the extent to which the unresolved contradictions and dialectical tensions in Hoover's progressive and corporatist thought, discussed in Chapters II and III, undermined his concerted attempt to "reconstruct America" before 1929, and the degree to which they remain debilitating features of similar ideas based on the voluntary cooperation of socially responsible individuals and nations. In addition, his influence on the affairs of the Treasury, Justice, Labor, and Interior Departments, and on governmental agencies like the Federal Trade and Tariff Commissions and the Federal Reserve Board, has not yet been adequately researched. Also, his stand on civil and human liberties as secretary of commerce and president, as well as the entire "southern strategy" of the Republican party in the late 1920s, has yet to be unraveled. The same is true of his very complex ideas and attitudes on foreign policy that evolved over the years. In particular his views on economic self-sufficiency and limited military defense for the United States, and how these concepts combined with his emphasis on peaceful economic cooperation and economic stabilization abroad to temper his ideas on the Open Door policy and on American expansionism in general, have not yet been fully sorted out or appreciated. The same is true of his attitude toward communism, especially after 1933. No adequate evaluation yet exists of his ambivalent relationship with pacifist, isolationist and anti-Communist groups or with certain revisionist historians after World War II, or of his role as a member of the Old Right and a leading Cold War critic.

Moreover, Hoover's disagreements with other Progressives of the 1920s over pollution, ecological, labor, conservation, and agricultural problems have yet to be discussed in any definitive manner, as is the case with most of his activities during the first eight months of his presidency *before* the Great Depression. Part of this deficiency to date has been the difficulty historians have had in understanding the brand of apolitical corporatism that Hoover actually espoused, and how that affected, for example, his labor and agricultural policies, as well as his views on antitrust revision and obligatory business codes that finally led to his condemnation of the New Deal. Most important, perhaps, is the need to determine precisely what role he unwittingly played in both the co-optation of labor as secretary of commerce and president and in the entire progression toward greater bureaucratization in government and business, despite his intentions to the contrary. His refusal to endorse unlimited use of federal power after 1929 must also be placed in perspective with his earlier actions that appeared to encourage greater centralization and rationalization of the political economy, and with his later recommendations in the 1950s for reorganization of the executive branch of government.

The Presidential Papers are probably the best organized of the major archival groups (Pre-Commerce, Commerce, Presidential and Post-Presidential). So far they appear to provide few new insights into how Hoover dealt with the Great Depression, though certain previously unknown details about his opposition to the Swope Plan, his decision to raise taxes, and his handling of the Bonus March have come to light. These papers are excellent, however, for research into Hoover's economic and political foreign policies, especially in certain geographical areas like Latin Amerca and with specialized problems like tariff policy. They also provide an abundance of new material on domestic issues not directly related to the Great Depression; that is, on the "uncompleted tasks" from his secretarial days that Hoover thought he could finish as president and energetically undertook during the first eight months of his administration, before the stock market crash in the fall of 1929.

To date, the Post-Presidential Papers are the least researched and possibly the most valuable, for their insight into Hoover's attempts as a private citizen after 1933 to influence foreign and domestic politics. His correspondence with such reporters and editors as Ashmun Brown, Theodore G. Joslin, Verne Marshall, Neil MacNeil, and Walter Trohan, as well as with several of his secretaries such as Lawrence Richey, George Akerson, and French Strother contains important new information. So does his correspondence with the following men: Hugh Gibson, Lewis L. Strauss, John Callan O'Laughlin, Arthur Kemp, James A. MacLafferty, Robert E. Wood, Generals A. C. Wedemeyer and Douglas MacArthur, Patrick J. Hurley, Edward Eyre Hunt, Ray Lyman Wilbur, William R. Castle, Jr., Arthur Vandenberg, Bernard Baruch, Robert Taft, and Presidents Truman and Eisenhower. There is even material of minor historical importance contained in his correspondence with Richard M. Nixon and various members of the Kennedy family.

It should also be noted that in addition to their correspondence with Hoover in the Post-Presidential archival material, the papers of Gibson, Wilbur, Castle, Wood, MacNeil, Marshall, Richey, and MacLafferty are also at West Branch, as are the papers of Gerald P. Nye, Burt Brown Barker, and Bradley D. Nash. Research for these years after 1933 will be even more profitable, no doubt, once the papers of Senator Bourke B. Hickenlooper and Admiral Lewis L. Strauss, plus the "raw files" of columnist Westbrook Pegler, are opened. The Hickenlooper and Strauss papers will be of considerable significance and interest because of the attitudes of these two men and Hoover toward the development and use of atomic energy.

The John Callan O'Laughlin exchange with Hoover is much more complete in the Library of Congress than at the Hoover Library. The same is true of his correspondence with some revisionist historians. Although the Hoover Library has the Charles C. Tansill Papers, they are most disappointing with respect to material about Hoover's relationship with post–World War II revisionist historians in general, as is the correspondence with Harry Elmer Barnes. However in the Barnes Papers in the Coe Library at the University of Wyoming there is a better selection of Hoover letters with both Barnes and Tansill on this question. While the correspondence in West Branch between Hoover and Charles A. Beard is intriguing, it is limited. It is to be hoped that the Beard Papers now in the possession of Mrs. Alfred (Miriam) Vagts (soon to be deposited in the Archives of DePauw University) contain correspondence between Hoover's friends and Beard that is more extensive than the Hoover-Beard correspondence, which except for a few confidential memoranda is complete at the Hoover Library.

By far the bulk of research material on Hoover's life now resides in the West Branch Library, except for his papers as U.S. Food Administrator, 1917–1919, and those on his relief activities during and immediately following World War I, which are housed in the Hoover Institution on War, Revolution and Peace on the Stanford University campus. There are also a number of valuable duplicates in both the Presidential Library and the Hoover Institution. Both, for example, contain copies of oral interviews, most of which were conducted by Raymond Henle beginning in 1966. Three hundred and nineteen have been recorded and the copyright on all of these transcripts in the Hoover Oral History Program is held by the President Hoover Library Association Inc. Lists of those which have been accessioned and opened for research can be found in the *AHA Newsletter* 10 (March 1972): 39; in *Prologue: The Journal of the National Archives,* Fall and Winter, 1972; and in *Historical Mate-*

rials in the Herbert Hoover Presidential Library (Washington, D.C., 1973).

Both also have what in Hoover circles is called the "Bible." This is a very informative chronological compilation of all Hoover's public addresses, statements, and articles from 1917 to 1964. In addition at both locations can be found the over one hundred file boxes containing documents on the two Hoover Commissions on the Organization of the Executive Branch of Government, and reprints of articles about Hoover. The West Branch reprint collection is by far the more extensive of the two. Hoover's correspondence with Woodrow Wilson during and after World War I is also at Stanford and West Branch. Finally, the Hoover Institution has selected Commerce and Presidential Papers, extensive documents on Hoover's relief activities during both world wars, the papers of Edward Eyre Hunt, one of Hoover's economic advisers, and those of Stanley K. Hornbeck, Chief of the Division of Far Eastern Affairs of the State Department from 1928 to 1937.

The Library at West Branch has a fifteen-page listing prepared by David Burner entitled, "Hoover Material in Other Archives." Except for a few thousand references to Hoover in the Diary and Papers of Henry L. Stimson, approximately a hundred Hoover letters to Colonel Edward M. House, plus a few others in several scattered collections at the Yale University Library, and a hundred or so items pertaining to his 1920 campaign for the presidency in the Ralph Arnold Collection at the Henry E. Huntington Library at San Marino, California, primary material on Hoover at other institutions is not extensive.

Turning to unpublished secondary works, my knowledge of Hoover has been greatly expanded by several papers delivered at conferences or seminars. Two by Ellis Hawley were particularly helpful. The first, given at the Southern Historical Association convention in November 1968, was entitled, "Herbert Hoover and the Economic Planners, 1931–1932." The other, "Herbert Hoover and the Expansion of the Commerce Department: The Anti-Bureaucrat as Bureaucratic Empire-Builder," was delivered at the Organization of American Historians convention in April 1970. Hawley has also contributed an essay on Hoover to the American Forum Series entitled, *Herbert Hoover and the Crisis of American Capitalism* (Cam-

bridge, Mass.: Schenkman Publishing Company, 1973), edited by
J. Joseph Huthmacher and Warren I. Susman. Other informative
papers were David Burner's "Primary Sources on Herbert Hoover's
Business Career," read at the 1970 convention of the Southwestern
Social Science Association, and his "Herbert Hoover: A Technocrat's
Morality," at the 1971 American Studies Association convention. An
expanded version coauthored with Thomas R. West was printed in
The Hofstadter Aegis: A Memorial (New York: Alfred A. Knopf,
1974), edited by Stanley Elkins and Eric McKitrick. At the 1971
Missouri Valley Historical Conference Frederick C. Adams delivered an original summary on the subject, "Hoover and American
Foreign Policy," while at the 1972 Organization of American Historians convention Evan B. Metcalf presented an interesting paper,
which dealt in part with Hoover's economic theories, entitled: "Economic Stabilization by Business: A Pre-Keynesian Survival in a
Keynesian World," as did Melvyn P. Leffler at the 1974 OAH meeting in his paper, "The U.S. and European Stability, 1921–1933" [sub-
sequently expanded and printed in *Perspectives in American History* 8 (1974)]. The most informative seminar paper I have read to
date is Carolyn Grin's "The Unemployment Conference of 1921: An
Experiment in Cooperative National Planning." I drew extensively
from this paper in Chapter IV. The published version appeared in
Mid-America 55 (April 1973): 83–107. One of the most stimulating
groups of papers about Hoover was delivered at the State University
College of Arts and Sciences, Geneseo, New York, in April 1973.
They can be found in *The Hoover Presidency: A Re-appraisal* (Al-
bany: State University of New York Press, 1974), edited by Martin L. Fausold. Another invaluable series of papers was delivered
during the course of 1974, in four Centennial Seminars held to com-
memorate Hoover's birth. Conducted at the Hoover Presidential
Library in West Branch, Iowa, four separate chronological antholo-
gies of these essays, covering his entire public career, will subsequently be published by the President Hoover Library Association.

I have also profited from reading the following unpublished dis-
sertations and manuscripts: "Aggressive Introvert: A Study of
Herbert Hoover and Public Relations Management, 1912–1932"
(Ph.D. dissertation, University of Iowa, 1970), by Craig Lloyd [sub-
sequently published by Ohio State University Press in 1973]; "Herbert Hoover and the Department of Commerce: A Study of Ideology

and Policy" (Ph.D. dissertation, University of Chicago, 1972), by Peri Arnold; "The United States and European Recovery, 1918–1923: A Study of Public Policy and Private Finance" (Ph.D. dissertation, University of Wisconsin, 1971), by Robert H. Van Meter; "Herbert Hoover and the Farm Crisis of the Twenties: A Study of the Commerce Department's Efforts to Solve the Agricultural Depression, 1921–1928" (Ph.D. dissertation, Northern Illinois University, 1971), by Gary H. Koerselman; "Herbert Hoover and the Armed Forces: A Study of Presidential Attitudes and Policy" (Ph.D. dissertation, Northwestern University, 1971), by John R. M. Wilson; "The Meaning of Industrial Conflict in Some Ideologies of the Early 1920s: The AFL, Organized Employers and Herbert Hoover" (Ph.D. dissertation, Columbia University, 1971), by Haggai Hurvitz; "The Politics of Financial Stabilization: American Reconstruction Policy in Europe, 1924–1930" (Ph.D. dissertation, Cornell University, 1973), by Frank C. Costigliola; "Progressive Pan Americanism: Development and United States Policy Toward South America, 1906–1931" (Ph.D. dissertation, Cornell University, 1973), by Robert N. Seidel; "The United States and the Problem of International Economic Control: The Private Structure of Cooperation in American Foreign Policy, 1918–1928 (Ph.D. dissertation, University of Iowa, 1974), by Michael J. Hogan; "The Struggle for Stability: American Policy Toward France, 1921–1933" (Ph.D. dissertation, Ohio State University, 1972), by Melvyn P. Leffler; "The Administrative Theories and Practices of Herbert Hoover" (Ph.D. dissertation, University of Chicago, 1963), by John Westrate; "Herbert Hoover's Use of Public Relations in the U.S. Food Administration, 1917–1919" (M.A. thesis, University of Wisconsin, 1969), by Leonard Dileanis; "Hoover and the Mississippi Valley Flood of 1927: A Case Study of the Political Thought of Herbert Hoover" (D.S.S. dissertation, Syracuse University, 1968), by Bruce Alan Lohof: "Morris Llewellyn Cooke: Progressive Engineer" (Ph.D. dissertation, Columbia University, 1963), by Jean Christie; "Secretary of Commerce Herbert C. Hoover: The First Regulator of American Broadcasting, 1921–1928 (Ph.D. dissertation, University of Iowa, 1970), by Glenn A. Johnson; "The American Engineering Profession and the Idea of Social Responsibility" (Ph.D. dissertation, University of California at Los Angeles, 1956), by Edwin T. Layton, Jr. [this has recently been published as *The Revolt of the Engineers* (Cleveland: Press of Case Western Reserve University,

1971)]. Extremely important for my discussion of Hoover's antitrust attitudes was "Relation of the Federal Anti-Trust Policy as a Goal of the Business Community During the Period 1918–19" (Ph.D. dissertation, Pennsylvania State University, 1963), by Robert F. Himmelberg. One of the most complete discussions of Hoover's political leanings before he declared himself a Republican in 1920 can be found in the appendix of "Partisan Positions on Isolationism vs. Internationalism, 1918–1933" (D.S.S. dissertation, Syracuse University, 1963), by Harold Tiffany Butler. Two interesting unpublished manuscripts to which I had access are "The United States and the World Court, 1920–1935," by Robert Accinelli; and "Herbert Hoover and Conservative Opposition to Truman's Overseas Military Policy," by Donald J. Mrozek.

Hoover's numerous published works and commission reports constitute a major source of information about his activities and ideas. Those I found most helpful for this biography were: *Addresses Upon the American Road,* eight volumes published beginning in 1936 and ending in 1961 by four different companies (Charles Scribner's Sons, volumes for *1933–1936, 1938–1940, 1940–1941;* D. Van Nostrand Company, volumes for *1941–1945, 1945–1948;* Stanford University Press, volumes for *1948–1950, 1950–1955;* The Caxton Printers, Ltd., volume for *1955–1960*); *An American Epic,* 4 vols. (Chicago: Regnery Co., 1959–1964); *America's First Crusade* (New York: Charles Scribner's Sons, 1942); *American Individualism* (Garden City, New York: Doubleday, Page and Company, 1922); *A Cause to Win: Five Speeches by Herbert Hoover on American Foreign Policy in Relation to Soviet Russia* (Concord, N.H.: Rumford Press, 1951); *The Challenge to Liberty* (New York: Charles Scribner's Sons, 1934); *Forty Key Questions About Our Foreign Policy* (Scarsdale, New York: The Updegraff Press, 1952); *After Dinner: Addresses by Herbert Hoover Before the Gridiron Club of Washington, D.C. with Other Informal Speeches* (New York: Charles Scribner's Sons, 1933); *America's Way Forward* (New York: The Scribner Press, 1939); *The Memoirs of Herbert Hoover,* 3 vols. (New York: Macmillan Co., 1951–1952); *The New Day: Campaign Speeches of Herbert Hoover, 1928* (Stanford: Stanford University Press, 1928); *The Ordeal of Woodrow Wilson* (New York: McGraw-Hill Book Company, 1958); *Principles of Mining* (New York: Hill Publishing Company, 1909); *America's Ideals versus the New Deal*

(New York: The Scribner Press, 1936). Hoover coauthored two books with Hugh Gibson, *The Problems of Lasting Peace* (Garden City, New York: Doubleday, Doran and Company, 1942), and *The Basis of Lasting Peace* (New York: D. Van Nostrand Company, 1945). Of all his published writings, Hoover's *Memoirs* remains the work which should be read most carefully for historical inaccuracies and misinterpretations because, as is often the case with such personal accounts, they reflect in some instances how he would like to be remembered rather than exactly what he thought or did.

The best published source for his public statements is *The State Papers and Other Public Writings of Herbert Hoover,* collected and edited by William Starr Meyers, 2 vols. (Garden City, New York: Doubleday, Doran and Company, 1934). The four most important commissions associated with Hoover's name are the two he appointed as president on Recent Social Trends and Recent Economic Trends, and the two he directed on the Organization of the Executive Branch of the Government 1947–1949, and 1953–1955. All resulted in multivolume reports.

A few edited accounts of Hoover's speeches and statements and conversations containing extensive narrative were also indispensable. This was particularly true of William Starr Meyers and Walter H. Newton, *The Hoover Administration: A Documented Narrative* (New York: Charles Scribner's Sons, 1936), and Ray Lyman Wilbur and Arthur Mastick Hyde, *The Hoover Policies* (New York: Charles Scribner's Sons, 1937). Less so, but still somewhat valuable was Theodore G. Joslin's *Hoover Off the Record* (Garden City, New York, 1934). Hoover's Post-Presidential Papers reveal that this book was edited severely by Hoover before publication; perhaps this accounts for the fact that it promises more than it delivers as a personal account of the president in action by one of his reporter-secretaries.

There are several autobiographical and genealogical works, plus contemporary essays about Hoover which should not be overlooked. The most personal and interesting is the privately published autobiographical account by Theodore Hoover called *Memoranda: Being a Statement by an Engineer* (Stanford: 1939). The similarity between some of the childhood memories in this account, written before Hoover started his own memoirs, and those he later recounted, leads to the interesting speculation that since Hoover so discounted life's trivia he might have been obliged to "lift" some from his brother, who seemed fascinated by it. *The Genealogy of the Herbert Hoover Family* (Stanford: Hoover Institution of War, Revolution and Peace, 1967), by Theodore's daughter Hulda Hoover McLean, updates the genealogical data in her father's autobiography. From this work, for example, one learns that Hoover's mother died a year later than all previous biographers have stated. Other autobiographical accounts worth consulting for references about Hoover are: *The Wartime Journals of Charles A. Lindbergh* (New York: Harcourt Brace Jovanovich, Inc., 1970); David Starr Jordan, *The Days of a Man:* vol. 2; *1900–1921* (Yonkers-on-Hudson, New York: World Book Company, 1922); Lewis L. Strauss, *Men and Decisions* (Garden City, New York: Doubleday and Company, 1962); Ray Lyman Wilbur, *Memoirs, 1875–1949* (Palo Alto: Stanford University Press, 1960); and Mary Austin, *Earth Horizon: Autobiography* (New York: The Literary Guild, 1932). Two of the numerous contemporary essays about Hoover that deserve reading are in *Prophets: True and False* (Freeport, New York: Books for Libraries Press, 1969; a reprint of the 1928 edition) by Oswald Garrison Villard; and *Big Frogs* (New York: Macy-Masius, 1928) by Henry F. Pringle.

Last, I relied upon published secondary accounts including biographies, monographs, and articles. Until the appearance of David Burner's biography and Martin L. Fausold's account of his presidency, the Hoover buff cannot afford to overlook the controversial reevaluation of Hoover's philosophy summarized by William Appleman Williams in the *New York Review of Books* for November 5, 1970 [subsequently reprinted in *Some Presidents: Wilson to Nixon* (New York: New York Review; distributed by Vintage Books, 1972)] and previously detailed by him in the following works: *American Russian Relations, 1781–1947* (New York: Rinehart and Co., 1952); *The Tragedy of American Diplomacy* (2nd rev. ed., New York: Dell Publishing Company, 1972); and *The Contours of American History* (Cleveland: World Publishing Company, 1961). There are three other seminally interpretive essays: "The Ordeal of Herbert Hoover," *Yale Review* 52 (Summer 1963): 563–83, by Carl N. Degler; "Herbert Hoover and the Crisis of American Individualism," in *The American Political Tradition* (New York: Alfred A. Knopf, 1949), by Richard Hofstadter; and "Presidential Planning and Social Science Research: Mr. Hoover's Experts," by Barry D. Karl, in *Perspec-*

lives in American History 3 (1969) : 347–409. But for the most part, the tendency has been for general interpretations and biographical accounts of Hoover to be either extremely hostile or eulogistic until very recently.

The best critical account of Hoover is the Walter Liggett book mentioned above. However, most of the hostile biographies were written after 1929 and are so vituperative that they serve little historical purpose, except to document the hostility toward him generated by the depression and to give credence to Hoover's complaint that there was a vicious smear campaign launched against him. Of the early eulogistic accounts Will Irwin's *Herbert Hoover: A Reminiscent Biography* (New York: Grosset and Dunlap, 1928), William Hard's *Who's Hoover?* (New York: Dodd, Mead and Company, 1928), Edwin Emerson's *Hoover and His Times* (Garden City, New York: Garden City Publishing, 1932), Herbert Corey's *The Truth About Hoover* (Boston: Houghton Mifflin Company, 1932), and Walter Friar Dexter's *Herbert Hoover and American Individualism* (New York: The Macmillan Company, 1932) are all still useful, as is Eugene Lyons' *Herbert Hoover: A Biography* (New York: Doubleday, 1964). First published in 1948 under the name *Our Unknown Ex-President* (a title Hoover did not like), this latest revision is even less critical than the first. In several respects the 1948 edition remains the better of the two, because the portrayal of Hoover is more realistic. For example, in 1948 Lyons matter-of-factly reported that Hoover had been convinced by William Ward, a Quaker and political leader from New York, that the best way for him to obtain a cabinet post would be to allow his presidential boom to develop. This and other calculating aspects of Hoover's public and private careers have been eliminated in the 1964 edition, resulting in an unbelievable, idealistic portrayal.

Of the most recent biographies written before the opening of the Hoover Library, by far the best in terms of balance and detail is Harold Wolfe's *Herbert Hoover: Public Servant and Leader of the Loyal Opposition* (New York: Exposition Press, 1956). David Hindshaw, a man Hoover seriously considered as a replacement for his press secretary George Akerson, has written a generally favorable and highly impressionistic account of his life entitled, *Herbert Hoover: American Quaker* (New York: Farrar, Straus and Company, 1950). An often overlooked recent biography is Carol Green

Wilson's *Herbert Hoover: A Challenge for Today* (New York: Evans Publishing Company, 1968). This book is based in large measure on interviews conducted in 1950 and 1951 with friends and associates of Hoover, most of whom are now dead. Of particular interest are those with financiers Eugene Meyer and Adolph C. Miller. All the notes and interviews for this book are currently on deposit at the Hoover Institution. The only biography to date of Hoover's wife is *Lou Henry Hoover: Gallant First Lady* (New York: Dodd, Mead and Company, 1969), by Helen B. Pryor. In writing this work Pryor had access to the now closed Lou Henry Hoover papers. Interviews I conducted with both Wilson and Pryor in the summer of 1971 provided interesting personal sidelights about the Hoovers.

In addition to this biographical material there are a number of monographs about specific aspects of Hoover's economic and political policies at home and abroad as secretary of commerce and president, and about his closest advisers and, in some instances, his opponents. While they vary in quality, all provide some valuable information. The following were written on the basis of research at the Herbert Hoover Presidential Library in West Branch: *Ideology and Economics: U.S. Relations with the Soviet Union, 1918–1933* (Columbia, Missouri: University of Missouri Press, 1974), by Joan Hoff Wilson; *American Business and Foreign Policy, 1920–1933* (Lexington: University Press of Kentucky, 1971), by Joan Hoff Wilson; *The President and Protest: Hoover, Conspiracy, and the Bonus Riot* (Columbia, Missouri: University of Missouri Press, 1974), by Donald J. Lisio; *The Hoover-Wilson Wartime Correspondence* (Ames, Iowa: Iowa State University Press, 1974), edited by Frances W. O'Brien; *The Politics of Normalcy: Governmental Theory and Practice in the Harding-Coolidge Era* (New York: W. W. Norton and Company, 1973), by Robert K. Murray; *Franklin D. Roosevelt: Launching the New Deal* (Boston: Little, Brown and Company, 1973), by Frank Freidel; *Aggressive Introvert: A Study of Herbert Hoover and Public Relations Management, 1912–1932* (Columbus: Ohio State University Press, 1972), by Craig Lloyd; *The Spearless Leader: Senator Borah and the Progressive Movement in the 1920s* (Urbana: University of Illinois Press, 1972), by LeRoy Ashby; *The Bonus March: An Episode of the Great Depression* (Westport, Conn.: Greenwood Press, 1971), by Roger Daniels; *The Revolt of the Engineers* (Cleveland: The Press of Case Western Reserve University, 1971), by

Edwin T. Layton, Jr.; *The Shattered Dream: Herbert Hoover and the Great Depression* (New York: William Morrow, 1970), by Gene Smith; and *Interregnum of Despair: Hoover's Congress and the Depression* (Urbana: University of Illinois Press, 1970), by Jordan A. Schwarz.

All of the remaining monographs used for this study were written *before* researchers had access to Hoover's private papers. They include: *The Poverty of Abundance: Hoover, The Nation, The Depression* (New York: Oxford University Press, 1965), by Albert U. Romasco [this should be read in conjunction with Murray N. Rothbard's excessively critical review, "The Hoover Myth," *Studies on the Left* 6 (July–August 1966): 70–84, and Rothbard's more balanced reinterpretation of Hoover's economic policies entitled, "Herbert Hoover and the Myth of Laissez Faire," in *A New History of Leviathan* (New York: E. P. Dutton and Company, 1972), edited by Ronald Radosh and Rothbard]; *Herbert Hoover and the Great Depression* (New York: Oxford University Press, 1959), by Harris Gaylord Warren; *Herbert Hoover's Latin-American Policy* (Palo Alto, California: Stanford University Press, 1957), by Robert M. Ferrell; *Herbert Hoover and Economic Diplomacy* (Pittsburgh: University of Pittsburgh Press, 1962), by Joseph Brandes; *Herbert Hoover and Germany* (New York: Macmillan, 1960), by Louis P. Lochner; *Executive Reorganization and Reform in the New Deal: The Genesis of Administrative Management, 1900–1939* (Cambridge, Mass.: Harvard University Press, 1963), by Barry Dean Karl; *The Fiscal Revolution in America* (Chicago: University of Chicago Press, 1969), by Herbert Stein; *Labor Politics in a Democratic Republic* (Washington, D.C.: Spartan Books, Inc., 1964), by Vaughan Davis Bornet; *Radio, Television and American Politics* (New York: Sheed and Ward, 1969), by Edward W. Chester; *Wesley Clair Mitchell: The Economic Scientist* (New York: National Bureau of Economic Research, Inc., 1952), edited by Arthur F. Burns; *A Scholar in Action: Edwin F. Gay* (Cambridge, Mass.: Harvard University Press, 1952), by Herbert Heaton; *Business Cycles: The Problem and Its Setting* (New York: National Bureau of Economic Research, Inc., 1927), Wesley Clair Mitchell; *idem*, "Intelligence and the Guidance of Economic Evolution," in *Authority and the Individual* (Cambridge, Mass.: Harvard University Press, 1937), from the Harvard Tercentenary Conference of Arts and Sciences: *Competition and Cooperation: The Emergence of a National Trade Association* (Baltimore: Johns Hopkins Press, 1966), by Louis Galambos; *The Great Contraction, 1929–1933* (Princeton, New Jersey: Princeton University Press, 1965), by Milton Friedman and Anna Jacobson Schwartz; *Prosperity Decade: From War to Depression: 1917–1929*, vol. 8 (New York: Rinehart & Company, Inc., 1947), by George Soule; *The Economic Lessons of the Nineteen-Thirties* (New York: Augustus M. Kelley, 1965), by H. W. Arndt; *Contemporary Economic Thought* (New York: Harper & Brothers, 1928), by Paul T. Homan; *The President's Cabinet: An Analysis in the Period from Wilson to Eisenhower* (Cambridge, Mass.: Harvard University Press, 1959), by Richard F. Fenno, Jr.; *Heir to Empire: United States Economic Diplomacy, 1916–1923* (Pittsburgh: University of Pittsburgh Press, 1969), by Carl P. Parrini; *George N. Peek and the Fight for Farm Parity* (Norman, Oklahoma: University of Oklahoma Press, 1954), by Gilbert C. Fite; *Caravans of Commerce* (New York: Harper & Brothers Publishers, 1926), by Isaac F. Marcosson; *Fall from Grace: The Republican Party and the Puritan Ethic* (New York: The New American Library, 1968), by Milton Viorst; and *Private Power and American Democracy* (New York: Alfred A. Knopf, 1966) and *The Decline of the Agrarian Democracy* (Berkeley: University of California Press, 1958), both by Grant McConnell.

In addition to the three collections of essays cited above in the American Forum series, or printed by the State University of New York Press and the Hoover Library Association, the following published articles were those most utilized in the preparation of this study: James S. Olson, "The End of Voluntarism: Herbert Hoover and the National Credit Corp.," *Annals of Iowa* 41 (Fall 1972): 1104–1113; *idem*, "Herbert Hoover and 'War' on the Depression," *Palimpsest* 54 (July–August 1973): 26–31; Geoffrey Blainey, "Herbert Hoover's Forgotten Years," *Business Archives and History* 3 (February 1963): 53–70; Kenneth Philip, "Herbert Hoover's New Era: A False Dawn for the American Indian, 1929–1932," *Rocky Mountain Social Science Journal* 9 (April 1972): 53–60; Lawrence H. Fuchs, "Election of 1928," in *History of American Presidential Elections, 1789–1968* (New York: Chelsea House Publishers, 1971); Louis A. Galambos, "The Emerging Organizational Synthesis in Modern American History," *Business History Review* 44 (Autumn 1970): 279–90; *idem*, "The Cotton-Textile Institute and the Government: A Case Study in Interacting Value Systems," *Business History Review* 37 (Summer 1964) : 186–213; James H. Shideler, "Herbert Hoover and the Federal Farm Board Project, 1921–1925," *Mississippi Valley Historical Review* 42 (March 1956) : 711–29; Ellis W. Hawley, "Secretary Hoover and the Bituminous Coal Problem, 1921–1928," *Business History Review* 42 (Autumn 1968) : 247–79; J. H. Wilson, "American Business and the Recognition of the Soviet Union," *Social Science Quarterly* 52 (September 1971) : 349–68; Kent Schofield, "The Public Image of Herbert Hoover in the 1928 Campaign," *Mid-America* 51 (October 1969) : 278–93; Robert K. Murray, "President Harding and His Cabinet," *Ohio History* 75 (Spring and Summer, 1966) : 108–25; William A. Williams, "The Legend of Isolationism in the 1920's," *Science and Society* 18 (Winter 1954) : 1–20; Edward and Frederick Schapsmeier, "Disharmony in the Harding Cabinet: Hoover-Wallace Conflict," *Ohio History* 75 (Spring and Summer, 1966) : 126–136; Gerald D. Nash, "Herbert Hoover and the Origins of the Reconstruction Finance Corporation," *Mississippi Valley Historical Review* 46 (December 1959) : 455–68; Donald J. Lisio, "A Blunder Becomes Catastrophe," *Wisconsin Magazine of History* 51 (Autumn 1967) : 37–50; Joseph H. Davis, "Herbert Hoover, 1874–1964: Another Appraisal," *The South Atlantic Quarterly* 68 (Summer 1969) : 295–318; Melvyn P. Leffler, "The Origins of Republican War Debt Policy, 1921–23; A Case Study in the Applicability of the Open Door Interpretation," *The Journal of American History* 59 (December 1972) : 586–92; Louis Galambos, "AFL's Concept of Big Business: A Quantitative Study of Attitudes Toward the Large Corporations, 1894–1931," *The Journal of American History* 57 (March 1971) : 847–63; Frank Costigliola, "The Other Side of Isolationism: The Establishment of the First World Bank, 1929–1930," *The Journal of American History* 59 (December 1972) : 602–20; Earl Pomeroy, "Five Early Letters of Herbert C. Hoover," *The Call Number* 27 (Spring 1966) : 1–12; Ellis W. Hawley, "Herbert Hoover, the Commerce Secretariat and the Vision of an 'Associative State,' 1921–1928," *The Journal of American History* 62 (June 1974) : 116–140; Richard N. Kottman, "The Hoover-Bennett Meeting of 1931: Mismanaged Summitry," *Anals of Iowa* 42 (Winter 1974) ; Gary Dean Best, "The Hoover-for-President Boom," *Mid-America* 53 (October 1971) : 227–44; Ronald Radosh, "The Corporate Ideology of American Labor Leaders from Gompers to Hillman," *Studies on the Left* 6, no. 6 (1966): 66–87; William R. Johnson, "Herbert Hoover and the Regulation of Grain Futures," *Mid-America* 51 (July 1969): 155–74; Gary M. Maranell, "The Evaluation of Presidents: An Extension of the Schlesinger Polls," *The Journal of American History* 57 (June 1970): 104–113; Virginia Gray, "Anti-Evolution Sentiment and Behavior: The Case of Arkansas," *The Journal of American History* 57 (September 1970): 352–66; Benjamin G. Rader, "Federal Taxation in the 1920s: A Re-examination," *The Historian* 33 (May 1971): 415–35; Stanley I. Kutler, "Chief Justice Taft, National Regulation and the Commerce Power," *The Journal of American History* 51 (March 1965): 651–68; Clayton R. Koppes, "The Social Destiny of the Radio: Hope and Disillusionment in the 1920s," *The South Atlantic Quarterly* 68 (Summer 1969): 363–76; and Helen B. Pryor, "Lou Henry Hoover," *Palimpsest* 52 (July 1971): 353–400; Calvin L. Christman, "Charles A. Beard, Ferdinand Eberstadt, and America's Postwar Security," *Mid-America* 54 (July 1972): 187–94; George W. Hopkins, "The Politics of Food: United States and Soviet Hungary, March–August, 1919," *Mid-America* 55 (October 1973): 245–70; Douglas C. Drake, "Herbert Hoover, Ecologist: The Politics of Oil Pollution Control, 1921–1926," *Mid-America* 55 (July 1973): 207–28; and John L. Shover, "The Emergence of a Two-Party System in Republican Philadelphia, 1924–1936," *The Journal of American History* 60 (March 1974): 985–1002; Michael Hogan, "Informal Entente: Public Policy and Private Management in Anglo-American Petroleum Affairs, 1918–1924," *Business History Review* 48 (Summer 1974).

Finally, Ruth Dennis, former Librarian at the Hoover Presidential Library, compiled an accumulative "Bibliographical Guide to the Life and Interests of Herbert Clark Hoover" of almost two thousand entries. This is the most complete guide to published secondary works (not including articles) that contain any references to his multifaceted ideas and activities. The current Librarian and Archivist Mildred Mather is keeping this file up to date. Ruth Dennis and Mildred Mather also organized approximately 150 boxes of articles about Hoover, by him or by others indirectly relating to his life. It is known unofficially as the "Reprint File" and is catalogued in chronological order and cross-referenced by author, title, subject, and periodical. It is available upon request by researchers at the Presidential Library in West Branch, Iowa.

Index